A World War II Story

Dad's Letters Home

Elaine Pelletier Holland and
Norman J. Pelletier

Bloomington, IN   Milton Keynes, UK

AuthorHouse™
1663 Liberty Drive, Suite 200
Bloomington, IN 47403
www.authorhouse.com
Phone: 1-800-839-8640

AuthorHouse™ *UK Ltd.*
500 Avebury Boulevard
Central Milton Keynes, MK9 2BE
www.authorhouse.co.uk
Phone: 08001974150

©2006 Elaine Pelletier Holland and Norman J. Pelletier. All rights reserved.

No part of this book may be reproduced, stored in a retrieval system, or transmitted by any means without the written permission of the author.

First published by AuthorHouse 11/28/2006

ISBN: 978-1-4259-5129-0 (sc)

Printed in the United States of America
Bloomington, Indiana

This book is printed on acid-free paper.

In Memory Of

Wildre Roland Joseph Pelletier

Born March 8, 1916

Died October 30, 1986

and
his beloved wife
Jeannette Marion Breton Pelletier

Born February 17, 1917

Died January 15, 1999

Letter to the Reader,
written by his daughter, Elaine M. Holland

This book was written in memory of Mom & Dad who experienced first hand the events and hardships of WW II as a young couple with a small child to raise. All of the letters written by Dad during his deployment were preserved by Mom who experienced the Depression Era and never threw out anything. Mom left these memoirs to her children who in turn felt they should be shared with others in order to have a personal sense of what it was like during this dreadful time when young men with families had to leave their wives and children behind in order to fight proudly for our country. Being of French Canadian descent some of the letters started with "Dear Face Laite" which is an affectionate French term for" homely face."

Mom was a beautiful woman and was small framed, around five feet one inches, compared to Dad who was a six footer and blonde, so this was his way of poking fun at her.

Dad sang in the choir at Our Lady of Peace Church in Berwick, Maine, and became friendly with the organist by the name of Annette Roy, and was also a good friend of her husband Ernest.

Annette is 94 years old and Elaine continues their friendship to this day.

One day Dad asked Ernest if Jeannette and Elaine could live with them and their sons while he served in the U.S. Army. As Annette tells the story, they had coffee after mass one Sunday and both parties agreed. After the war Dad and Mom stayed in Berwick to raise their family.

Dad entered into the US Army on August 4th, 1943, when I was 6 months of age, and he did not see us again for three years, until his separation in January 1946. He served eight months and four days in the South Pacific and nine months and nine days in the Foreign Service Association Pacific Theater. One of Dad's jobs in the Army was that of a French interpreter since he spoke the language fluently. He was a member of the 208th Army military police. His active duty ended on January 16th, 1946 and his grade rating at separation was Sargent, Tech 4. He separated at Center Fort Devens, Massachusetts, and returned to the Portsmouth Naval Shipyard where he was employed both before and after the war as a Calker, Chipper and Flangeturner. His classification while employed was 1st class and he retired from the Naval Station after 28 years of service.

I am now in my 60's and still have my father's US Army ring and wear it often. I also still have the grass skirt Dad brought back home for me from the South Pacific.

My brother Norman was born later in December 1946, and before her death Mom made sure Norman had something of Dad's from war time and that was the diary that Dad kept during the war.

Dad's childhood was not easy. His family consisted of nine children who were brought up by a single parent, his mother Clementine. His father died of pneumonia at the age of thirty-eight.

Dad's formal education ended in the 8th grade at St. Michael's school in So. Berwick, Maine in order to work and help his mother with finances. As Dad recalls he was detained another year in the 8th grade, even though it wasn't needed the nuns at St. Michael's knew he would be expected to work, and would not be allowed to continue with his education.

Mom also had an unusual childhood. She was one of 16 children, second to the oldest, and had to terminate her formal education at the sixth grade level in order help her mother take care of the children and household due to a fire that destroyed the family home. The way Mom told the story she had a wonderful childhood even with the absence of material wealth. There were good times, but also times of tragedy and loss. One evening when a kerosene lamp was being filled and lit, a fire broke out and burned the entire house. Not only did Mom and her family lose everything, but one of Mom's brothers died in the fire. Some years later another sibling died of scarlet fever. After the fire, Mom had to quit school to take care of her brothers and sisters while her mother went to work. When she turned sixteen, she went to work and her mother stayed home with the children. She worked at a mill, several shoe shops and eventually began working for the General Electric Company in Somerworth, N.H. She continued to work there for twenty - eight years.

Mom was working at General Electric at the time of her marriage. She cashed in a life insurance policy that she had through the company to pay for her wedding. As Mom recalled, I remember her saying that those years while Dad was gone were very difficult. After the war the couple was able to settle into married life.

After retiring from the work force, the couple remained active. They were very busy doing gardening, cooking, and Dad made many wood projects. When he was ill he asked what he could make for his granddaughter on a special occasion , and I suggested a cedar chest. We still have that piece and treasure it. The most important aspect of this stage for them was the enjoyment of spending time together. Dad was a wonderful cook, and the one meal I absolutely loved was when he cooked his bean hole beans, as well as a ham shoulder in the ground. It was succulent, and we all enjoyed it so. Another meal the entire family loved was his annual lobster bake where he would cook on the open fire in the month of August after selling his fresh vegetables from the garden. They both worked so hard in the garden but loved the fruits of their labor.

We did that annually for years, and looked forward to having the entire family together, and having a good time. In 1985 Dad became gravely ill and was diagnosed with leukemia.

Mom and Dad stayed married until his death in 1986. Mom lived another twelve years, and died one month shy of her eighty-second birthday.

My parent's outlook on life and the way they faced each new challenge, their faith in God, a positive attitude, strong work ethics and a sense of humor were how I fondly remember them. I strongly believe that the combination of genes, culture, and childhood/adolescent experiences contribute to shaping our personalities.

Their young adolescent years as carefree teens were almost non existent due to family circumstances, but their lives were meaningful and well-lived regardless.

My parents were generous, honest, and loving. We miss them dearly, and are thankful for the wisdom, spirituality and life experiences they provided for us, as well as giving us an openness and willingness to grow as individuals. I became a nurse and practiced in college health, and Norman became a high school teacher and school administrator.

These are the compelling letters that Dad wrote during war time. His memoirs are true gifts of human compassion, love, loneliness for his family and at the same time a testament of his love for his country. Norman and I truly hope that this book will give you a better understanding of what veterans sacrificed for the love of country and the separation of family and how the two came together during the years of World War II.

At the time that the World War II memorial was built in Washington, D.C., Norman and I entered Dad into the World War II Memorial Registry of remembrances for participating in the war, and helping our nation win the greatest military victory in history.

Norman and I want to share Dad's memoirs so that future generations will better understand what sacrifices were made by the men and women of the armed forces in order to make this a safe country for all to live in.

What we see here is the stuff of history . . . invaluable documents of rare authenticity that provide a window in the life of an ordinary man from New England who served our country. It tells a personal story of a brave man's experiences as a husband, father and soldier.

Letter to the Reader,
written by his son, Norman J. Pelletier

Firstly, I remember how little he spoke to me about WW II. He never attended local parades on Memorial Day—even when I participated as a scout or as a bike-decorated observer. He never attended town activities on July 4th holidays. I never remember speaking to him about the war and his activities and experiences in it. At a young age, I could not explain why he did not. Later, I thought that maybe his experiences were such that he did not want to remember it.

My mother often related how he wrote to her and to Elaine some heartfelt letters about how he missed them. I was not born yet.

The only times that I heard him speak about his war experiences were when he met with our neighbor, Mr. Walter Osgood at Christmas season. Mr. Osgood would present himself to our doorstep with a full bottle of whiskey. They would sit at the kitchen table with two glasses and drink the whiskey straight. I would eagerly sit so as not to be noticed. Indeed, I was not noticed. I was an invisible observer to experiences that only they could understand. I knew it and they knew it. They spoke of times and people honestly and with emotion—sometimes laughing and sometimes almost crying.

I don't remember one story from Mr. Osgood but I do remember some from my father. One time, during Basic Training in the Army, he was among soldiers who were crawling between and under barbed wire. All the while, machine guns fired live rounds just above the heads of the crawling soldiers. All at once, my father noticed a snake move just in front of one of the soldiers and he jumped up at once out of fear of snakebite. The machine gun bullet hit its mark and the soldier died instantly.

Another time, he was among troops who boarded the troop ships in California. Some soldiers who knew what they would be sailing to, jumped from the ship while boarding. Military Police were right on hand to fish them from the water and put them back on the ship. After leaving port, he saw others jumping ship with no land in sight. In those cases, the ships just kept heading towards the South Pacific. Those troops either drowned or were eaten by sharks.

The last experience that I can remember was the time when he was chosen to leave his ship headed to the D-DAY Invasion. He was just walking around the ship one day when he heard an officer ask if anyone spoke French. He said he did. The next thing he knew, he was headed to an island off the coast of New Caledonia. He became a military policeman, carrying out duties typical of policemen everywhere. He dealt with rapes, murders, burglary, etc., as well as dealing with military matters and translating.

The poignant times came when they each talked of someone they knew who died or when they discussed those who were ordered out of their unit with no explanation. Sometimes soldiers were shipped out without them. Others were taken to another whole theater of the war. When they talked about those men, sometimes their eyes glossed over. A sad silence permeated the room. They swallowed more whiskey. Then they would continue their release of sad or horrifying ideas for a total of about three hours.

Very little of the bottle was left by the end of the meeting. A simple shake of the hands, an understanding of each other's experiences, would end the annual ritual. My father never talked about the war other than at those times with that man. I felt it a privilege to be there as the observer. Next year, they would do it again. I would wait until the next Christmas season when they would reveal new stories with a new bottle of whiskey.

Photographic Prologue

Father and Mother just after getting married

AUG-1943
Father and Mother holding Elaine.

DEC-1943
Father on Leave before going overseas.

Father in his Military Police Uniform.

Father and his buddies in the Military Police.

Father's U.S. Army Ring.

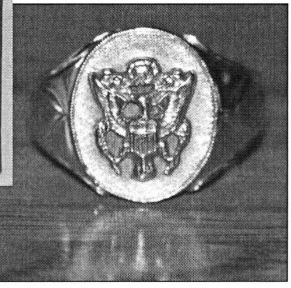

xvi

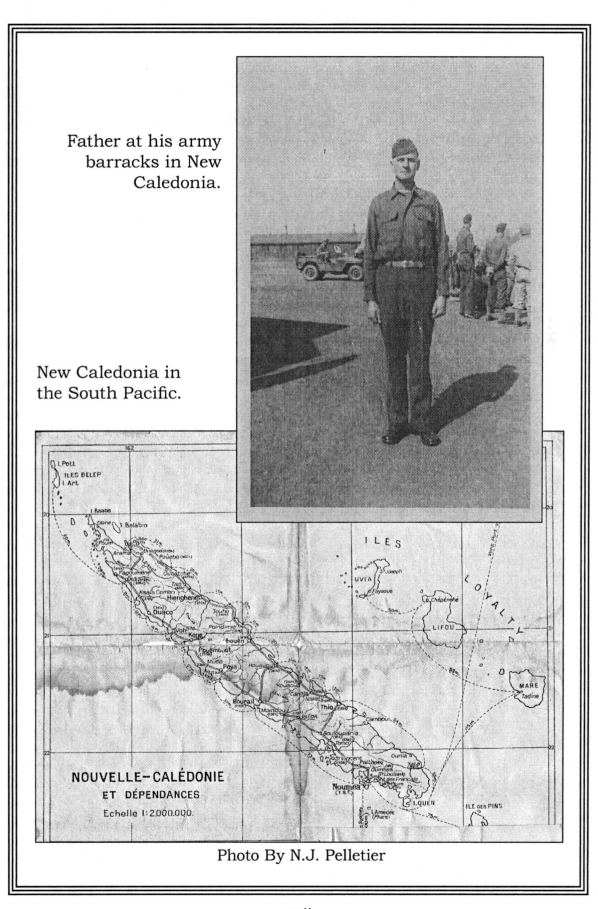

Father at his army barracks in New Caledonia.

New Caledonia in the South Pacific.

Photo By N.J. Pelletier

The Base at New Caledonia.

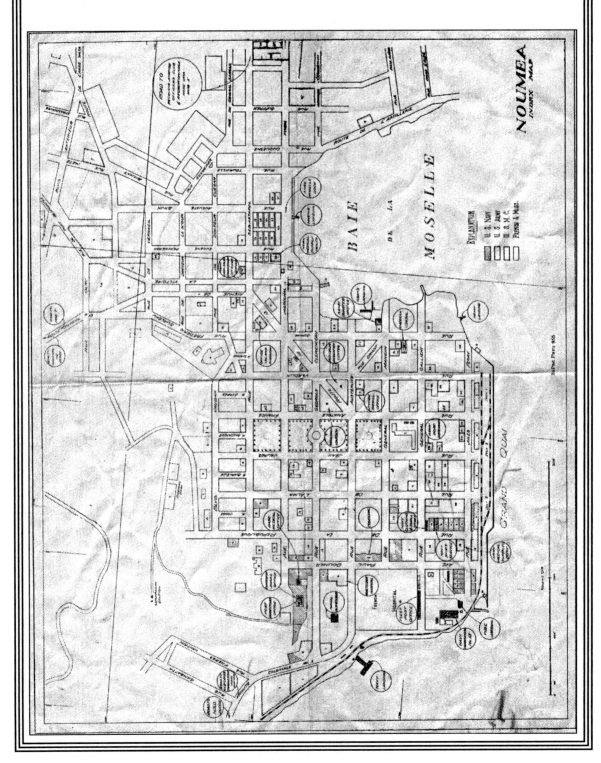

Dad's Letters Home

No. 255   1/6 7-'45

Dear Face Faite:

    I've had so much good news to-day that I just don't no where to begin. I should start by giving you a good whipping by letter, but you've been so good too me that I just can't bring myself to do this.

    So, too start in, first on my list is your very nice package. Yes I finally received it to-day. Was I happy, well that's putting it mildly. When I saw your name on the package, I just tore into it and didn't stop until I found that watch. And what a watch. I've written so many words

— 11 —

words about that watch that I'll bet they could fill a book. I put it on right away and it fits just right on my wrist. Although I didn't want you to spend so much money on a watch, I'm certainly glad I got it now. It would be useless to try and thank you, so I guess I won't attempt it. Not now at least, but some other time.

Besides that watch the next best thing was that diary of Rene's. I wish I could have gotten it for the first of Jan. but nevertheless, I'll have use it. I'll have to site Rene to-night and thank him.

You must have had quite a time

—111—

finding those cigarettes. From what I hear, they are hard too find at home. We have no shortage here, we have all we want, and much cheaper than you can buy them.

The socks and hankies, I can always use. They were nice. And thank you for everything else there was enclosed.

Now — I'm going to let you in for a big secret. Are you ready? Read this carefully and don't faint. The big reason why that package did not get here in time was because you put the wrong A.P.O. number on the package. Instead of A.P.O. 50__2__, you had 5__9__0. Simple little mistake isn't it? And yet, by just switching those two last numbers, it was enough to delay it for two months or more. It traveled to three different A.P.O. numbers before it even got to this island. It's a wonder that you didn't get it back. I guess you were a little over anxious to get everything just right and in your anxiety a little slip like that was overlooked. But anyway, all's well that ends well. I got it at last and that's all that matters. Thanks honey, for everything.

Now that our story of <u>the package</u> is settled, and to top off my good fortune I received three letters from you and one each from Anette and Fern. I won't try to answer all of them to-night, cause

- V -

I've already did a lot of writing to day and my fingers are sore. I think I'll save them for some day when I don't receive any.

Little wonder that I didn't hear from Medee if he lost my address. It's the same with me, I lost his address as well as all the others. So if you'll send me his I'll rite to him. And when you have time you can rite the others down and send them to me. Medee must be seeing plenty of action over there.

Guess I'll close for now, don't want to write everything in one letter. So long for now, Until I can do it in a better way, thanks again for everything face laite.

Your loving Wilbré

No. 256. Feb. 8-'45

Chere Pace faite:

Hello honey, after getting all that mail yesterday, I didn't get any to-day. But that's alright, I can stand a few days without mail now. I'm still quite happy about receiving that watch and other things. So far it keeps perfect time.

Well I guess I can answer your letters now.

I see Elaine is always anxious to go out of door into open air. You should take her out more often. She'll make an outdoor girl and have rosey cheeks. It would do you a lot of good if you went out more often. From what you say, you don't step out very often. Remember, all work and no play is bad.

In regards to writting mother, I write to her at least once every week. As I told you before, it takes much longer for a french letter to go across than one written in english.

-//-

So your expecting to be laid off most anytime? Don't worry to much about that, you could stand a nice long vacation anyway. And it won't hurt my feelings if you didn't work any more.

When I get back, I will take you swimming as often as you wish, I promise. And not only that but I'll do anything you ask for,— so help me. You seem to be having a little trouble sometimes to make Elaine mind you. Well, I guess all kids are not angels all the time, And I don't agree with you at all when you put her to bed without her meal. There must be other means and ways that you could punish her. Like standing in a corner for instance. But please don't take her meals away from her. How would you like to go to bed without eating dinner, would you like that? The next time she's bockey, I hope you

—111—

have another way to punish her.

I sure enjoy the way you explain every little detail of your saturday chores. I like to read about those little things about you, Elaine and home. Keep right on in the same line. And besides enjoying reading all about that, your letters are much longer.

I'll be waiting for those pictures you took of Elaine on her birthday. And by the way, if you have an extra one of those folders with pictures of we three,— I'd like to have one. But don't buy any extra ones just for me. And speaking of pictures, I've found a camera that I can use any time I want to. All I need is films. So if you can buy some films (univex film No. 00) and send them to me, I'll send you lots of pictures.

I guess that's all for now, so long honey and take care of you both.

Love Always Wilbur.

No. 357   Nf. 10-45

Chere Face Suite!

    Hello honey, didn't get any mail again today so I'll answer one of your old ones.

    I see Elaine's birthday was celebrated in great style. What with all that cake and ice cream and the gifts she had, she must have had smiles all over her. I'm glad you were there at least, to help make that day a great celebration. Next year, we'll make it a family affair.

    From what you say, the weather must be a little chilly or am I putting it mildly. 15° or 20° below zero is nothing to sneeze at — I don't suppose. But I'd sure like to share it right now.

    I don't doubt but it will be some time before Lula hears from Laurent. She hasn't

—11—

answered my last letter yet.

I still maintain that you should go out more often. I can understand that in that cold weather, one doesn't feel much like going out. But you never go out, surely once in a while would not harm you.

Yes I do wish that it was Elaine's birthday more often, so that you would make your letters longer. Four pages is quite a lot for you to write, but if I had Elaine, I'd do the same every day. Good wife huh?

This is my fourth letter today, and it's about time for me to run out of words. So in signing off, so long and take care always.

Love Always Wilbur

Feb. 10 - '45

Hello Mr. & Mrs:

Received your very short letter a few days ago and also your valentine and picture.

There must be something wrong with you, for that letter was very short. What's the matter, are you too busy with hairdressing or is it that man of yours too active? If it's the latter reason, stop feeding him eggs and cream for a while, and I'll bet that will dampen his ardor. As for myself it will take more than that to stop me once I get back again, at least for a while.

I finally received that package, and that much talked about watch. The reason for such a long delay was that Jean had addressed the package to the wrong A.P.O. 530 instead 503. It was a small oversight, but enough for it to travel thru 3 different A.P.O. numbers before it got here. I also received a diary book from Rene. All in all, everything was swell, especially the watch and I'm greatly relieved and happy that I received it.

The picture of Emile and his deer was nice, I'll admit, but wait until you see mine. It must have been quite cold at the time, cause that dead deer seems to be frozen standing up.

If Conrad and Lionel can have furloughs more power to them. I don't expect mine for a long time to come.

Am still at the old job. There's nothing much different, just working day after day.

Hope the body (yours & Bill's) are in good condition. No new developements yet?

So long until next time, from your inlaw — As Ever, Willie.

P.S. Did you notice that Cpl.?

No. 258   Feb. 12 - '45

My Dear Face Suite:

Hello honey, I hope your in the best of health and Elaine also. What with all that cold weather and snow your experiencing at this time, I can well imagine how difficult it is too keep well. I sure like to be there with you. But that goes without saying. I heard to day on the radio about your big snow storm. Eighteen inches is quite a lot. I hope you take good care of yourselves.

Its been four days now since I've received a letter from you, and I miss them more than I can ever reveal on paper. But when I do get them, they more than make up for lost time. You always seem to rite just what I like to read, — about you and Elaine and all your little activities. If I could only make my letters as interesting as yours. But then, that's asking quite a lot.

-11-

I received a V-mail from Bill Elliot to day. He thanked me for that request and said that at a later date, maybe he could sing that request for you on another station. So, I hope your keeping time with his programs, you might still hear it.

I also received a letter from Camille to day. We're still keeping up that old argument about who has the best looking daughter. Of course I always win, at least I think so. He expects a great change at the yard most any day. He also told me about Andre being in L.A. and going for his final examination soon. I'm sorry to hear that. I hope everything turns out as well for him as it did for us.—That is, as well as could be expected.

I'm having a little trouble writing this letter t-night. Those damn bugs seem to be thicker to night than usual. I hate to act like an old crab, but they are thick. I shouldn't complain to much, for I've been in places where they were much thicker. But you no, the better off one is, the less he realizes it. I guess I'm getting spoiled.

That diary that Rene sent me is very nice. I'll try to keep it up as much as possible. My memory is very poor, so that's one way I'll be able to remember some of the things.

It's been only four days since I've heard from you and Elaine but it seems like ages. Should get some news to-morrow, - I hope. Sure miss your face Cutie. Have opportunity to contact lots of females, but so help me, no soap, just don't care to bother. Too many memories of past happiness to start a double life now. I no it's the right thing to do, pretty hard to teach an old dog new tricks. That's me.

So long for now, take care always,
Always yours Hildor.

No. 259 Feb. 13-'45

Chere Face Laite:

I hit the jackpot in the mail to-day, received four letters from you and one each from Alice and mother. The latest one from you was only twelve days old and that's pretty good, considering the time it usually takes.

Glad to hear you finally received Elaine's birthday card. I'll be waiting to hear whether you received the other surprises.

Elaine seems to be the head attraction as usual. I'm always glad to hear she's well and happy, but when you mention something about her health going wrong I start worrying. So you'd better keep a close watch on that babe, and that goes for yourself as well. Especially in that below zero weather you've been having lately. Brrr, I'd sure like to be there.

So they finally caught up with Bill Vachon?

- 11 -

He's been pretty lucky so far, too bad they had to catch up with him. — I'll bet there's still plenty Hervey's in town.

I still haven't got a picture of myself to send you. I've been waiting for one I had taken three months ago. One of my tent mates sent it to his wife to have finished and it hasn't come back yet. As soon as I get it tho, I'll send it.

That must have been quite a shock too the young couple who live on the Boulanger farm. Loosing it by fire I mean. I sure wouldn't want that to happen to ours. I can well imagine how the fire department was so prompt in putting out the blaze. They always were an efficient little gang.

You never did tell me when Meggie's wife was expecting. Be sure to tell me all about that shower. I will rite to Mesee now that I have his address. I guess he knows now what it is to receive letters. And as time goes on he'll realize it all the more.

Mother tells me that Andre has chosen the marines. He'll be a sorry guy within two days I'll bet.

Am always in good health, and not working hard. Am still satisfied as far as my army job is concerned. Won't be at all surprised if my satisfaction is cut short. That's the way the army usually operates you no.

Guess that's about all for now, so long and keep warm.
Love Wilson

No. 260 Feb. 14-'45

Chere Face Faite:

Hello honey, received three more letters from you today. Was sure surprised. Also a couple of Valentines from Alice and a letter from Annette.

You certainly got me beat if you write as many as nine letters in one afternoon. In regards to your not writing another letter after the war, I feel the same way. As a matter of fact, I'm surprised more and more every day that I rite so many letters. I never thought for one minute that I'd be writting to you most every day. But then again, I never thought one could miss his loved ones so much either. A daily letter is very little to compensate for all the pent up lonliness. I hope you never stop writting to me, at least till I get back. Then you can stop anytime.

-11-

I'd sure like to see some of that snow your having. Gosh you make me homesick when you mention snow. It's so hot here sometimes that I have to take salt tablets most every day. I hate them for they turn my stomach. But if I don't take any I get much sicker, if that's the proper word.

I got a kick out of reading one of your letters to-day, where you stated as to how that package was mailed etc. I'd like to see your face when you read why it was so delayed. I'll bet the next time you'll pay attention to my A.P.O. no.

Thanks for St Laurent's address. When I have time — I'll drop him a line. As for that fellow who bought our car, I don't even remember his name. I'd write to him also but not until I can get his address.

So glad to hear about Pauline receiving a letter from Laurent. It must be a long wait between letters.

- /// -

Yes, the war news have been encouraging lately. It can't last much longer now honey. Keep your chin up and before you no it we'll be all together again.

I think I'll rite to McKee to-night. It's been so long since the last time. I was all caught up with my correspondence a few days ago, but now I have three or four letters to answer. You don't hate to rite any more than I do.

I guess that's all for now, solong and take care.

Love Always Wilbur

No. 261   Sep. 15 – '45

Hello Race Suite:

     Received two more letters from you to-day and one from Florida. I've been getting so much mail from you the past few days that I don't no where to start in answering. So I'll just take one at a time.

     I see by your letter that my name is on the board in Berwick. That's the second place, it's on the board in So. Berwick also. I never knew I was so popular.

     In one letter you said that you had a week off and I was glad. But to-day's letter says that they've changed their mind and I didn't feel so good. I guess they will have to fire you before you take time off. That big girl sure is smart according to what you say. It hat a gal. Sure takes after the old lady I think. Fern told me about that cup

—11—

that she fought for her birthday. It must be pretty nice.

I never thought about writing to Medee's wife. It would be to late now. But I will send her a note anyway. I wrote to Medee last night.

I don't think I'll rite to René anymore until I hear from him. You no, he'll probably have a chance to meet Medee on his new island. I'll mention it to both of them the next time I rite.

I can imagine how he feels after seeing white people again. I had the same experience only I wasn't away quite so long.

I received the 'Ice-Capades' program that Alice sent me to-day. It was very nice. Let's hope next year we'll see them together huh?

I guess I'll close for now, solong and take care honey,
 Love Wilbri

P.S. enclosed are a few pictures which were taken and given to me by a tentmate. Will have others in a few days.

No. 262 Dec. 17-45

Happy Birthday Dear Faite:

Another birthday and another day closer to being together. I could mention a lot of nice things for this day, but the first sentence is about the best I can think of right now. I hope you liked your flowers. I couldn't think of anything to send you from here, so I hope they helped to brighten up your day a little more. I also sent a couple of cards. Well, your the same age as I am to-day, but I'll be ahead of you in a couple of weeks again.

Received another letter from you to-day and one from Fern. For the past week mailed has been getting here pretty fast. Let's hope it keeps up.

Glad to hear you had a good time at the shower. I hope everything turns out all right.

In reference to the "Hit Parade", I haven't heard it for several weeks now, because I always worked on saturday night. This is the first saturday

- 11 -

I'd listen to it. Of course its transcribed but there isn't much difference. I don't have my easy chair to sit in, nor the nice radio you have, nor do I have a wife to sit and listen with me. But then, I can't have everything can I?

So glad to hear you put on a little weight. You could still put on a little more tho. I'd like to have something to squeeze when I get back. You'll need plenty of armor I assure you.

I guess I'll make this short for now. Will rite more to-morrow.

Be sure and take good care of you both for me.

Love Always Wildré

No. 264   Jy. 18-'45

Dear Face Suite:

Hello honey, it's Sunday afternoon on this side of the world and a very nice day it is. As I'm not working this afternoon, after dinner I had a short nap and upon awakening, I figured it was time for your daily letter.

The sun is beating down on the tent and it's quite hot inside, about 90°. It's a little warmer than Berwick I bet. But outside there's a nice breeze and makes me think a lot of Berwick in the good old summertime.

I'm feeling fine and I hope you are also.

I didn't receive any mail from you for two days now, but I shouldn't crab too much tho. I had beaucoup mail last week. I'm never satisfied when it comes to getting mail from you.

On Florita's letter yesterday, she says that her and Pat will take a cottage at the beach

— 11 —

this coming summer and she wants to keep Elaine while you work. I don't think much of the idea and I don't think you will either. She's not old enough yet to be kept by everyone who takes a fancy to her. It would be alright if you both stayed there and it would do you both lots of good, but Elaine alone — I don't think much of it. Maybe by then you'll be out of work and you may be able to accept that offer, — I hope.

I had my picture taken last week, and this time I'm going to send the roll to Mom and have them finished. I'll be sure to get them then and she can send you mine. The negatives will be on the way this coming week.

Take good care of our big girl face Kate. There will never be another one like her you no.

That's all for now, so long, from me with love to you and you "Willie".

A World War II Story: Dad's Letters Home

No. 264 Feb. 19-'45

Chere Face Suite:

Hello honey, this is the third day without mail from you. It seems to comes in bunches now. I have no more of yours to copy from so I don't have very much to write.

Enclosed you will find a picture of myself that was taken a couple of days ago. One of the boys developed it himself and it didn't turn out bad. It was taken while I was standing in front of my New Caledonia home at high noon. You can see that the sun was shining brightly and the temperature was about 90° or more. Some difference from Warwick huh? You can also see for yourself that I'm not very skinny. My cloths are all too small for me now. I guess I'll have to start doing a little manual work to reduce. Some change since I first got here.

-11-

I received a letter from René to-day. It was a V-mail. His new A.P.O. No. is 70. Medee's is 74, so they can't be too far apart. Maybe on separate islands but still in the Phillipines. René seems to be in pretty good spirits about his new home. He tells me about seeing white women and having real eggs for breakfast. I can imagine how he feels after staying in the jungles for so long. I felt the same way when I first got here, but I wasn't away from it all as long as he.

Well I guess that's about all for to-night. I'll try to rite more to-morrow. So long and take care of you both.

Love Always Wilbré

No. 265   Feb. 20-'45

Dear Face Laite:

Received one letter from you to-day and also one from mother.

I answered René's letter this afternoon, the first since he's been at his new address.

Enclosed you will find some pictures taken a few days ago. As for the negatives enclosed, I'd like to have some finished and enlarged. I was going to send them to Vern, but I've been promising you pictures for so long that I thought of sending the first batch to you. Now here's what I want. I'd like ~~eight~~ (8) sets finished and have them enlarged to the same size as the one of the two boys which I have enclosed as a sample. Send me ~~7~~ sets back, for the fellows want some, and send the other set with the negatives enclosed to

-11-

Mrs. L. C. Rickson
1358 Davis Ave. N.W.
Grand Rapids, 4, Michigan.

Rickson is the fellow who owns the films and camera and he'd like to keep the negatives. Instead of sending his set across and back again, you might as well send his to his wife. It won't take so long for her to get them that way. You can have a set made out for yourself and also keep the negative of mine if you want to. It's going to cost you quite a bit for this time, but after this I'll send them to Fern.

Changing the subject a little, you people sure are getting a lot of snow this winter. It must be nice sleeping in that cold. I'd sure like to have some for a change. Does Elaine still toss her blankets on the floor? I remember when she was little, you had to pin them down every night.

Glad to hear that you turned down Florida's offer to live with her. At first I thought that she was inviting you but it turns out that you have to pay half expenses. It's no good either way. Your much better off to stay with Mom for a vacation I think.

I'll find out over here if I can rite to Tousainte. I doubt it tho. Lula must be glad to hear from him.

Well I guess that's all for now. Hope you got everything straight on those pictures. I've been bragging about how much faster you can get them than Kickson's wife. So you'd better not let me down.

Solong and take care
Love Wilbu

A World War II Story: Dad's Letters Home

No. 267   Feb. 21 -'45

Chere Face Laite:

Received two letters and one card from you to-day. That newspaper clipping that was enclosed with the card shows just much snow there is in Maine. I haven't seen so much snow since I was going to school. That was a long time before I ever met you. Take good care of yourself and Elaine in all that snow and cold weather.

Don't tell me that you finally went to a show. How did you do it? Did Annette lock you outside? She should do it more often if that's the only way to make you go out. I no it's pretty tough to be alone all the time honey, but it can't last forever. We'll be together again before you no it.

Glad you liked the cards I sent you. Am anxious to no if you got the flowers okay. I'm still not sure if your birthday is on the sixteenth or the seventeenth. Remember, every year I always had

-11-

an argument with you on that point. But I didn't forget your birthday, I never will.

Your sure getting pretty smart on that job of yours. I'd better hurry up and get home or else you'll be wearing the pants.

I get a great kick out of you writing me about the watch. I guess it wouldn't have done much good even if you did insure it, what with that wrong A.P.O. No. I'll bet the next time you send a package you'll make sure of the right No. huh?

Glad to hear your feeling swell all the time. Elaine is always the main topic of conversation, as well as attention—I see. As long as you both stay that way, I won't worry.

Solong for now, until to-morrow, solong
love, Wildie

No. 267								Feb. 22-'45-

Chere face cute:

Hello honey, how are you and that big girl to-day? Are you all being buried in the snow? From all indications, I should say you've had enough.

I was sure surprised to hear about Andre leaving his wife. I haven't the slightest idea what could have provoked this freak. No matter what it was or who was to blame, he's at fault as far as I'm concerned. There's no excuse on his part for leaving his kids. That's just like somebody hitting him in the face and then he taking it out on somebody smaller than he. I don't care what happens to he or his wife, but I hope the kids make out all right. They have a long time to live yet and I'd hate to see their lives spoiled. By the way, Alice told me about this. I may sound like I'm giving you hell, I hope your not afraid

- 11 -

But this won't happen to us, we no better. You told me before that I was a pretty good husband, but just you wait and see how really good I can be once I get out of this army. The army may not have taught me much of anything, but I have learned one thing at least; that is to appreciate the ones we love and home in general.

Say, I've been on the same subject so far. Maybe I talk to much huh? — could go on and rite some more on that subject but I guess thats enough for now.

Can't seem to think of anything else so I guess I'll close. Solong for now, take care,

Love Always Wilbur.

A World War II Story: Dad's Letters Home

No. 268 Feb. 19-'45

Dear Sweet Suite:

Hello honey, this is the bad half again. Haven't received news from you for a few days now, and I'm at a loss again just what to rite you.

I received a letter from Florida yesterday and in it, was enclosed two pictures. One of the family and the other of Lorette and the Buick. Lorette sure has grown up since I last saw her. She's taller than her mother. Sid and Florida seem to have aged somewhat. But then they can't stay young forever I guess. The pictures were very nice. I'm still waiting for some of yours and Elaine. Haven't received any for quite a while.

I must make an effort to rite Fern to-day. Been putting it off for a week.

-11-

—I still rite as many letters as usual. To many to suit me, but then if I didn't rite to other folks to keep me busy, I might get into trouble.

We're continually having excellent weather here. If it wasn't so far from home, this would be a nice vacationland. But that's all. I wouldn't want to stay here forever.

Hope Elaine is growing prettier every day. I'd sure like to see her. You also of course. I'll be in for a great surprise when I get back — I'll bet. I try to imagine sometime, just how she will look, but that's hard to do. I don't have to imagine for you, you'll never change, — I hope.

So long for now honey, take care

Love Always Wilder.

Feb. 24 - '45

Hello Good People:

You must be quite busy not to remember whether you wrote to me or not. But I like it that way, you rite more often.

Thanks for that cup you sent to Elaine on her birthday. I'm sure she'll remember her old aunt and uncle when she gets to the ripe old age of reasoning. That won't be long now according to Jean.

I received my first letter from Rene in the Philippines last week and answered right back. He's tickled with his new home and I don't blame him much. He might meet up with Medee yet. As for me, I don't think I'll see him unless there's a great change. (Vern send me some film.)

For Jean's birthday, I gave her flowers thru Mr. Elmer Graves in Somersworth. I don't no

-11-

if she's received them yet or not. She'll be surprised I'll bet.

Has it really been three years since you've been swimming? I think you've got your dates mixed up, or else I have. At any rate there's nothing to stop you this year,—or is it to early to predict? Hope you have better luck this time. Too bad — I can't show you how it's done.

Why do you have to get up so early in the morning? Are you working or is it that course in hairdressing? Don't be too ambitious, Enjoy some of that freedom you still have. I'll show you just what I mean someday.

Guess I'll cut this short for now, more next time. Solong, so so ver.

Wilbur.

No. 269   Feb. 25-'45

Hello Honey:

I received quite a surprise yesterday. The letter that you wrote on the 16th got over here in seven days. That's the quickest I ever got one.

In it I read all about your surprises which happened the day before your birthday. Did you like the flowers? I knew they would surprise you. It was easy to send them to you. All I had to do was mail a money order to Mr. Elmer Graves and request that he deliver to you flowers for such a date.

But what I can't understand is that request of "Always" you heard over the radio. I didn't ask for that. Probably it's Mr. Graves who requested that over the Portsmouth station.

-11-

Tell me more about it in your next letter.

That big girl seems to be pretty smart according to you. I'd sure like to have her become a singer. At the rate she's going now she can't miss. If you encourage her and help her she'll learn fast.

You should be ashamed of yourself for thanking me so much. That's the very least I can do for you to repay everything you've given me, and for everything your doing for me every day. I'll never be able to give you enough no matter how much I try.

Well, I guess that's about all for now. Until to-morrow, solong and take good care of you both.

Love Always Willie.

No. 270   Feb. 26 - '45

Chère Face Laite:

Received two more letters from you to-night. They were a little old compared with the last one I got, but was glad anyway.

That must have been quite a snow storm you had. It sure crippled the industries for a few days.

You and Elaine must have had a nice supper at Annettes folks. That girl can sure eat according to you. She seems to have and like everything you give her. It's a good thing you no her capacity or else she'd be sick all the time. And don't worry, we'll have that chicken farm one of these days. That's a promise.

According to your letter of the 12th, you received a lot of mail that day. Had you got the birthday card okay. But best of all, you got the flowers. Aren't you glad I surprised you with them instead of telling you in advance? I think that's what I'll do from now on. As long as your not near me to coax, it will be easy.

Glad you finally got word from Savigne's wife. Enjoyed reading her letter and could comment on it but I guess I won't. Hope they have a chance to see you soon. I'm enclosing it with this one.

Gosh, I don't no what to rite any more. I haven't been across so very long, but yet I can't seem to think of anything any more. I use to be able to knock off a letter in ten or fifteen minutes, but now it takes me an hour and sometimes longer. If I could tell you what I do everyday it might be different, but I can't and that's that. Oh for the day I won't have to rite another letter. But until that day I'm going to make an effort to rite as often as usual. That's the least I can do for my face Lute. That's the best ending I can think of for this letter. So until to-morrow Solny, Love Wilbur.

No. 271   Feb. 27-45

Hello Honey:

Just received two more letters from you and one from Annette.

Glad to hear that Elaine got so many Valentine cards. She's pretty young to be so popular.

Now I no how come you heard that request of "Always" over the radio. It was Annette who requested it in my name. She told me so on her letter. That was very thoughtful of her.

Well, well, imagine you getting in a fight with some big fat woman. I can't imagine such a picture as that and I hope it wasn't as bad as it sounded. You had the boss on your side so you must have been right. You must have changed since I left. If I remember right when you got angry with me, you never talked at all. I'll have to change tactics with you I guess.

-11-

If ever they want to put you in that paint shop, don't you do it. I don't want you to kill yourself just to earn a few dollars. On the next letter, I want you to promise that you'll quite if they want to give you that job. And let me no which shift your on now.

I think I'll go and make my Easter duties this coming sunday. It's about time I go anyway.

Had a little rifle practice to-day. The first time for quite a while. I'm pretty soft now, and what little training I get now will do me good. I could stand to loose about 35 pounds. I don't no for sure but I must weigh about 300 pounds at least, and that's much to fat, specially in this climate.

Well I guess that's about all for now, solong and take care honey,

love Wilbur

A World War II Story: Dad's Letters Home

No. 272   Feb. 28 – 45

Dear Mace Faite:

    Although I didn't get any letters to-day, I have a lot to say to you anyway. This doesn't happen very often because I can never think of anything to rite.

    First of all I want to thank you for the nice card I received, and best of all, the pictures that were enclosed. Elaine seems to have grown still taller since you sent the last pictures. I can tell by the suit she's wearing. It's already getting small for her. And she looks like 'her highness' sitting at her special table. That picture came out pretty good even tho it was taken inside. You look pretty good your self in that snow beside her; with that same big smile always present. I could do some sitting myself if I had the chance you no. Annettes' boys don't seem to have changed much.

-11-

According to those pictures, you sure have a lot of snow up there. And that old picture of Elaine and I was nice. I'd almost forgotten what I looked like at home. Thanks for everything, but keep those pictures coming whenever you can.

Well, I didn't have that watch long before I put it out of order. I dropped it on the floor this morning. After getting up I wound it up as usual and about nine oclock she stopped running. Well I soon found the trouble. I wound it up to tight and broke the main spring. I don't no if it's the fall or winding it to tight but anyway she won't go. I've always been hard on a wristwatch and that's the reason I asked you for my pocket watch. But I liked this one tho, it kept good time and it was a good watch. When I found out it was broke I was so damn mad that I almost sold it

— III —

for $50 and send you the money. But I hated to do that, after you had gone to so much trouble to get it. At any rate, — I'm going to send it back to you and see if you can have it fixed. — I'd suggest that you find out the address of the manufacturer and send it direct to him. Because Mr. Tibbetts may not be able to get the parts or else if he can it would take a long time. By sending it to the company and with it request that they in turn send it to me direct by airmail after it's fixed, it would save time and money. For they would charge me for the parts only. And by impressing upon them that this watch is vitally important to me and to the war effort, I'd get it all the quicker. If you can't do anything about getting it fixed, send it back to me anyway and — I'll try to get it fixed somehow. I'll send it in a few days.

-IV-

Well, I guess I've said enough for one night. I still have something more to say but I'll save it for tomorrow. If I put everything down in one letter, there's nothing to talk about in the next day.

So until to-morrow solong and take care of you both.

Love Always Wilbre

No. 273   Mar. 1 - '45

Chere Pace Suite:

Hello honey, how's the better half to-day? Fine — I hope. Haven't had any news from you for a few days now.

In yesterday's letter, I told you about somethin' that I had to say, but my letter was long enough. Well it's a good thing that I kept that for to-night cause I can't think of anything else to rite.

Two nights ag', the 26th, I went to a gendarme's home and had supper with he and his family. The same place where that baby had wet my pants, that I told you about a few weeks ago. That same baby is 9 months old now, and I was supprised to see she had grown so much. She made me think a lot of Elaine, cause Elaine was about that same age the last time I saw her. She has curly dark brown hair and dark eyes, she has white skin and very chubby. She looks

-11-

a lot like Elaine. No, she didn't wet me this time.

The supper was pretty good, but far from being the same thing that you use to do. We had roast beef, french fried potatoes, asparagus, soup bread and dessert. For drink, we had red wine, that's still the main drink at meals. It wasn't at all the same as our good old home. Heres the way we ate.

First of all when we sit at the table, there's a small glass of punch to drink, they call it an apetizer. Then we have soup. Then the asparagus is served with some kind of hot sauce. After that's done, we eat the french fries, then the beef covered with gravy. Each of these is served separately and is eaten with bread, — no butter of course. For dessert we had cake and canned pears and peaches. Everything was very good but I didn't like the way it was served separately. I rather have mine the American way. Of course if I'm invited again, I won't turn

-111-

it down. I like to eat to much. Well, I guess that covers about all of it.

Haven't sent my watch yet, but will the first chance I get.

Oh yes, I must tell you about these damn roosters here. The reason why I just thought of that was that I just heard one crowing. And here it is 10 o'clock at night. It seems that they crow more at night than they do in the daytime. Most any hour of the night — wake up and can hear them crow, especially on a moonlight night. Maybe it's the climate or something. I sure long to be where roosters crow when they are supposed to crow, — early in the morning or in the daytime. But I guess I'll have to put up with these roosters for a little while yet. So until I can meet up with them, so long and take care.

Love Always Wilbur

No. 274   Mar. 3-'45

Hello Honey;

Received two more letters from you to-day. If you think your glad to receive letters from me, you must no how I feel to get yours. So if we both feel the same way, we won't let each other down and stop writting. I'll admit, some times I skip one day but I've got a good excuse. I haven't got Elaine to talk about like you have. But this doesn't happen very often.

Glad to hear that you won't have to work nights any more. And also your having a week off. — I'm sure it will do you lots of good. I can't believe that your as crabby as you claim. Or have you changed so much? You say it's because you've been working to steady. Well, this won't happen when I get back. And I'm not afraid what I'll have to put up with either. I guess we'll

-11-

get along alright, and I'm not worried a bit.

You certainly had a happy birthday from the way you sound on your letter. Maybe next year we'll be able to make it still happier.

Glad to hear you visited Nula. Elaine seems to be the masculine type and Roger the feminine. Well, I'd rather see her tall than a little shrimp, — no reflection on you now. I'll bet your proud to have her that way also. Am I right? What a gal, she certainly will make a good farmer one of these days. But don't make her grow too fast cause I'd like to see what she looks like the way she is now.

Solong for now, take care of you both,

Love Always H Ide

No. 375   Mar. 3-45

Hello 'ma Suite:

    Received another letter from you and a birthday card from Annette to-day. Your letter was almost a month old but that's all right, I was glad to get it anyway. I've already received other letters from you which were dated much sooner.

    In Annette's card she had a picture enclosed of her family, taken on Richard's birthday. I was glad to get it cause I haven't got any like that. The card also was very nice. I can't send her or Ernest any cause I don't no their birthday. But I guess they understand.

    The pictures that you mentioned in to day's letter, I guess I've already received them, and it wasn't so very late. So don't be angry over a little thing like that. I'm used to waiting. Ever since I've been in this army, I've waited a lot of times and I'm not there yet. I'll wait as long as I'm back where I belong I guess.

Hope you and Elaine are feeling well. Be sure and take good care of yourselves. There wouldn't be much to go back to if anything ever happened to you and she.

I'm always in good health. I'm not in any danger. I like my work, that is as far as Army is concerned.

War news seem to be quite favorable, hope it continues that way. It won't be long before we'll be together again.

Guess I'll close for now, until tomorrow. Solong and take care.

Love Always Walter.

No. 276   Mar. 4-'45

Dear Face Faite:

Got another letter from you today. Mail has been coming in pretty good the last few days. It was written on your first day off I guess, cause you mentioned it being pretty nice to stay home. Won't it be nice to stay home all the time? You will sometime soon you no. I can't recall to clearly just how it was in the good old days, but what I do recall, it seems that it was a nice way to live. Let's hope those same old days are not to far off. I guess we're both quite anxious, so I won't say that I'm more anxious than you are.

I see that Elaine's bank account is increasing all the time. When we get back to normal living again, we'll see if we can't help her out more. It would be nice if at her eighteenth birthday she would have a nice sum to give her. By that time, she probably would no what she wanted. Of course that's thinking pretty far ahead, but then

-11-

I'm predicting a bright future for her also.

Speaking of money, your doing quite a bit to increase our own pile. It's no use of me to try and say tribute to you. It just can't be put down in words. Maybe someday I may try to show my gratitude but I no I'll never succeed. Until then, all I can say is thanks.

I see that your still having trouble finding shoes to suit you. If I don't get there soon, you'll be going barefooted. I can still pick them out for you you no.

Glad to hear that Lula has been receiving news from Tousaint. I can imagine how much better she feels. But I don't see how she knows where he is in Germany. It must be just hearsay. I'll try to look it up on the map.

Well I guess that's all for now, so long for now,
Love Always Hildre.

A World War II Story: Dad's Letters Home

No. 277   Mar. 6 - '45

Chere Face Faite:

I didn't receive any mail yesterday and I didn't rite any either. Not because I didn't get any but I did'nt feel like writting anyway. To-day was my day off anyway and I thought I'd have more to talk about. I'm sitting in the shade of my tent while writting this, trying to picture this same setting that we have in the good old summertime in Berwick. Of course one has to close his eyes to do this, cause what I see before me is far from being the same picture that we have at home. At any rate, it's nice to daydream. And one has time to do a lot of that sometimes.

The weather is very nice over here. We have rain sometimes, but they have that in the best places. We haven't had a hurricane yet, but I'm told that there's still time. That is Mar. + April. After those two months, the danger is over until next ~~summer~~.

I can't get use to calling our winter months summer and visa versa. Last week the schoolchildren summer vacation was over and they started going to school again. And here's another thing, they started this simester on a Friday. They don't go to school on Thursday and Sunday and the hours are altogether different than ours. Everything is topsy turvy it seems, but still the kids goes to school. There are countless other strange customs but I won't attempt to put them all down now.

I sent my watch home today. I don't no yet whether it went airmail or otherwise but I'll let you no. I could have had it repaired over here, but I was afraid it might have been spoiled. That's a chance we take when it's fixed here. When I get it back, I'll be more careful with it.

Haven't received any mail yet today, to early in the day.

Hope your enjoying your vacation. It must feel pretty nice to stay in bed in the morning for a change. Wish you could do that all the time. Some day soon, I'll see that you do just that.

Solong for now, take care of you both
        Always Willie

No. 278 —   Mar. 7-'45

My dear Jacquite:

First I don't get any mail,— then bang, I'm swamped. I'm not kicking mind you, just telling you what it's like over here concerning the mail situation. To-day, I received three letters from you, one each from mother, Alice, Everett and Vern. After putting in quite a day's work, all this mail was sure welcome.

Glad to hear about Conrad getting a furlough. If you think he found a great change in his girl, think how I'm going to feel when I see that big girl of ours again. Gosh, I don't think I'll believe it. If Conrad is going back to the camp you mentioned, there's no doubt but he will be heading across soon.

About that trouble between André and his wife, mother has mentioned that to me already. And Everett also. So it's not much of a secret anymore.

-11-

And as for André's army life, I'm afraid he's going to find it a bit difficult compared to his old civilian life. That guy is in for a lot of surprises.

I've known about his trouble for a month now, but didn't like to mention it to you. I don't like to think, much less talk about such things. We could talk about that subject for days and still find no sensible solution. You see, we have a pretty nice partnership, you and I, and I don't want to think for a minute even, what a farce marriage can be made of. So let's not worry to much about those things, the farther away we stay from such things, the better I'll like it. Personally, this is the last I'll mention of this thing of André's. Don't you ever worry about this half face laite, your half is the only one I ever want.

I see your taking good care of my old cloths. You think of everything don't you. It will save feel good to get into them again. I wonder who's hoping the most, you or I, for me to get into them again. I'm pretty hard to beat.

I got a kick out of your saying how Elaine acted like a little lady, eating her ice cream. I bet she'd also. That was quite a walk for her, all the way back from Somersworth. I'll bet Roger couldn't do that. Quite a pair of gals I have there. I could use a little biting right now. I can imagine all the bruises in our family on the big day soon. Can't you picture yourself walking around all black and blue?

Had you finally found a pair of shoes.

The watch I mailed yesterday was sent air-mail. You should get it with this letter.

Still talking about those flowers huh? Wait until next time. So long for now, take care,

Devotedly Wilfré

No. 279   Mar. 8- '45

Hello Face Faite:

    Another day, another letter to the two girls back home, letting them no that I'm still thinking of them.

    Glad to hear that you spent a day with Al. Must be nice to talk to your old friends about old times again. She must have been happy to see you again. You should go visit more often. You'd have someone to fix your hair. I see that your still up to your same tricks, having her fix your hair.

    So you think Elaine is taking after me huh? I hope she's not to much like me. I don't want her to be an old maid. But that's not a bad vice she has, preferring the radio and a book. Don't you worry, when we get together again, we'll have a merry Oldsmobile and I'll take you both riding anytime you want to go. That's a promise.

I suppose Joe Gagnon is still happy go lucky as usual. Tell him to take a drink for me. Hope he doesn't get called.

It's unusually warm to-night. As I'm writing this, sweat is rolling right off from me. Maybe we're due for a tropical storm.

I bought a few cards of New Caledonia this week. I'll send them to you a few at a time.

Well I guess that's about all for now. Until to-morrow, solong and take care. Love Always

Wilbre.

P.S. Almost forgot, I'm 29 winters old to-day or had you noticed the date. No comment except that I firmly hope for a Berwick birthday on my next.

No. 280   Mar. 10 - '45

Hello Face & Faite:

    I didn't rite to you yesterday, because this morning I wasn't working and I thought maybe I'd have more to talk about. But I was wrong, I don't no any more now than I did last night.

    Well, the weather here is very warm now. It's almost as bad as Guadalcanal and believe me, that's hot. It won't be for long though, in another month or so it will be nice again. I don't suppose your complaining about the heat in Berwick, – or are you?

    You no, I never received an answer from Medee or Rene. They must be pretty busy or else they would have answered.

    Vern must be pretty busy in her new

-11-

work. She doesn't write as often as she used too. But then she's always full of business, when it's not one thing it's another. In her last letter, she said that you were going to spend three weeks with her this summer. Is that true? I can hardly believe it.

I don't believe I ever told you before, but the 30th of this month will be just one year ago that I sailed from Frisco. I can't recall all that has happened in this past year, but this much I do. I remember very distinctly that it was with a heavy heart that I last glimpsed the shores of California. I didn't no then what the future had in store for me. I still don't no, but the last year wasn't so bad. It could have been much worse, and it was for some fellows. I've been very lucky, and no one knows it better than I do. I hope next year I can say that this was only a bad dream, and wake up in Berwick. Solong, Love, Milore

No. 281   Mar. 11 - '45

Hello Race site!
        I received so much mail yesterday and to say that it will take me a week to answer them all. But I'm glad anyway, we never get to much mail you no.

        So you think that my last french letter shows some improvment? Wait till you read the one I wrote to Annette. I'd site to you in french more often but as you already no, it takes much more time for them to reach you. I no how much you like to get mail also, so I won't site to often in french.

        Glad to hear about our brand new niece who was born Feb. 25. I also received a card from somebody in So. Berwick telling me about it. I don't no who sent it. I'll site her a few lines in the next few days.

        Well you finally got a picture of me huh. I'm glad you liked them. But you did not mention

-11-

anything about the negatives. Remember, I asked to have a set finished for me? Hope you don't forget that cause I've been bragging about how you can have them finished in a hurry. Let me no. how you make out. I'll try to send you more pictures soon.

The way Elaine gets excited over my pictures you'd think she really knew me. Maybe she does and I don't. I'm sure if she were put in my presence, I could not recognize her. So if she really does recognize me by my pictures, I won't have any trouble with her.

So you noticed my ring too huh? Do you think I'd throw it away or hide it? You should be ashamed of yourself for doubting me. I don't want eny of those navy yard marriages that you talk about. Remember, you and I still have a date to fulfill. I wouldn't want to spoil that for all the chickens on this rock, I could tell you a lot about these chickens but it might not pass the censor.

I received a short note from Elmer Graves, telling me about the flowers you received. Wait until the next time you get some. I have another surprise for you on the next big aniversary.

Well I guess I'll close for now, time for me to go to bed. It's about 3 in the morning in Berwick, so I guess you must be in dreamland already. Solong until tomorrow, with love always,

Wilbur.

No. 282   Mar. 13-'45

Hello Honey;
 I have five letters to answer and I couldn't think of a better way to start in then yours first.
 First of all I want to put you straight on this furlough business. Don't hope to much about my coming home on a furlough in 18 months. I don't no where you got that story, but it isn't true. I no some fellows here who have been here for over two years. I don't want to discourage your hopes now, because it's nice to live in hopes such as yours. I do the same thing, but I'm not counting the months, and I won't guess as to when I'll be able to go home. In the army, especially in wartime, we can't make to many plans. We just have to wait and

-11-

hope and pray that the coming day will bring the end of war. Once that's over with, then we can anticipate a real home coming. But until then, lets not be too optimistic.

I hope you rested up on your week off. And I don't think it's laziness that caused you to be so tired after that week off. You must be really tired and I think you should stay at home all the time. Or at least more often than your doing now.

Don't feel to bad because you didn't send me a birthday gift. You did send me a card and that was plenty. It was enough to let me see that your always thinking about me. You've already done more than anyone else for me. All that you've given me in the past is more than I'll ever repay.

Solong for now, take care of you both.
Love Always Wilbur.

No. 253   Mar. 15 -'45

Hello 'ace Lute:

Received another letter from you to-day. In it you mention those last pictures I sent you but you still don't say anything about those which I asked you to finish for me. I hope you had them finished for me.

So you think I look like a big shot on that last picture huh? Well I'm not, but it's true that I'm not working very hard. I wouldn't be so damn fat if I were. When one is used to working with brawn and suddenly changes to a little brains, well something is bound to happen. I'm not kicking tho, I like this work better than any other I've ever done in the army so far.

I wrote a few lines to McKee's wife to-day. It was about time, I've been putting it off for the last few days. By the way, McKee is now at the same A.P.O. as Rene now. Alice told me about it in a letter I received from her to day. They might still meet over there yet.

I've written so many letters this week that I don't no what to rite anymore. Some fellows write one letter and then copy all the others. That's all right as long as nobody catches up with them. Personally, I couldn't do that. I'd rather not rite.

How's that big girl getting along lately? The other day, I met a little girl who was two and a half years old, and she could talk very good french. So now I no about how big Elaine is and if she can talk as good as this little girl, I no about how she acts like. But then, there's no if about it, she must be brighter than anyone her age, or else she would'nt be Elaine.

So long until to-morrow, Love Always Wilbre.

No. 284   March 16 1945.

Hello Face Laite;

Have not received any letters today but I guess I'll write you a few lines anyway.

Not having very much to do I thought of writting it this way. This is the first slack period I've had on this job since I've been here, and it seems odd to be this way. I almost feel guilty to take my money for doing this, but not completely though. When I get to feel that way there is usually something that turns up and I'm busy as hell all over again. That, my dear face laite is the army.

I caught a little cold somehow a few days ago, it's not very much, but enough to make me feel uncomfortable. I guess this tropical climate has thined the old blood stream and it does not take much of a draft to catch cold, especially me. But I think I'll live through it.

We've been having quite a lot of rain the past few days and the weather has cooled off somewhat. It was sure hot before the rains came though. Back in Berwick spring must be in the air again, and it must be nice to behold. Maybe next year I'll be there with you to take in all the beauty of a real coutry. I miss so many things (outside of you) that I'm quite sure to be contented with very little when I get back.

Well I guess this is about all for afellow with not much to say, until tomorrow solong and take good care of yourself and that big girl.

ALWAYS YOUR OWN

WILDRE'

No. 285   Mar. 17-'45

Hello Face Faite:

Received another letter from you to-day and also one each from René and mother. It was the first time I heard from René since he's changed address. It was very long and interesting too. I must try to answer him right away.

You mentioned on your letter that you had spent the same day you wrote at your mothers. I can't figure it out. You were supposed to be working on that day were'nt you? But that letter was dated the seventh and the previous one I received, the third. When I get the others maybe things will be more clear.

Elaine seems to have had a good time with Donald. Has she changed her ways or was that one of her lighter moments? We'll see how she reacts at that birthday party you were supposed to attend at Al's home.

And I'm anxious to hear about Lignon's wife. That's another bit of news that is

-11-

baffling, because letters come all mixed up.

Didn't feel so hot to-day, that damn cold sure lays a man down. Maybe it's because I haven't had one for so long. A whole year is a long time without a cold for me.

We're still having lots of rain, seems like fall rains we have back home. Shouldn't kick to much tho, we've had nice weather ever since I've been here.

Well, can't think of much more to write about, so I guess it's time to close. Oh yes, you didn't mention anything about finishing my pictures yet.

So long for now, be careful

Love Wilbré

No. 286   Mar. 19-'45

Hello Face Suite:

Haven't received a letter from you for three days now. I'm due for another batch, maybe tomorrow.

My cold is still hanging on but it's not to bad. Outside of that I'm feeling swell.

Tomorrow, I'm going to visit some of my old pals in the old outfit. It may be the last time I see them for a long time. The two addresses I sent you to keep for me are two of the best friends I had. After the war we will go to their home states for a visit. The one from Kansas lives not far from Larry Sullivan. And speaking of Larry I wonder what he's doing now. I never did hear from him. Anyway, we have a lot to see and do, you and I, after this is over with. We'll have to decide whether we want to take that big girl along, what do you think?

-11-

I wrote to Rene yesterday, the first time for quite a while. He seems to be on the move all the time and I guess there's a lot to be done.

It finally stopped raining this morning. We had enough to last a little while.

I can't find anything else to talk about, so I guess it's time to close. Maybe tomorrow I'll have more to say. Take care of yourself and that big girl. Solong for now,

Love Always Hilde

No. 287   Mar. 20-'45

Dear Face Suite:

Just received another letter from you today, and also one from Alice.

Glad to hear you got another week off. And don't worry about this summer, you can still take your vacation in Conn., even tho' you won't have any time coming.

Alice told me all about you and Elaine going to see her. She sure is crazy about Elaine. But who wouldn't be.

After telling me everything you do on Saturday nights, I can imagine just what your routine is. It must be very monotonous and lonely, but cheer up honey, one of these days, I'll see what I can do to change that routine. Our day can't be so very far away.

Well, they finally caught up with Bill huh. They've been pretty lucky so far and I don't think

-11-

think they should feel to worry. But personally I don't believe he'll pass the physical anyway. Martha Roy's husband has been lucky also. And for Lacasse, that guy's full of — up to his ears. He is not 33 years old. How can he be when not so long ago, just before I came into the army, he was only 23 years old. He hasn't aged ten years in a year and a half that's sure. He's just another fine example why a lot of fellows already in army are so bitter. Oh well, why think about it.

Saw the picture "Here Comes the Waves" last night, it was pretty good. You ought to see it.

That's all for now, take good care of you and you.

love Wilbur

No. 288   Mar. 21 - '45

Dear Face Laite:

Received two long letters from you to-day and one from Annette.

So sorry to hear you and Elaine couldn't go to the party. After all the preparation you made and then you had to cancel everything. I hope that rash Elaine has is not to bad. It could be something she ate or drink but don't wait to long to change doctor if LeBrun doesn't do her any good. It may be the same thing you had once. Remember how you were? no doubt you still have the same thing. They never could cure yours, but if Elaine also has the same, don't you spare any time and go see the best doctors there is, for both of you. It looks to me as if her rash is the same as yours cause you also never had any fever and you use to itch just like her. Keep

-11-

a close watch of her and be sure to let me no how it turns out.

It must have been nice at the party if the place was all decorated. It would have been nice to see how Elaine would have acted with all the kids. Cheer up honey, this war can't last forever. When we're home again it will be one continuous party and we'll enjoy it all the more.

I see you got my watch alright. It didn't take long to get there. When it's fixed once more, try to send it back air mail so I can get it much sooner. And don't worry, I wouldn't sell it for anything. I was only kidding you.

It must be nice to see your leading men working again. I can imagine how degrading it must be to them. Don't you worry about loseing your job. You need a long rest anyway to build up the lost energy. You'll need it when I get back. I gues thats all for now, will rite longer tomorrow.
Love Mildre.

No. 289   Mar. 22-'45

Dear Face Faite:

Received another letter from you today, the one you had written on Mar. 8 and had the pictures enclosed. Those are the best pictures of you both yet. Especially the one with you and Elaine with the flowers. You seem to have put on weight and Elaine is as plump as always. The two of Elaine in her grass skirt were very nice. She looks almost like a real south sea native, only much fatter of course. And I noticed the bed in the background. It looks familiar, haven't I seen that before? I guess so. All of the pictures were nice, now I'm ready for the next batch. You don't no what it does for morale to see those pictures. It makes one lonely and long for home all the more, but

-11-

they are sure nice to look at.

I hope Elaine's rash is much better. Be sure and let me no how that turns out.

Oh yes on one of your pictures you didn't have on your ring and you mentioned it on the back. What's the matter, got a guilty conscience? ha. ha. Don't worry, I'm trusting you. You'd better be good or <u>else</u>.

Are you kidding when you say that Elaine can sing better than you can? I can hardly believe that. If that's true she must be a genius or something. But don't worry about that, I'll kind of like you a little better even tho you can't sing. I could even love you if I tried. I think I'll try it when I get back. ha. ha.

-111-

I received a letter from Medee today the first one for a long time. I guess he doesn't like it very well over there, I don't think I would either. I answered right away.

You still haven't mentioned anything about those pictures I asked you to have finished. I sent them to you Feb. 19 and I should have them back now. You'd better get on the beam and send them back or else I won't be able to brag about your fast service anymore.

That's all for now, Solong and Take care of you both.
Love Always, Wilbur

No. 290 Mar. 23-'45

Hello Honey;

Well, I got two more letters from you today. I still have one of your old ones so I'll start with that one first.

First of all, I hope that Elaine is better. Gosh, if you take all her food away from her, how is she going to live. You can't just take all the best foods away from her, she'll get weak. I agree that to much sweets is bad for her, but don't take away such foods as potatoes. Just because they are cooked in that water doesn't mean that they do her harm. When the potatoes are boiled the water also is automaticaly boiled. If that rash is caused by something she eats, you won't no what it is unless you take away first one of her foods for a period of about one week. If one doesn't

—11—

do the trick, give her back that food which you held from her and try another. But don't take them all away at once. That's a good idea, about boiling the water. But I still think her rash might be the same as the one you had once. Don't forget, if Le Bien don't do any good, change doctor. And don't wait to long. I'll be anxious to hear how this turns out, so be sure to let me no.

That article in the Free Press about me is only a bit of army publicity, which was issued thru the personel section. That's the same thing I wrote you about before.

When you get this letter be sure to listen to that 'V-mail music' program on station W.H.E.B. I'm sending a request especially for you and Elaine. That song 'I'll get by' that Elaine knows so well, I don't seem to no.

- 111 -

I think I'll request it on our own local station and hear what it sounds like. Ever since I've left our domicile, I haven't paid much attention to music. All we have mostly are records anyhow. We have programs that are transcribed also but somehow they don't sound real to me.

Well I guess that's about all for tonight. Could rite some more but I'll save it for tommorrow. Solong and take care of yourself and that big girl.

Always Yours Wilbré

No. 291   Mar. 24-'45

Hello Honey:

Before I go any further, I hope you excuse the pencil. I left my pen at the office, so for a change I think I'll rite to you in pencil. I write better in pencil anyway, don't you think so?

Well, what do you no, I got another letter from you today and also one from Florida. I received my share of mail this week.

In reference too the something that you mention, that Vern sent me for my birthday, well I haven't received it yet. And I don't think she is smarter than you are. You did send me those pictures on my birthday and that was better than any other gift you could have sent. All I ask for is pictures, and as long as I

-11-

receive a few every now and then, I won't ask for anything more.

Well, I see you've been playing housemaid on your time off. And you seem to like it too. You probably had the same feeling doing that than I would have if I had a furlough right now. But you had better keep in good shape anyway, because I'll be getting back soon and I want the same cook and maid when I do. Gosh, I won't believe it when <u>the</u> day is here.

If Elaine misses Annette now, it will be hard when she leaves her for good. But she'll have me then too keep her busy and you too, because you'll be back to your old job and you'll be with her all the time. She seems too like the open air a lot, that big girl. When I get back, I'm going too take her hunting. I'll make a good tomboy out of her, and I'll bet she'll like it. Speaking of hunting, I'm being interrupted at this moment by one of the fellows who's trying to describe to me various bugs that's flying around in the tent, and I'm not the least bit interested. But I give a few nods and pretty soon he drops the subject because he notices that I'm not paying attention. I really haven't changed much you no, I still have some of my old traits.

Well, it seems that writing with a pencil does make me write more. I think I should use one more often, don't you? But it's late anyway, so until tomorrow I guess this will be all. Hope Elaine is better, be sure and let me no.

So long and take care,
Love Always, Hildré.

No. 292   Mar. 25 - '45

Dear Face Laite:
           It's still saturday in your part of the world, but over here it's seven oclock at night, and I just got back from mass. This may sound funny too you, but too me it's not. In the past year and a half I've been to mass at most any time of day or night. Over here I usually go at the 6 oclock mass because I have to work. And I also made my Easter duties tonight. I had to go without supper, but once won't kill me. I'd been putting it off for so long that tonight I made an extra effort and finally did go.

In one of your previous letters, you stated that saturday night was the loneyest one of the week for you. Mine is sunday. I don't no why, maybe it's going to church that makes me that way. It's when I'm at church that I think most of you. You used to have my prayer beads handy when I'd forget them, or if I did have them, you'd flash that smile of approval. When I didn't kneel right, you'd remind me. Or if my glance was ever sidetracked from the alter too some good looking chicken just coming down the aisle, you'd be there to pinch me, and I'd be sure to have a blue spot for the next three or four days. You see how well I remember you? Don't ever think that I'll ever forget you. I still want all of you, — even with your pinches. I hope you don't teach Elaine how to pinch or I'll be blue all the time.

Alice told me all about your trip over there. She still marvels at the way Elaine puts away so much food, and how pretty she is etc. I don't believe I quite no what we have in that girl. I'm sure anxious to see first hand just what she is.

—111—

Sorry to hear about Joe Gagnon's wife. Hope she gets well soon. Nice of you and Annette to help her.

Our radios finally went on the fum huh? They lasted quite a while. When we get together again we'll get a new one, so don't worry to much about that old one. That's only one of the several new things we'll get. I won't tell you all my plans now, it would take to long to site down.

I see your doing all right in boosting the bankroll. Don't harm yourself doing it, your health comes first.

Hope Elaine is better, be sure too let me no.

Well, I guess thats about enough for to-night,

Solong, take care,

   Always Yours Willie

No. 393   Mar. 27 - '45

Chere Dace Laite:

This is the second day without mail, but I shouldn't kick. I received so many letters from you in the past week that I'm still answering from that batch.

From your last letter, I got a great kick from reading about how Elaine was so crazy about corn on the cob. That's your fault because you always about the same thing. Remember? But that's not a bad fault. I only wish I could be there to see her. Although I'm not there to see her, I'm glad you are. Give her all she wants so that she grows up to be strong as well as beautiful. And if she becomes a singer, she'll have everything. With all these good traits, how can she miss. What a gal.

—11—

So – you finally got around to making apple pie again? Well it's best to keep in practice cause it won't be long before I get back. Even if you have maids and cooks in your postwar household, I reserve the right to call upon your services too make apple pie. If only I ever wrote all the plans and ideas I've had since leaving home, what a book that would make. I don't think I'll ever attempt that, I'll save it all for the future when I can tell you all about it.

Well I guess that's enough for now, solong and take care. Hope Elaine is better.

Love Willie

No. 394.　　　　Mar. 28 - '45.

Dear Face Laite:

Just received five letters from you, one each from Alice, Florida and Butch. You can imagine how glad I am. I won't promise to answer all of them tonight but I will in time.

First of all, I think I'd better tip you off about that postmaster of yours Mr. Hurd. Three of your five letters that I received were post marked the 16th. I figured that maybe you mail your letters in that outside box and he probably does not look in it but once a week. You ought to shape him up. No wonder I get my mail in bunches.

Glad to hear that you finally have some nice weather. Over here, our winter is coming on. But it's never cold tho. As a matter of

-11-

fact I'm sick of the same climate. Give me the four seasons of Maine anytime.

I see Elaine put in her two cents' worth in one of your letters. Boy what a gal she must be, yeh yeh and all.

It didn't take you long to have that watch fixed. I'll be glad to get it again, and this time I'll be more careful. It would have cost me about ten dollars over here. Too have it fixed I mean. Thanks face laite.

I see you had a flue monday on the week of the fifteenth. To top it off they had to put you on nights. Cheer up honey this can't last forever. Take good care of yourself if you have to walk home late at night.

Elaine seemed to have had a good time at your mother's. You should go out with her as often as you can. She would get used to a lot of those things that she's afraid of. Boy, am I anxious to see her. Everytime you talk about her in your letters I can almost picture what she looks like. But almost don't count. It's a good thing you sent me those pictures once in a while. I believe I told you that I had received those last pictures. They were all very nice. The fellows didn't believe that you were my wife. They said you looked like a schoolgirl. So you see, you can believe me if I should rite a few mushy words about you now and then. Elaine must take after somebody and I'm sure it can't be me.

We haven't had any hurricanes yet, but there is still time. Don't you worry about a little hurricane doing me any harm. If that's all I had to think about, I'd have a clear

-IV-

conscience all the time. For instance, if I were still with the old outfit I'd be much worse off than I could be here. At present, I don't no where they are or where they are going. But I no that I'm better off than they will ever be. Some of the fellows will rite me to let me no where they are.

I guess it's time to close for now. I still have some more of your letters, but I'm saving them for another day. I should rite to others but don't feel so hot to-night. So until tomorrow solong and take care. Let me no how Elaine is getting along with her rash.

With love to you and you

Wilbe

No. 295 Mar. 29-'45

Hello Dear Suite:

  Here I am again, trying to answer another one of your letters.

  I'm just reading the letter on which you were telling me about Joe Gagnon. He seems to be still having his ups and downs. But he can't be doing to bad if he can sell and buy that car the way he's been doing. You no, about that injection birth you talked about, I don't think much about it myself. Joe's wife is a good example of a doctor not knowing his business. It takes a specialist to administer something like that, and even then I wouldn't think much about it. You can tell Joe that when we get together again, we'll have another clambake and another quart of whiskey just for the two of us. So you didn't think we had had so much to drink that last time we had a

-11-

clambake? You learn more about people every day don't you? Even your own husband. And I never cheated on you either. You were with me at that clambake but you probably forgot to count the drinks I had.

How's that big girl and her "ah gee" getting along nowadays. You'd better watch her french or she'll be forgetting it before you no it. I hope her rash is better. Be sure and let me no how she is.

Sorry to hear you have to work nights again. Take care of yourself. Tell me if you have to walk home alone after work, so I can worry about you. I sure hate to have you walk home all alone.

Glad you got those pictures finished. I don't see how it cost you so much. If they cost 8 cents apiece for eight sets, they would cost $5.12, and not $6.72 as you said it cost you. But anyway the fellows will pay me

— 111 —

for them. The next time, I'll send the money in advance, with the pictures. But thanks anyway face laite.

Well, I guess thats all for now, solong and take care of you and you for me.

Love Always Mildre

No. 296   Mar. 30 - '45

Chere Face Laite:

Another aniversary is almost over for me. March 30 of last year saw me leave the coast of God's country for parts unknown. I've covered a lot of miles in this past year, most of them on water of course. I don't no what the next twelve months has in store for me, but I hope one of the things include a return trip to where I come from. Don't we all hope for the same? I've accomplished one thing in these past months if nothing else. 296 letters is nothing to sneeze at is it? Especially coming from a guy like me. I never thought for a minuite that I could ever manage to rite so many words. True, some of those letters were quite similar to each other, but I did rite them and I'm patting myself on the back for being so good. Now on the other

-11-

hand, I'll bet you wrote one every day. I never kept count but I'm sure you did. And your letters were and still are so full of news, that I'd much rather received one every day than have anything else. I'd gladly go without a meal anytime to get that letter, no fooling. Maybe I could have written more often, but gosh, sometimes when there are times when I don't get mail for days, it's almost impossible to rite every day. But I will try to do better in the future, and I firmly hope your letters come as regularly as they have been.

Well, today is "Good Friday" over here, there isn't much change except that all churches are holding services at all hours of this day. Hearing religious music over the radio only makes one more homesick.

Received two more letters from you today. One of those letters was addressed as follows.

-111-

Cpl. Rene Breton 31328096 - P.M. Section 209 M.P.Co.
I got it alright but my name sure isn't Rene Breton. I don't no what you were thinking about, but if you insist on writting my address wrong, the army will be giving me a furlough to go and shape you up. Now you don't want that to happen, do you? Maybe it's war nerves, But take it easy face Caite, your working to hard. I received two letters from Fern this week and they also were not addressed right. I don't no whats the matter, maybe it's a desease. You no, when a letter is not addressed right, it has to go thru a lot of hands and very often we don't get them. So get on the ball Mrs. Pelletier and address those letters correctly, or I'll be sending my love letters to Annette, — by mistake.

So long for now and take care —
Love Always Hildie.

A World War II Story: Dad's Letters Home

Mar, 31-45

Hello Yourselves:

Received your birthday card and letter a couple of days ago and thanks for remembering.

First of all, I'd like to get one thing straight. You no, I like you and I like to get your letters. Your very thoughtful, kind, considerate and a lot of other things I like about you. But,— for Jehovah's sake get my address right whenever you rite to me. The next time that you don't put down my right address, I'm going to blow my top. Now you wouldn't want me to go crazy would you? Think of the wife and kid, what would they do without me? (don't answer that) If that package you sent me has the same address

—11—

on it as these last few letters, I don't expect to get it for six months if at all. I don't no whats the matter with you civilians but lately I've been getting mail two and three months old, and only because of a wrong address. So get on the ball Mrs. and get that address down right.

Now that we've cleared that up, lets turn to more urgent thoughts. So they finally have Bill in 1A huh? I'd bet you a good bottle of scotch he doesn't pass. (Said scotch payable within first week after my discharge) Even if he did pass, I don't think it would be for long. Your right when you say that you won't be the worse off. Take Butch for instance. According too his letter I got yesterday, he also is 1A, and he has two kids,

But I'm sure there are some who are still worse that he is. A good thought to keep in in mind is that your never alone in misery, there's always someone worse off than you are.

Glad to hear that your still busy with your hairdressing. I hope you never have to use that trade in the manner you mentioned on your letter. I'd like to say more on that subject, but I guess time will take care of that.

Time to close, so until next time solong.

From the same old crab Wildor.

P.S. In case you overlooked the envelope, here it is again Cpl. Wildor Pelletier 31398096
P.M. Section, 209-M.P. Co. A.P.O. 502
% P.M. San Francisco

No. 297   April. 1 - '45

Hello honey:

    Easter Sunday to-day over here,— a memorable day, and yet, going thru the daily routine of existance as part of the army, the full meaning of this day cannot be recognized,— at least not by me. As for the spiritual part, I attended mass at the cathedral this morning and the ceremony was very nice and inspiring. The Bishop officiated at mass with several priests acting as assistants; the church was decorated and the choir was very good. It was a civilian mass of course, I thought of going because it had been so long since I had been to a civilian mass. Mass lasted one hour and a half. I wonder where I'll be when the next Easter comes around. On the last one, I was on the boat coming across, this one I was here, the next, — who knows?

-11-

Guess what, I received a letter from Mary this week. It had been months since I had written her and she finally decided to answer. But better late than never I guess. I got so many letters this past week, that I don't no where to begin answering.

Glad you like your night job. But take care of yourself walking home all alone.

I seem too have a lot to say, but just can't find the right words to put down. So I guess I'll close until tomorrow. Take good care of yourself, and hope Elaine is better.

                Love Always, Wilbr

No. 298   April 2-'45

Hello Honey:

Haven't got any letters for a couple of days, but I still have some of your old ones to answer yet.

Well, I see that you've been enjoying some good weather for a change. I'm glad to hear that. Over here, we can't say the same, cause the weather is always the same. Once in a while we have rain to break the monotony, and when it rains we have mud but never any snow. By the way, it's raining right now and I guess we have all the bugs in the South Pacific in our tent. They sure are thick.

So Conrad's A.P.O. is New York, well, at the rate it's going over there, it will be all over before he gets there.

Glad to hear you went bowling again. But you'd better get more practice if you want too

-11-

beat me. Anyway, you need the exercise. It does you good to have some fun once in a while. As for me, I'll wait till I get back so that I can catch up with you.

I'll be anxious to see those pictures you had finished for us. And I'm sure that Rickson's wife will answer your letter cause from what I gather from his letters from her, she's very nice.

Butch and Al sure are having tough luck. Maybe he can get a deferment if Al is going to the hospital. Hope they make out alright. Better take care of yourself face Caite, if anything happened to you, I'd be worrying all the time.

Say, at the rate she's going now, Elaine will be talking english before french. It's a good thing I'm not there cause she probably would learn something she shouldn't. And I could teach her to play football, she's big enough. Or maybe I could take her fishing and hunting. I'll bet she would like that. I'm sure anxious to get back and try that with her. Of course the boss would have to okay that program.

Yes, I no that Harry Snow that works with you. And I did work with him in So. Berwick. He's a pretty good old fellow. Give him my best regards.

Well, I guess I'll close for now, tomorrow is another day, and I don't want to run out of words tonight or I won't no what to site then.

Glad to hear it was only the water that was bothering Elaine. Take good care of her for me, and don't forget about yourself.

Always Wilbe

No. 299   April-3-'45

Hello Face Faite:

Didn't get any mail again today, but maybe will get some tommorow.

I have a day off today, and I'm spending it by writting to most everybody I guess. This is my fifth letter already. It's raining again, it has been for the past three days or more. It's not steady, one minute the sun is shining and the next it rains.

I bought another souvenir to put in my box today. I can't buy everything at one payday because everything cost so damn much. But the package will be ready to mail before our next aniversary. So don't be too anxious to get it. The next time you think about it, measure your wrist with a piece of string and send it in

—11—

one of your letters. I want to get you a nice bracelet for your watch. They are made of tortoise shell and are very nice. I'm also going to get one for myself. There are lots of things I want to get yet, but I won't tell you what they are.

Hope your making out alright on the night shift. Take care of yourself when you walk home alone after work. And watch out for that big girl too. Hope her rash is okay.

There isn't much more to say so I guess I'll close for now. Don't quite remember the date for "Mother's day", but am mailing a V-card anyway. Solong face laite.

Always Wildie

No. 300   April 4 -'45

Hello Honey:

Received three more letters from you today, the first in three days. But I guess I'm lucky at that, some fellows don't get any mails for weeks.

Well, I see Elaine is still afraid of a lot of things. The only cause I can figure out for that, is that she doesn't go out often enough. I don't blame you of course, because you have enough to do already. But I hope she gets over that soon. It's not normal to be afraid of everything like that. Take good care of her, cause we can't find any more like her.

Don't worry if my letters are slow getting to you from now on. More and more men are coming this way you no, and the fighting fronts are getting further away also. The fellows that are doing the fighting get priority on mail and it's only right that they should. So do I bitch about the mail being slow, but I should no better.

They are sure catching up with a lot of married men back there. Even Willie O. huh?

Nel must be glad to be changing camp for a change. He is much nearer home now. I don't think that he will ever go across. As I remember correctly, he can't hear so well. But then, you never can tell. There were fellows worse off than that and they came across with me. I don't wish that kind of luck on him tho.

Well, I guess I'll cut this short for now, so until tomorrow, solong face laite,

Love Always Wilbie,

No. 301   April- 5 -'45

Hello Dace Laite:

    This is the bad half again, wondering whether I can think of a few words to put down. It's funny how the mind works sometimes. On some days there's a million things I could rite about, and on others it's impossible almost to even think.

    I couldn't quite make out on your letter whether Fern got her package back again or lost it. At any rate I hope she didn't loose it. From what I gather, there was six dollars worth of goods in it.

    It's been quite warm today. After a lot of rain we had to cool off the last warm spell, I thought that the warm season was over with. I sure could use a little cold weather. They can give this tropical climate back to the natives, as far as I'm concerned. I'd sure like to smell some Maine

-11-

pine once more. But I guess I'll have to wait a little longer.

How's yeh yeh getting along these days? Is her rash alright now? Be sure to let me no if you heard your request and hers also over the Portsmouth station. I asked for her favorite song you no, "I'll get by".

As for me, there isn't much change. Always in good health and always at the same job. Oh yes, I often think of our farm, in fact I even dream about it. I wake up at night all in a sweat, dreaming that I'm working on the farm. I just can't wait to get home, I'm building already, even tho it's only a dream.

Solong honey, until tomorrow,
                    Yours Always. Wilbur

No. 302 April 7-'45

Chere Face Laite:

Received a letter from you today, the first in the last three days.

Sorry to hear about Elaine being scared of everything and that you put her to bed for being that way. I think your mean, because it isn't her fault if she's afraid. As I said before, it must be because she doesn't go out often enough. You won't cure her by putting her to bed or spanking her, it's by going out with her as often as possible and using a little patience that will do the trick. At least that's what I think. Why don't you try my way and see if it works. But whatever you do, I'm all against punishing her for something she can't help.

Well, that first hot dog roast you had

—11—

must have ~~eaten~~ tasted pretty good. There are many times when I think of the roasts we use to have, especially lately. Gosh, I don't think I'll ever stop eating when I get back. You'll have to stop me just like you do Elaine now. I'm warning you in advance so that you'll no all about me when I get home.

Butch told me about being in 1A. He said he'l let me no how he made out one way or the other. I hope he makes out all right. You see, we're not to bad off when it comes to comparing positions. We could be in that same predicament or even worse. I guess we could be a lot worse off.

And about all those places we're going to visit, we will take that big girl with us.

-111-

I was only kidding when I said we'd leave her behind. There will be no parting, not any more. We'll have a whole lifetime to make up for what we lost time, and we sure are going to make up.

Well honey, I guess that will be all for to-night. Until tomorrow, solong and take care of you both.

Love Always Wilbie

No. 303   April-8-'45

Hello Honey:

This is another one of those nights when I can't think of anything. Can't think of anything but home, but I can't put all my thoughts of home on paper, it would take to long and besides I don't feel like writing a book.

Seeing that there's not enough gossip to ~~talking~~ talk about, I just thought of ~~something~~ that I did over a year ago. I was wondering if you ever opened those two letters I wrote to you ~~and~~ Elaine shortly after I got back ~~from~~ camp from my furlough. Remember, I said or rather asked you not to open them until Elaine was eighteen? I often wonder if you ever opened those letters. You said you wouldn't, and I trust you, but

-11-

I can't help but think that you might be curious. The next time you rite, tell me if you still have them. But don't you dare open them. A promise is a promise. When I get back I might change my mind and let you read them,—but just maybe.

I hope your getting along okay on the night shift. Take care of yourself face laite. Be sure and let me no how that big girl is, and also how she's getting along in her slang english.

Well, I guess I'll close for now. Hope I get mail tomorrow. Solong honey

Always Love Wilbr

No. 304   April-9-'45

Hello Honey:

    Received three letters from you today and also a card from André.

    In reference to that clipping about the pretty girls at A.P.O. 755 or 502 that you had enclosed, here's what I have to say. I must admit that there are some very pretty girls here, now mind you I said some, but U.S. servicemen have been here long enough to have goffled them all up. It's very seldom that you'll find a nice girl who will have anything to do with the average dogface. They stay at home neath their mother's skirt. There's another type of girl that most anybody can make most any time. For that type, a fellow has to be drunk or quite hard up in order to get near enough to even smell their breath. But that's only minor, if he goes so far as touch that type of flesh, he'll most likely wind up in my department. He goes to a hospital and so does she,— if we can catch her. All in all, if one wishes to stay healthy, he won't monkey with that type of feminine charm. I'm no saintly body and never did claim to be perfect, but anytime such a reckless thought as explained above enters my mind, I only have to recall the poor unfortunates that passed before me,— then I don't pass, I detour.

Glad to hear that Ned had another furlough. He's sure been lucky so far.

So Elaine is getting used to the farm after all huh? If you go there often enough she's sure to like it more and more. But don't you scold or punish her for being afraid, or I'll spank you. How would you like that?

-111-

The next time that I send films home to be developed, I'll send them to Fern, and I'll enclose the money too. If I sent enough to be developed, and have you pay for them, your bankroll would go down fast.

I wonder how those fried clams tasted, the ones you spoke of in your letter. You should go more often and have an extra order for me. That's only one of the little things I miss.

Well, I guess thats all for now,
Solong for now,
Love Always Wilbur

No. 305   April.10-45

Dear Face Faite:

    I didn't get any mail today, but I still have one of your letters from yesterday to answer. So I won't have to wrack the brain too much in search for words.

    I'm sure glad to hear that Elaine hasn't got a permanent rash. For a while, I thought sure it was the same as you had once. I'll bet you won't give her any more of that juice.

    Don't worry about that layoff you were talking about. Even if they did lay you off, you have plenty of money to hold you and Elaine until I get back. But if you insist on working, I'm sure you won't find it very hard to get another job. And before you do that, I hope at least that you will take a long vacation, and I don't mean two weeks only. As long as there's money in your pocket don't be afraid to spend it. It's okay

— 11 —

to pinch a penny, but when it comes to living, that comes first.

Glad to hear your getting along nicely in your new job. And the weather seems to be on your side for a change also. It's almost as warm as it is here.

Rickson tells me that his wife has received the pictures that you sent. We should be getting ours soon, and also my watch. I miss it very much.

I'm taking a sunbath while writing this. It's my day off. I don't have the chance to get a tan like I use too. So on my day off, I just sit around or lay around in the sun and usually get cooked red.

Well I guess I'll sign off once more. So long until tomorrow, With Love Wilbur

No. 306   April, 12-'45

Hello Face Suite:

Haven't received any mail for three days now. I didn't rite to you yesterday because I just didn't no what to write. I don't do that very often, but when there's nothing to talk about it's pretty hard to put down on paper. You wouldn't want to receive a couple of sheets of blank paper in an airmail envelope would you?

The last letter I received was from Alice. In it she mentioned about going over to see you on Easter sunday. She keeps telling me how pretty Elaine is, and her kids are all crazy about her. I don't think I realize what we have in that big girl. She must be just about tops. It's about time I should be getting more pictures of you two. You no the

-11-

last pictures that you sent me of Elaine in her grass skirt, that was the best of her so far. She looked just like a glamour girl, with her long hair. And yours, well, you never change. Your always the same to me, only a little better every time I get new pictures. You seem to have put on a little weight, and it makes you look just like a schoolgirl. But don't stop gaining, by the time you get to weigh 300 maybe I'll have to start courting you all over again. There's no danger of that tho, going as high as 300 I mean, I know you well enough by now to no that you'll never weigh that much.

Well, I guess that's all for now, until tomorrow, solong and take care,
   Love, Wilbur

No. 307   April 13 - '45

Hello Honey:

    Another day without mail but there was plenty of news over here, and back home as well I guess.

    We got the news of the presidents' death this morning and that's all we've been hearing about all day over the radio. I guess that bit of news came as a shock to most everybody. I was surprised for sure. All the flags were at half mast, not only American but also the French and English. It only leaves us to wonder just what happens next. Time will tell, no doubt.

    Well, I've got another supper date for tomorrow. I'm going to the same home I was at before. I told you about it a while back, remember?

-11-

It must have been two months ago that I was there. I'm anxious to see if the baby has changed much. She looks so much like Elaine, and she is about the same age as she was when I left. The baby is not so tall as Elaine but otherwise I think she looks just like her. She was eight months old the last time I saw her, the same age as Elaine was when I left. In two months she must have grown quite a bit. At any rate, I'll tell you all about it on my next letter.

I met a fellow today, that used to be in my old outfit. When we landed on the Canal he was transferred to another outfit and I hadn't seen him since then, almost a year. I found out that he was on this island just accidently and I looked him up. He was sure glad to see me and I also. He was a buddy of mine ever since I went to North Carolina. You no, before I left him on the Canal, I loaned him $15, and after I had left we wrote to each other. But he lost my address soon after and never wrote to me anymore. On my last letter to him, I had told him to forget the money he owed me, that after the war, we would go see him. He lives in Colorado. Well, today, he wanted to pay me back that money but I refused. I reminded him that I was still going to see him after the war and he would spend more than $15 to keep us for a week. So the deal still goes, we will go there for sure. But that's only one stop. There are many others, for instance, take

—14—

Marstella from Kansas, and Ciotti from Pennsylvania, those are more places we will go to. So you see, I have a lot of plans in the making. I hope we can carry them thru.

Well, here I am gaffing like an old maid tonight. I get these moods once in a while, but they are not bad moods for I manage to rite a little longer letter. I'm sure you don't mind.

Solong until tomorrow, from the old man always, love Hildré,

No. 308   April-15-'45

My Dear Face Faite:

    I finally received a letter from you today and also one from Annette. It had been about four days since I received any mail. As time goes on, there will be longer periods without mail I'm afraid. I think I've already explained the whole situation to you.

    Well, I had a very nice supper last night, at the same place I told you about before. We had roast beef, french fries, fresh cucumbers and asparagus, soup and dessert, and a few other things I can't remember now. I took the baby again and boy has she grown. She's not so tall as Elaine but she's fat, just like a little ball. She even walks now, and she's only ten months old. She still looks a lot like Elaine, but her features are changing. All in all, I had a nice time and I'm more lonely than ever as a result

—11—

of such a nice evening. I'll never be satisfied till the real thing comes along.

On your letter today, you mention that you went on the farm again. I'm glad to hear that because it's good for you to go out more often.

I see your getting acquainted quite well with your fellow workers since you've been on the night shift. I'll be getting jealous if that keeps up. So you'd better mend your ways.— Of coarse I'm just kidding you. I no that you wouldn't do anything that I wouldn't do. You'd better be good or _else_, its my turn to say that there will be a divorce,— see.

Well I guess that's about all for now, until tomorrow. Solong and take care of you both.

Love Always Wilde

NO. 309   April 16, 1945.

Chere Face Laite:

    Much too my surprise today I received four letters from you and one from Camille. As a result I hardly no where to begin answering.
    First of all, you seemed to have gotten a cold almost at the same time as I did, even though I was not anywhere near you. Could be that I relayed mine to you by remote control huh? Or is that possible. Even if it were possible Elaine would'nt have suffered from the same effects. At any rate I hope your both feeling better.
    In reference to that article I supposedly mentioned to you to look up in the LOOK magazine, about life on this island, I remember telling you about that quite some time ago. But I think I failed to mention just you should look up that article. If you noticed closely that article was about an officers' club and not enlisted men. But even so, there was nothing mentioned about Wacs stationed on this island, because there are'nt any over here. The article you saw must have been about New Guinea perhaps. At any rate don't you go getting ideas about me. I can hold up my end of the firm, we incorperated on August 31, 1940. In other words, when the day comes that I'll be unfaithful to my four foot two brunette from Berwick, I'll be sure to let her know the first one. I've never been that hard up yet and I don't intend to be .
    Glad you liked those cards I sent you. Don't let the nice pictures on those cards fool you. There's not a place in the South Pacific as pretty as those cards make out to be. They are used mostly to attract tourists. I'll admit there are places on this rock that are nice to see, but as a whole it's nothing to brag about. Some day when I have nothing more important to write about I'll give you a brief description of this place, and you will no doubt change your mind.
    I have not received my watch yet nor the pictures either. I should be getting them soon.
    By the end of this month I will have my box ready to send to you. I'm not telling you just yet what it will contain but I'm sure you will be quite surprised. It has taken me long enough to get this together, it should be good.
    I sent a typewritten letter to mother last week, the first I had ever written that way. I'll bet she will be surprised. It is't very often that I have the time to write one like this. I have the the time today so here is yours. I hope you can make sense out of it.
    Solong for now and take care of that cold.

                LOVE ALWAYS
                    WILDRE'
                    Wildré

P.S. Just thought I'd add a few words to make this look real. Somehow or other a letter written by typewriter does'nt appeal to me.

No. 310   April-17-45

Hello Honey!

    Was glad to hear that Fern and Bill came down to see you again. I don't suppose that she's changed very much. She seems to be always busy with her hair-dressing course. Look at all the money I'll save by having her fix your hair.

    So Elaine doesn't like crowds huh? I wonder who she takes after? And she even takes care of you when you go out. What a girl she must be. I only hope she stays that way. And when it comes to liking her home sweet home, I heartily agree with her, and so do you, so how can she be any different.

    So you think Fern has some nice cloths? Just wait till I get back, you'll

—11—

have some much better. You no how I took care of you before huh, well thats nothing compared to what's in store for you. I keep telling you now, that you should spend more on yourself but you always have some excuse to give me. I'll fix that when I get back, and that's a promise.

As for mailing your letters in Somersworth. I don't think it will make any difference. So don't go out of your way just to mail a letter. The mail situation will get worse as time goes on, and there's nothing we can do about it. And nobody can force you to write & mail either, not at present anyway.

Walking back home in that rain didn't help your cold I'll bet. Be sure to take care of yourself face laite. They won't make any more Bretons like you, and I'd hate to start looking for another one like you. As a matter of fact I don't think I'd even try. You gave me the run around for three long years, remember? That was a long time for a man with my patience. It was worth every minute of it tho, and now I want to hang on too every last hair of you.

That's the best thought with which I can close this letter now. Solong and keep well always

Love Wildee.

No. 311   April-18-'45

Dearest Face Laite:

After I got through writing to you yesterday, I received another letter from you. It took only five days to get here. I always look at the date on the envelope and I was very much surprised when I saw it took only five days. That's a record for me so far.

I see your still boosting that bankroll. What are you going to do with all your money? You could certainly have a good time if you wanted too. But I guess there's no danger. We'll make up for lost time tho, when I get back, don't forget that for a minute.

Well you finally got a new permenent huh? You see, no matter what I tell you, you won't do it. So you do need a man to make

-11-

you do those things. ha. ha.

I see that you and Annette have started your spring cleaning. I always did hate to see the furniture scattered about when it came time for your spring cleaning. But I'd sure like it at this moment, or any other time from now on. After the cleaning was over with, it was always nice to see everything take new life again. It was almost like starting housekeeping all over again. Ho, hum, that was the life, — and will be again soon I hope.

I just got back from a movie a few minutes ago. I sat thru it all in the rain, not alone of course, there were many others. Even tho I could find other means or source of entertainment, I find this is still the best that I want over here. In your last letter you mentioned about being very lonely. Even tho I'm not in your shoes, I'm still the other half and I also am very lonely. I'm not trying to belittle you, far from it. I may not tell you in my letters how much I miss you or love you very often. But it's not because I don't think about it, it's simply because I just don't no how to say it. You no I was never much of a smooth talker, in fact I never talked very much. I haven't changed any you no, not much anyway. Thoughts of home are always uppermost in my mind. There's hardly a minute that goes by that I don't think of home. And when I speak of home, I mean you and Elaine and all the other things that goes with it. So keep that chin up face lite, if we both hold on tight enough there's nothing on earth that will make us let go. I'll always

—IV—

hold on to my end of that partnership and I'm sure you will also. Don't let a little thing like a couple of years apart change your mind. Look at all the other years we have ahead of us. Is it a bargain? Thanks face laite, I knew you'd understand.

Well, I seem to be preaching again. I don't mean to you no. But I mean what I said, all of it. There's lot more to be said but as I said before, just can't express myself on a letter especially. Hope I sound reassuring enough. If not I'll have to see the general for a furlough I guess. Now you wouldn't want me to do that would you?

Solong until tomorrow face laite,
Devotedly Wilbe

No. 312   April, 19-'45

Hello Honey:

    Didn't get any letters from you for two days but I still have one of your old ones to answer.

    I quite agree with you that that big girl is nobody's fool. So she can count up to ten all by herself huh? On most every letter, you have something new to tell me about her. She'll be out-smarting us before we no it at this rate.

    Glad to hear you had another day off. The more you have off the better I like it.

    According to Conrads' new address, it won't be long before he'll be meeting up with a few Germans. Hope he makes out alright.

    I'm anxious to see those pictures of you and Elaine in your new skirts. I'll never turn down pictures you no. I realized that it's hard

-11-

for you to get films, but whenever you have pictures don't be bashful to send them. When I have to many to carry around I'll send them back to you.

I received a letter from Medee and Kene to-day. Medee is still on the same place and I guess he's pretty busy. Kene sent me four pictures of himself taken with some girls. He seemed to be quite happy and he has grown too. He said that he might move again before long. He sure has seen a lot of territory in his young life.

I guess that's all for now, so until tomorrow solong and take care.

Love Always Wilbré

No. 313   April 21-'45

Hello Pace Faite:

    Received eight letters from the folks yesterday. Four were from you, one each from Annette, Fern, Alice and Florida. The worse part of it is, that I have to answer them now. I'm sure tired writting, but if I want to receive mail I'd better answer.

    So Elaine likes to go walking huh? I can just picture her walking through the snow with those short legs. She should walk more often, so that she would have strong legs. I hope her cold is alright, and yours too.

    Yes I know Rose Norman that works with you. And She's just everything you say she is. Stay away from that, it's no good.

Well, people nowadays say that anything can happen and I guess that's quite true. So it's not surprising if Marie finally got what she wanted for so long. She must have been disappointed tho, to find herself in that condition after adopting a baby. Too bad she had to loose it. Maybe next time it will turn out different.

So you have your mail delivered to you in bed now huh? That's what I call service. I'm glad your getting along okay with the Roys. You must be, to be getting that kind of service. But you'll get even better service when I get back.

Too bad you won't be home to listen to your

-111-

request, but Elaine will be there to listen to hers anyway. The next time I send one, I'll make sure you'll be home to hear it.

Haven't received my watch yet, nor those pictures you had finished for me. Should be getting both any day now.

I'm always in good health but the days are getting longer all the time. There's not much change otherwise.

Guess I'll sign off for now. Solong until tomorrow, and take care.

Love Always Wildre.

No. 314   April 22-'45.

Hello Face Lite:

    Was glad to hear you've finally received some mail. You don't sound so good when your not getting mail. You've been used to getting your mail more regular than I, and that's the reason I don't mind it so much. Don't loose faith in me, cause I'll always write as I have done in the past.

    Glad to hear your cold is better, take care of yourself and that big girl.

    I like the way you tell me all the gossip that goes on around town. It's not gossip really, it's more like getting a first hand account of what goes on about town. In case I've never told you before, your letters are number one on my list. Not only because your my number one girl, but also because your letters are

-11-

really the best. You seem to tell me all about the news about ~~twice~~ the first one. In other words you scoop all the other people and your also more thorough in description of same. I'm not telling you this to flatter you but I'm really serious.

By the time you get this letter, there may be a slight change in my address. Instead of 209 Co. it will be 208 Co. I'm not leaving the island, just changing company. So I guess it's safe to say that from now on, mail my letters to 208 M.P. Co. Don't forget now, 208 M.P. Co.

I guess that's all for now, solong and take care of you both.

Love Always Wilbur

No. 315   April 26-'45

Dear Face Faite:

If you haven't received many letters for the past few days, I hope you haven't worried too much. This is my first letter in four days. There's been quite a lot of change the past few days, and thru no fault of my own, my correspondence had to cease during that time. However, I'm still at the same A.P.O. number, but for the time being you'll have to address my mail to the address I have on the last page. Of course, I can't tell you what this change is all about, the mail is still censored you no.

My mail will be all screwed up for the next month or so, and as a result I don't expect to receive many letters until everything is straightened out again. But in the meantime I'll still be writting to you as usual.

Well, I received a whole batch of letters from you this week even tho I didn't write any. I also received a letter from most every-

- 11 -

body else I guess. I won't attempt to answer those until I'm more settled this. At present, I'm living like a field soldier and trying to keep clean enough to work at the office. I don't mind doing one of those things at a time, but the two together is a full time job.

In one of your letters, you had enclosed those two pieces of string that you had measured your wrist with. I'm glad I got it because now I can get that bracelet for your watch. Just wait until you see it. As for buying something for me, I wish you wouldn't. You'd doing more for me now than I deserve. All I want of you is what I left behind; and that big girl too of course.

Speaking of Elaine, I see she was not quite so scared the last time you took her on the farm. You just keep on going out more often with her and she'll be alright. Let that be

-111-

a lesson to you. The idea of putting her to bed and scolding her just because she was afraid. Just wait until I get back, you won't get away with something like that. —— I'll spoil her for sure.

So you laugh at the way I express myself huh? And just because I mentioned the office. Well, I'm not a big shot by a long shot. I guess it's just a habit I've got, mentioning "the office". And if you like my writing in pencil, I'll do it more often, but it's not dignified or polite.

I hope you and Elaine alright. Take good care of you both. So long for now.

Love Always Wilbré

My address
name
Provost Marshal Section
Hq. Co. Island Command A.P.O. 502
℅ P.M. San Francisco

No. 316   April 27 - '45

Hello Pace Suite:

    This is your bad half again trying to answer some of those letters I received this week.

    Glad to hear you received the "Mother's Day" card. It wasn't much of anything but better than nothing at all. Just goes to show you that I haven't forgotten those special dates. Last year I believe I sent you a card from Guadalcanal. Maybe next year I'll be home to give you one personally.

    Elaine seems to be learning the english grammer faster than I am french. I hope she doesn't grow to fast, I'd sure like to see her as she is now. I'm missing out on a lot, but at least your there to see it all. And your doing a good job of reporting to me her every actions.

    I had not heard about that big fire in

-11-

So. Berwick. I don't seem to remember Theresa Dagan, but I'm sure I no her. Its been quite a while since I've lived in So. Berwick, and the kids that I knew than are married to-day. Anyway, that must have been quite a shock to her, loosing the baby.

Was glad to hear your cold was better. Take good care of yourself, especially walking home at night after work.

It seems that I have a lot to write about but am just not in the mood tonight, or maybe it's something else. So I guess I'll sign off until tomorrow. So long face laite

Love Always Wilde

P.S. Am enclosing a malaria control calendar for May. How do you like it?

No. 317   April 28 – '45

Hello Dear Faite:

Received two more letters from you today. I sure received a lot of them this past week.

I'm glad to hear that your spring cleaning over with. I was all in just reading about it. It probably didn't help you any tho.

You mentioned that there would be a big change in another week or two at the shop. Don't worry over that job because I still say you don't have to work if you don't want to. But if you insist you won't have much trouble getting another job. I do wish tho, that you would take a long vacation before getting another job. No need hurting yourself just for a little extra money.

I realize that working and taking care of that big girl is quite a job, and you haven't got much leisure time. When I told you that Elaine should go out more often, I didn't mean that you should devote your all spare time just to take her out. But you yourself keep telling me that you seldom go out, and I figure

— 11 —

that that was the reason why Elaine was afraid of most everything. Then when you do go out with her she can't help of being afraid. In a way its a good thing she is afraid. If she were like you when I first met you, I'd be worried all the time. Remember when I used to tell you to be careful all the time? Oh well, we'll make up for a lot of things when we get back too normal again.

As for that bet that Medee made with me, I guess you no what it is. I'd explain it to you more in detail but there's still a censor who reads my mail. Anything that's personal, I'd rather keep to myself for now. Its alright for you to write about anything because nobody reads your mail but me.

I guess that's all for now, solong until tomorrow and take care.

Love Always Wilfred

A World War II Story: Dad's Letters Home

No. 318   April-30-45

Hello Face Laite:

I didn't receive any letters today but did get something just as good. — I finally got my watch and the pictures you had finished for me. The watch runs swell, it doesn't loose a minute. But I'm afraid to wind it now for fear of breaking the spring again. I'll be careful from now on. The pictures were all swell except mine. I look like an overgrown hog just fat enough for killing. I'll send it to Rene anyway along with the others. I've promised him some for a long time. Thanks face laite for everything. That's something else to pay you back for.

If Elaine likes to sing so much, I guess I'll have to teach you how so that you'll be able to sing when she says 'chante maman'. Just wait until I get there, she'll get all the singing she wants.

- 11 -

I haven't written to anybody but you for about a week now. People must be wondering what's the trouble. I'm still not settled yet, and until I am, I don't believe I will write to them. Everything is all mixed up, my cloths I mean, and different surroundings, living on the ground. At any rate I hope it's not for long.

I received the chronicle and free press today, and I saw for the second time that article they had written about me. I also read where George Nadeau was home from the South Pacific.

Guess I'd make this short for now, somehow or other, I can't get in the mood to write a long letter.

So long for now and take care.

Love Always Wilbre

No 319   May-1-'45

Dear Jace Laite:

I finally got settled down today, don't no how long it's going to last tho. From where I am now, overlooks the ocean and if I could close my eyes to some of the things, there is a nice view to be seen. I'm further away from my work than I was before, but we're all alone here and it's pretty quiet. The view is a lot like Ogunquit or York Beach. The weather also is about the same, — always windy and it's cool even tho the sun is shining. It's to bad there aren't any clams over here or I'd go and dig some up. But I can't have everything can I?

Was sorry to hear that Marie had to go to the hospital. I guess there's not

-11-

much hope of her having any babies of her own. I must write to her soon. I've been meaning too but just didn't have enough time. As a matter of fact, I owe a letter to most everybody now.

Joe Gagnon and his wife are sure having a lot of tough luck. Even tho he hasn't been called yet, he hasn't been any luckier. I guess we are quite well off and don't appreciate the full value of what we have. As much as I hate the army, I'd rather stay in it an extra ten years than have you in the same condition as Joe's wife. So you'd better take good care of yourself and that big girl. I don't want anything to happen to you two.

I won't give you hell if you address my letters wrong once in awhile, but if you

-111-

do it all the time like Fern did for awhile, I'll sure tell you a few things. But I don't think I'll scare you very much tho, you don't scare that easy.

One of the fellows took my picture yesterday, and when I get it I'll send it to you. I have some more to be finished, but this time I'll send them to Fern so it won't cost so much.

I guess it's time to close for now, I want to site to some of the others. Until tomorrow solong,

Love Always, Willie

A World War II Story: Dad's Letters Home

No. 320 May-4-'45

Hello Face Faite:

Haven't received any mail for the past three or four days now, and words are beginning to fail me again. I didn't write to you yesterday on that account. The longer I stay away the worse it will get I'm afraid. I think that from now on I'll write to you every two days. Then maybe I'll be able to think of more to put down. As it is now, very often I skip a day because I just don't no what to write about. Or else I'll rite a V-mail one day and an air mail the next. Don't give me hell now, because I'll try to do the best I can. I no you like to receive mail honey, but gosh when there's nothing to write about I can't just send you blank paper in an air mail envelope can I?

Well, there are a lot of changes taking place on this part of the world. You may have read about them in the newspapers. Of course there are

- 11 -

some things that they don't print and neither can I tell you. If I could, I wouldn't worry about being able to site a daily letter to you. Nowadays one's address is subject to change from day to day over here, now that the Germains are folding up. The Japs are'nt licked yet, not by a long shot. But it shouldn't be long now tho.

Well, I wonder how that Yankee (Elaine) is getting along in her english learning? Is she still picking up new words? And by the way, I should be getting some new pictures soon, huh?

Hope your not working to hard face laite. Take care of yourself and that big girl.

Guess I'll sign off for now, solong

With Love Always
Hildre.

May - 4 - '45

Greetings To My Inlaws:

It's been a hell of a long time since I've written to you, but I hope you don't mind to much. You no very well that I've always been faithful in writting to you whenever it was possible. The reason for such a long delay this time was that I've been moving around again. I'm still on the same island but changed location. Don't ask me why because by now you should no that I can't divulge any such valuable information. Please notice my new address on the envelope and take for granted that that's where I live, — for the present at least. Some day I'll have a lot of little secrets to tell you about. You no, when I or rather we go down Walnut Beach way and sponge on your hospitality, (including your best liquor and food.) In the meantime tho, I'll have to be content to just dream about it.

And now to get down to business and answer your last letter. First of all, in case you don't no, I'm a forgiving person you no so you don't have to apologize for not having much time to write to me. What with your hairdressing classes, housekeeping and last but not least, having such a thing as a ~~husband~~ hanging onto your neck in your spare moments, I don't doubt for a minute that all your time is quite occupied. So you see, I understand perfectly. But I don't blame you, on the contrary, keep right on as you are. I'd do the same thing if I were in your shoes. Have your good time while you can.

Jean told me about you going home over Easter. What do you think of that big girl now huh? I'm afraid to brag about her to you because you might think I'm ruffing it in. I'm not really you no, but I can't help mentioning her

-111-

I guess. Do you flame me?

So 4F Hervey and his Annette are looking like bigshots huh? Well, I'm not envying them any. He's still on my shitlist as far as I'm concerned. I don't want to have anything to do with him.

Sorry to hear that Bill is 1A, but then those milk legs should keep him near you. I wouldn't worry to much if I were you. You get gray hair young if you worry to much.

Too bad you lost all that money from the package you sent me. Thanks anyway for having such good intentions. (I didn't no you cared) When I can gather up something nice for you I'll send it to you.

Time to sign off for now, so until next time solong and don't work too hard.

As Ever Willie

P.S. don't forget my new address.

No. 321   May-5-'45

Hello Pace Laite:

    Still haven't received any mail yet. I guess I won't for a while either. Until the mail from my new address starts coming mail will be pretty scarce. Time sure drags by when I don't receive mail.

    From the news we heard over the radio this morning, it won't be long now before everything is over with in Europe. Maybe by the time you get this letter. That end will come as a great relief to everyone, but I hope they don't forget that on this end there's still a war to be won.

    I've received four letters from Florida since I last wrote to her. She must be wondering whats the trouble. And it's been a long time also since I last wrote to Butch. I must write

—11—

to them soon.

    I've had my watch for a week now and I haven't broken the spring yet. It keeps very good time and I'm sure glad to have it. now about and army ring

    I thought that I'd be able to fill my package on this payday, but I guess I can't. But I'll send what I have anyway and later on I'll send the rest. There will be two or three nice articles in this one that you will be able to wear. Just wait till you see them. I can just picture how curious you are. ha. ha.

    I guess that's all for now, so solong for caite and take care of you both.

                Love Always
                   Wilde

A World War II Story: Dad's Letters Home

No. 322   May-6-'45

Dear Pace Laite!

I was just wondering what you could be doing on this sunday morning, and I thought this was a good time to write to you. It's not sunday really for you, it's still saturday but you will be getting up in a few hours, then probably go to church at ten, then I hope, you'll enjoy a nice sunny May sunday with that big girl tagging along. Beside doing that I can't say what else is on your program, because I've been away too long now, you may have changed routine since I left.

As for me, I'll go to work this noon and tonight, go to church at 6. Nothing new, always in the same rut day after day. From where I'm sitting, while writting this, there's a beautiful view looking out over the ocean. The water is so blue you can almost think that some

-11-

blueing was put in it. Beyond a little way, there are two little islands sticking out of the water. They make you think of sore thumbs on a big hand, like mine maybe. There are also a few sailboats dotting the water, and the breeze coming coming off the ocean is just right for a sailboat ride. But no matter how nice the scenery or everything else connected with it, nothing can take the place of anything meaning home. One can look and admire but his thoughts always looks much farther, and home is the picture he can always see. What I'm trying to say is that I miss you and that big girl terribly. period. Need I say more?

Well, I'm going to break and tell you what I'm sending you. There's a necklace and earings to match, a bracelet for your wrist-watch, these are made of tortoise shells and I'm sure you'll like them. Then there are two pins, and a set of glass holders and one for the pitcher. They are made of some kind of wood I forgot the name now. That's all there is for now, my bankroll couldn't stand any more. As for the bracelet for your wrist watch, you don't have to take it to a jeweler to have it put on, I'm sure Ernest can do it for you. You just have to fasten it on one end and the other can snap on. Tell Annette to send me her wrist measurement like you did and I'll get one for her also. I'm sure you will both like that the best of all. Your package will be on the way this week.

I guess I'll close for now, solong honey and take care always.

      Devotedly Willie

No. 323   May-7-'45

Dear Pace Laite:

Hello honey, this is your bad half again, trying to put down a few thoughts I have in my mind. I won't put down everything that I think about because that's next to impossible, but here's a few anyway.

I saw a swell movie tonight, one of the best I've ever seen. The name is "Hollywood Canteen". I don't know just what it was, but there were a lot of things explained in it that I try to tell about and I somehow never can put down on paper. At any rate it was very good and I hope you see when it comes around town.

I went to mass last night at six oclock, and upon entering the church there seemed to me as if something different had been added. I started looking around and I didn't have to look much

-11-.

before I noticed right in front of me, the statue of the Blessed Virgin, all decorated. It was so nice that I said to myself, I'll have to tell face laite about it. Just picture the same statue in your church, decorated with satin cloth of blue and ~~yellow~~ white from the bottom to about six feet over the top, with a crown of little lights on top and also on each side of the statue, and flowers of every kind and color mixed in, and last of all, the foot covered with another design and more flowers. The statue was of regular size but with the decorations, it must of been about eighteen feet tall. I can't explain it all so that you could get a clear picture, but this will give you some idea. Of course this was because it was the Month of May. Maybe one of the reasons that it awed me so was because I hadn't seen anything like that for

-111-

a long time, almost two years. If I start gapping at things like that now, what am I going to do when I see you and Elaine again? You'll have to pinch me to make me believe it.

You may think it odd for me to write like this, maybe it's because I have nothing else to write about, or maybe it's because of loneliness, or of other things. I haven't received any mail for almost two weeks and maybe that has something to do with it. But whatever it is, it all adds up to meaning that I never thought one human could miss another so much. It seems that everything I see now, reminds me of home. One of these days I'll be seeing the real thing. It won't be soon enough to suit me tho.

Solong for now and take care of you both always.

Love Always Wilbr.

No. 324   MAY, 9, 1945

HELLO FACE LAITE:

    Well the war in Europe is finally over. There's been all kinds of celabrations going on over here, people have been parading the streets all day yesterday and this morning. Flags of all Allied nations are waving from most every home and also from civilian cars. Yesterdays' activities were toped off with a torchlight parade, and this morning there was a ceremony held in the main park at the statue of the French Soldier. This afternoon everyone seems to be indoors celabrating thier own individual parties. Every other civilian is in an inebriated condition or probably will be before the day is over. The municipal and business functions will be closed for three days. As for the American servicemen, I guess the average man is glad to here the good news but outside of that it's just another day for us. They are not doing much celabrating, in fact I have'nt seen any. It's nice for those fellows over there to celebrate and be happy, God knows they have earned it. I only hope that we are not forgotten over here and that it won't be to long Before the other half of the battle is finally won.

    There will be a pontifical high mass at the Cathedral tomorrow night with a Bishop officiating. Attending that mass will be my way of celebrating.

    I'm sending your package today with this letter. I'll try to send it airmail so that you can receive it sooner. I'll let you no tomorrow whether I was able too or not. I did'nt include the glass holders because it would have been to heavy airmail. I'll send them in the next package.

    Hope you and that big girl are okay. We have'nt got much longer to wait now, we'll soon be together again and won't be worrying about you any more. So until then take good care of you both for the old man.

                  LOTS OF LOVE

                      WILDRE'

No. 325   May-10-'45

Dear Face Faite:

Haven't received any letters for two weeks now, but I'm not doing bad writing to you. A few days ago, I said that I wouldn't write to you every day any more, because I couldn't think of anything to site. Ever since then I skipped one day only. I guess the habit of writing every day is to strong, but you won't mind it I'm sure.

I sent your package today, — airmail. So you should be getting it about the same time as this letter.

I just got back from mass a few minutes ago, the mass I was telling you about on yesterday's letter. There were two ~~bishops~~ Bishops and about six priests or more officiating. Well, instead of trying to explain it all, I'm enclosing the program that was given us that explains everything. The church was all decorated and it was all very nice. Wish you could have seen it. But I was thinking about you and Elaine all through the mass tho, and maybe that helped a little.

My mail must be going all over the South Pacific now. That's the biggest headach in moving around. I don't expect to receive any mail for at least another two weeks. When I do, it will be in bunches.

I'm having an awful time trying to write this letter. The reason, — there's an argument going on in my tent concerning serviceman's wives left at home in the states. One side says these wives are unfaithful, the other says they are. The latter seems to be winning the argument, that's the side I'm on. That's one reason why I can write every day to my woman. I haven't the least headach or worry about her faithfullness. Knowing this and keeping it in mind, will help me to hold my end of the borgain always.

Solong for now, take care of you and you,
Love Always Wilbré

No. 326   May-12-'45

Dear Pace Faite:

I was pleasantly surprised this afternoon, and the reason, I received four letter from you. I didn't expect any for another week yet, but I'm sure glad to get them. Now maybe my mail will come again as it has before.

Most of all I was glad to hear that you and Elaine were alright. I was only two weeks without mail but I was worried as hell about you. It was glad also to hear you were working days. And as I said before don't worry about being out of work. Let me do the worrying for the time being. You don't want to get gray young do you?

I see you write quite a few letters also. When I get out of this army I don't think I'll ever write another.

Sorry to hear you couldn't hear that request I asked for. But I'll send another one soon.

Now that your home nights you'll be able to listen to it.

I'm still at the same job. I can't tell you why I had to change address, but I can say that nothing has changed in regards to my work. There's a few changes taking place and I can't say when this change will affect me. So if you don't here from me for a few days at a time, it will probably mean that I'm pretty busy. At any rate don't worry I'll be alright.

So Elaine has found a friend huh? How can she be without with that great personality. And as for my bragging about her to my dear brothers, if they can't take it they can sure leave it. At least Alice is on my side and she doesn't mind telling me so. So I guess I'll keep right on bragging about her and you too. They are only jealous because she is better looking and

—111—

smarter than their own kids.

 Tousaint should be getting home pretty soon now that everything is over with in Germany. He deserves a discharge after what he's been thru. I envy his going home but I don't envy what he's been thru. I'd rather stick it out a little longer as I am. And as for this discharge business, don't get any ideas about me going home in a hurry. My turn will come but there are a lot of others ahead of me. We'll just have to take what they give us and not be too optimistic. In this way there will be know broken hearts. So cheer up face laite, I'll get home as soon as the next guy. Just keep on being the same until then for me and that big girl.

    Lots of love Wilbr.

No. 327   May-13-45

Hello Vace Laite:

It's sunday night over here. I just got back from church and now the rest of the evening will be spent writting to you and Florida. At this moment I'm listening to the radio playing "Always". Whatever I may be doing, when that song is being played within hearing distance I can't help but pause and listen. Sentimental aren't I?

I also received some pictures from René. Some of them were taken with some Philippino girls. He's getting to be quite a romeo. The next time I write to him I'll send him some of mine.

You seem to be fattening the bank roll all the time. I don't no what I'd do without you. How did you ever fall for a mug like me anyway. I'll never figure it out, but I'm

-11-

glad you did. And don't worry about me noticing anything wrong about the way you handled everyday affairs. Anything you do is okay by me and always will be.

Today was the feast of "Jeanne d'Arc", a french national holiday, and there was more celebration over here. There was a ceremony in town and also a military parade. All the army and civilian big shots were out and if I had had a camera I could have taken some nice pictures.

I guess I'll close for now, so until tomorrow solong honey and take care of you and you.

Love Always
Wilbré

No. 328   May-15-'45

Dear Pace Laite:

I haven't any more of your letters to answer and I hardly no what to write, but I'm going to make an effort anyway.

I have a day off today, the usual Tuesday and there isn't much to do except write a few letters and loaf around.

Yesterday I was officially informed as too how many points I had. I have 46 and in order to be eligible for possible discharge I would have to have 85. So you see there are a lot of other guys ahead of me. But that 85 is subject to reduction at any time. It's not permanent and you never can tell when it will be lowered. I no the army well enough by now to know that nothing is

-11-

definite. Just keep your fingers crossed and before you no it, it will be my turn for that return trip to the states.

Florida was telling me on her letter that she had seen a nice farm not far from Lover, and that she was sure it was just what we wanted. Well, maybe it is but whatever we do, we won't let anyone influence us when we get ready to buy a farm. I no just what I want and I'm sure you do also.

Hope you and that big girl are okay. Is she still learning how to speak english? And do you think she'll no me when I get back? I'm sure anxious to find out.

Solong for now and take care.

Love Always Wilbre

No. 329   May-16-'45

Hello Face Faite:

After writting to you yesterday I received a letter from you and today I got another long one. So I guess mail will be coming as usual from now on.

Was glad to hear that Lt Lawrence is able to stay home with his family. Some guys are lucky that way. I was wondering what would happen to Andre, now that there's a change. He might have a chance to get out.

So it seems nice to be home on saturday night again huh? I hope that I'll be able to make your saturday nights a little more so soon. I've completely forgotten by now, just how it feels to be at home on a saturday night or any other day. But even so, I'm sure it can't be anything but the best feeling and you can't imagine how much I'm looking forward too

- 11 -

experiencing such a feeling. Such a day is'nt so very far away, and I guess until then we'll just have to dream about it.

I enjoyed very much reading about the jaunt you and Elaine took to Salmon Falls and So. Berwick. You explained everything in minute detail. Of all the people who write to me your the tops. Not only because you happen to be my wife but you are really the best letter writer.

That big girl must be quite tall and strong to walk as far as you mentioned on your letter. But are you sure that Medee's baby is as pretty as Elaine was at her age? I can hardly believe it. Alice saw that baby and she didn't mention anything about that. Maybe your just being polite, because I'm sure Elaine has it all over her.

-111-

And as for Theresa being a good cook, well,— you weren't so bad yourself you no. In fact, for the short time you were housekeeping you had it all over your mother, and she's been married a long time. And nobody showed you how either, you, or rather <u>we</u> had to <u>taste</u> and learn the hard way. Remember those beans? Boy, how I'd like to be sampling some of your chow again, or better still a bite of you now and then. Ah, me, that's home as I remember it.

So Bisson is still in Germany, huh? He must be still in the engineers. If I remember correctly his Elaine was born a week before our Elaine. And yet ours is bigger than and taller than his. That big girl of ours must be just about perfect. I don't think I quite realize what we have there. Can

—IV—

you imagine now why I do so much bragging to those brothers of mine? And if I can brag that much about her when I don't hardly no her, just think what I'll do when I really no her. I'm happier everyday to have her as a girl and not just another boy. And besides, I'll bet your glad she's a girl even more than I do.

I could go on and on tonight it seems, talking about you and Elaine. But instead, I'd better save some of that talk for tomorrow or I'll be skipping another letter, and I no you won't like that. So until then, goodnight face laite and take good care of yourselves,— for me.

Lots of Love
Wildre

A World War II Story: Dad's Letters Home

NO.　　　　　　　　　　MAY,18,1945

Hello Face Laite;

Have'nt received any letters for a couple of days but thats to be expected for a while. At any rate I'm goin to rack my brain for the next hour or so in order to try and fill this page with nonesense.

At the present time excitement is at a low ebb over here, there's quite a change since I first took over this job. Everything is just routine now. Even the location where I live is so quiet in comparison with the last place. However there are still a few choice bits of excitement happening now and then, and I wishI could tell you about them. Then, maybemy letters would be a little more intersting. But you know the army. Usually after I'm through work and return to my canvas domain it's so quiet that I think I'd go batty if I did'nt occupy my time by reading or seeing a show. Anyway, it's better to keep busy regardless of the circumstances.

I have'nt heard from Medee, Camille or Everett for quite some time, and I'm just aching for a good argument. Maybe I can get them riled up a little more about that big girl of ours By the way, I'm anxious to see those new pictures that you took of Elaine. You know, the ones you took of her in that new dress. I also had my picture taken and the negatives are ready to send to Fern for developeing. I'll let you no when I do send them.

You must be having nice weather up your way about this time of the year. What with the trees and the grass and everything else getting green. Over here everything is green all the time except when there's a dry spell, then nature's Crops are not so green.

Well, what do you think of my typwriteing ability by now huh? Outside of a few misspelled words and other mistakes it's not too bad is it? Or am I bragging again.

Solong for now FACE LAITE and take of YOU and YOU for me.

　　　　　　　　　　　　LOVE ALWAYS

　　　　　　　　　　　　　WILBUR

No. 330   May-20-'45

Dear Face Laite:

    Still haven't received any mail yet but I'm hopeing tomorrow.

    It's sunday night again over here and I just got back from mass. I also went to confession and communion tonight. I'm getting to be quite religious huh? I went only one month and a half ago, and now again tonight. Believe me, it's quite a sacrifice to go to communion at the six P.M. mass. Each time I go, I have to fast from noon ~~that~~ miss supper. But sometimes I'm lucky enough to get a couple of hamburgs. Anyway I shouldn't complain, because I've been a lot hungrier before now and probably will be again. Just goes to show that one is never satisfied.

    Well, I got hold of a couple of films

yesterday and I can borrow a camera too. So I'm going to take lots of pictures in the next few days and send them to you as soon as I can. Now, with a promise like that you should send me another new picture of you and Elaine. Is that a bargain?

I got a bright idea today and the best part of it is, your going to share it with me. I'm going to suscribe to the "Yank" magazine and have it sent to you. You civilians can't buy it and there are a lot of interesting articles in it for you to read. So I'm sure you'll be happy to receive it every week. You will probably start getting it sometime next month.

I guess that's all for now, so until tomorrow solong honey and take care.

Love Wildi

May-21-'45

Dear Mr. & Mrs:

Haven't received any mail from you for so damn long that I've a notion to believe you've kicked the bucket. I hope thats' not true. Not having anything better to do, I decided to let you no that at least I was still alive.

I don't remember now whether I informed you about my new address. But at any rate if you will notice the address on my envelope, that is the correct way to send my mail for the time being. Outside of the change in address there's nothing new. Same old job, same old routine and the same old me.

The last time you wrote to me I believe you said that Bill was in 1A and about ready for his physical. But since then I don't no whats happened. I hope he didn't pass anyway.

-11-

A few weeks ago I sent some negatives to Jean so that she could have them finished for me. Well, she did alright but it cost her a small fortune. She said that If I sent them to you from now on, you could have them finished for two cents apiece or not more than four cents apiece. Well, I'm enclosing some more negatives this time, so that you can have them done for me. On payday, I'll forward a money-order to cover the cost. Now you don't have to do this if you don't want to, but if you want to keep the great love of an adorable in-law, you'd better comply. ha. ha. In case you should decide to have them finished, I'd like to have 7 sets finished, and send them back with the negatives. Or better still, send me 6 sets and send the 7th set to Jean. She'll want to get a set as soon as possible. And as for you,

—111—

you can have one set made out for yourself if you want too, and if you send me your set, I'll ~~make~~ mark them in back so that you can no what and who they are. Now,— do you understand what I've been trying to tell you? I hope so.

Well, I guess I'll close for now and will try to rite more next time. Anyway, there's a dirty argument going on in the tent and I'm anxious to get in my two bits. Solong for now, and take care.

As Ever,
Wildie.

No. 331   May 22-'45

Chere Face Laite:

It's been over a week now that I haven't received any mail and, needless to say it's a long time between letters. It just goes to show you that there's still a war on over here and it has too come first.

I took a whole roll of pictures yesterday. I still have another roll left and I was going to take some more today, but it had to rain and on my day off at that. I want to take some of that french cop I told you about before, and also of his grand daughter. If you remember, I told you about her before. She must be about a year old now. I haven't seen her for a long time.

I wrote to Fern yesterday and I sent her some negatives to have finished for me. I told her to send you a set direct to you when they were finished. You may not no what some of them are, but if you send them to me, I'll mark

– 11 –

them for you. I hope you'll like them.

I hope you and Elaine are fine. I was wondering that maybe by now you've been laid off. If you have don't worry about it. You no what I've told you before. Elaine must be growing up as fast and smart as ever huh? I need not say how much I miss you both, I guess you no after all this time.

As much as I'd like to write a longer letter, it just doesn't seem possible. Unless I talked about the weather all the time. So I guess I'll close for now and maybe tomorrow I'll rite a long one. Solong and take care,

Love Always
Willie

No. 332   May-23-'45

Hello Face Faite:

Just a few lines to send along with the enclosed photograph. If you remember that when I first got here on this island, I wrote a lot of things about the engineers. Well, this picture is what I was bitching about. I helped build this building. We got a few nice words from the Commanding officer for the nice penthouse we built for him and his click. I hope you like the picture but whatever you do, don't ever show it to me. I can't help but recall all of the bitterness that went into building this place. I'm sending it to you in hopes that maybe it will make you happy in some way. Save it if you want too, but put it someplace where I'll never find it. Solong and take care of you and that big girl.

Love Always Wilbie

No. 333   May-24-'45

Dear Face Laite;

After going without mail for the last ten days, I was more than pleasently surprised today to receive two letters, one from you and Alice. I was so damn glad that I read yours over four times so far, and I guess I'll keep it until I get another one from you. I don't no what's holding up the mail but these delays are sure making me appreciate those letters.

So the spring weather is drawing you in the wide open huh? I say this because you mentioned on your letter that you had taken a walk with Elaine. I can just imagine you two walking down the street and Elaine calling hi to everybody. Do you think she'll no me when I get back? She won't have much to go on, just a few pictures won't amount to very much. With your help I shouldn't have much trouble tho,— I hope.

-11-

As for the picture enclosed, I saw that in a magazine and, outside of the blond hair the little girl made me think of Elaine. How do you like the nonesense, or is it?

Glad you liked the description I gave you of that statue, but I'm sure I didn't do it justice.

If by telling you of the pictures I see is the only way I can get you to go out, I'm going to name you one in every letter. Your excuse of not enjoying anything just because I'm not around is not good enough for me. So you'd better be good and go out more often. I appreciate your being good and true but you just can't stay cooped up all the time. This can't last very long now, so keep that chin up honey, we'll be back in the old groove before you no it.

Was glad to hear you had another week off. Hope it happens as often as possible, having a week off I mean.

—111—

Alice tells me about the lobsters and clams they buy at the beach and then having a feast at home. Haven't tasted good food like that for so long that I've almost forgotten what it tastes like. Sure makes my mouth water to read about it. She also said something about Elaine, she always mentions her. Nice to no somebody agrees with my boasting.

Guess there isn't much more to say, so until tomorrow, solong and stay the same. always.

Love Wilbur

No. 334   May-26-'45

Hello Face Faite:

    Talk about a surprise, well, I got about eight of them this afternoon in the form of letters. Five from you and one each from Annette, mother and Butch. I had to read yours over three times already and I'm not thru yet. I have so much to tell you now that I hardly no where to begin, so in order I won't get the cart before the horse I'll start with the oldest letter first.

    Rene may be lucky to have a pretty nurse to work with but he's got nothing on me. There are plenty of pretty girls to be had over here if one was interested. But as you well no I'm not interested, so I might as well be in the jungle. Do I convince you of my faithfullness? I had better or I may find myself divorced of both wife and child huh?

-11-

I'll make a note of that last sentence because a thought just struck me that it would make a good subject to talk about. It also concerns some of the people living here. But I'll save that for another letter.

Even tho you had a week off from the shop, I see you've been keeping busy. Putting your winter cloths away and taking care of the stored furniture; boy you sure no. how to keep busy. Always the little bee, never quiet. Pourtant, I'll anchor you down one of these days.

I quite agree with you that Elaine would look pretty good in a knit suit like you mentioned. But how about getting a suit of your own. It's alright to pinch a penny, or wait for me to pick it out for you, but you've

— 111 —

been waiting long enough now. Won't you please buy yourself something? How about it!

Elaine must be getting along pretty good with Ernest for him to be giving her piggy back rides. What a gal.

As for that crack you made about the air-mail paper, well, it could be used as you mentioned and as a matter of fact it's been done before, — by yours truly. But at this socalled Subtropical paradise that hasn't been the case so far. But whatever made you think of such an idea anyway. Oh you unpredictable females! I could go on and on but I guess I'll save some for tomorrow. So long and take care. Always the same for the same two girls.

Love Wilbré

No. 335   May-27-'45

Dear Face Faite:

    Sunday afternoon again and time to sit down to rite you another letter. I'm sitting by the radio listening to a championship ballgame as I'm writting this. It sounds almost like the big leagues back home, but only almost. The environments quickly bring you back to reality. But it sounds like a swell game and if I wasn't so lazy I would have gone to see it, instead of lazing around my canvas domain. (tent).

    I'm sorry I disappointed you when I said that I was going to rite to you every other day. I knew you wouldn't like that too well and I was sorry I said that afterwards. So I guess I'll try to do as I have in the past. Okay?

    Got a great kick out of reading about Elaine liking her music so well. I can just imagine her sitting at the piano. I wonder what makes her like music so well. Anyway I'm glad she is that way, who knows, maybe she'll be a great opera star some day. Any boy can become president but not any girl can become a good singer. That takes brains and beauty and she has a good start already.

Was glad to hear that Bill got another six months, I'll bet Fern is also. Long time no hear from that babe. She's probably all tied up in her hairdressing.

I was just thinking that, right about this time my two brunettes must be sleeping the sleep of the faithful, while over here its only three oclock in the afternoon,—but a day ahead. Sometimes in the morning, the news announcer from Frisco begins his broadcast with, good afternoon folks. It's six thousand miles from

-111-

here to Frisco and about thirty five hundred miles from there to Berwick. Add that up and that gives you quite a few miles. It's little wonder then that mail gets here so slow. But then again, it also gets here pretty fast sometimes.

I'd like to write some more, but I've been translating so damn much these past few days that my fingers are pretty sore. So until tomorrow, solong face laite!

Love Wildré

A World War II Story: Dad's Letters Home

No. 336   May-28-'45

Hello Race Suite:

Received two more letters from you yesterday and also one each from Florida and Butch and Annette. I have enough ahead now to keep me busy for awhile. The two I got from you were very old, I guess they got mixed up somewhere.

Glad you liked the Ascension mass program. Too bad you couldn't see it, but when I get back that's another must on our list we'll have to do.

So you too talk about your husbands at the shop huh? I wish I could listen to the conversation you girls talk about, but don't say the same about ours, it probably would be a little rougher language. But I can assure you that no matter how rough it is, there's nothing bad said. How can there be. And as for having some of your coworkers vouching for you, that's not necessary in the least. I've never doubted you so far, so why should I start in now? So you can tell your women freinds that their word is not necessary, okay?

I was glad to hear that you received your package. It certainly didn't take long did it? I'd like to have gotten you more, but that stuff costs like hell and the only way I can buy it is a little at a time. I'm glad everything fit okay especially the bracelet for your watch. As for the two pins, the NZ means New Zealand because they come from there. If you remember a while back I asked you to send me the measurement of Annette's wrist so that I could buy her a bracelet like yours, but you never did. If I don't get it within a few days, I'm going to get her something else, maybe a necklace. I've never sent her anything yet and I feel that I should, what do you think? As for me, you don't have to send me anything, unless you could wrap yourself up airmail, that would be okay. But otherwise I have everything I need. There's no need to tell you this is there, you'll send something no matter what I say. Thanks anyway face laite.

Glad to hear that Elaine is getting along better with the ducks and chickens on the farm. Just keep on going there and we'll make a farmer out of her yet. I can imagine her being dead tired after running around in the open air all day.

So long until tomorrow face laite,

Love Always,
Wilde

No. 337 May-29-45

Dear Pacefaite:

Here I am again, trying to answer some of your letters I received in the last few days.

Was glad to hear that you finally went to a show. But on the other hand I'm not so glad because you said that you probably won't go again for another six months. I don't no what I'm going to do about you, there's not much I can do now but I'll certainly fix you up when I get back. Why don't you try taking Elaine with you once, maybe she would take my place? How about that?

In your letter, you mentioned that Florence Perrault was going to sing in a minstrel show, but you didn't say where or when. She's a very good singer. I think she was in the same show as I was the last time I played. That was in Salmon Falls, do you remember?

You no, the last letter I received from

Florida, she said that I must have changed or something because I didn't sound the same as usual on my letters. Do you think the same, if so, you sure haven't mentioned it to me. I wrote to her yesterday and I assured her the best I could that I haven't changed in the least. See if you can convince her. It seems to me that if I had changed you would be the first to notice.

In reference to my being over here instead of Europe, the reason was told to me shortly after we landed by some reliable authority. But of course that's another deep secret that will have to wait to be told. I can say tho that it was to satisfy the whims of one person that we came here instead of <u>there</u>.

Solong for now face laite, until tomorrow

Love Willie

No. 338   May-30-45

Dearest Face Faite:

    Another Memorial day away from home, the third to be exact; will we be apart on the next? Well, for the first time since I've come over, I'm going to venture a guess, but only a guess mind you. I really believe that by next year at this same time, I'll be home,—that is in the States, or at least on my way. Let's wait and see how near right I am huh? I'm putting this down in my diary so that I won't forget.

    There wasn't much going on over here today, except a short ceremony at the military cemetery. But back home there must have been parades in most every town. I thought about that today. Remember the Memorial day you were peeved at me, I don't remember how it all started, but you were mad enough so that you wouldn't come to the parade with me. I'm sure it was all my

—11—

fault tho. But I promise I won't get you angry any more, am I forgiven?

Hope your mother is better. Didn't no she was sick until I read your last letter.

How's that big girl getting along lately? So you had to put away that horse because she was getting to big huh? She must be big for her age. I get a great kick out of reading your letters about her. How she likes music and talks english. From your description I can almost see her, all except her face. I'm sure I couldn't recognize her in a crowd because she must have changed so much. But you, you haven't grown or changed any,— I can tell by your letters, and I could pick you out anywhere anytime.

Solong until tomorrow, take care

Love Wilbre

No. 339   June 1-'45

Dearest Face Laite:

I started the first day of June by receiving five more letters from you and one from Alice. The mail is sure coming in now, although not every day. I'm so bursting with different things to tell you that I don't no where to start now. That's me all over, either I have a lot to say or nothing at all.

In reference to those colored pictures that Mrs. Rickson promised to send you, it was her husband who asked her to do so at my request. They are all paid for, and I'm sure you'll find them nice.

I don't doubt for one minute that you are sick of those sandwiches. Remember before you were married, you used to say the same thing. Now that your married it's still the same old routine. Well you were a couple of years without eating sandwichs but the war had to come along

-11-

and make you eat them again. Well, it won't be long now honey, before you'll have your hot dinners again and this time there won't be any interruption.

On one of your letters you talked only about what you and Elaine did on a day spent at Florida's. That's not bad, on the contrary, that's very good. I don't have to tell you all over again just what I think of those letters. All I can say is, thanks. Keep those kind of letters coming, they do more good than anything else you could possibly do.

Now that you've already sent that package, you could at least tell me what's in it. You talk about me being mean, but I always told you what was in the package before you received it. How about that?

It was sure glad to hear that Tousaint was on his way home. I envy him very much now, but I didn't when he was prisoner. He'll probably get discharged too. Be sure and let me no when he gets home and tell me all about him. I'd sure like to

- 111 -

write to him, maybe I will, and address it to his home. As a matter of fact I'll do that tomorrow. He'll probably get it while home on furlough at least.

I had another civilian dinner last night at the same place as the last. You no, the french cop I told you about before. You'll be able to see what he looks like soon because I took his picture last week, and I'll be sending them home soon. Oh yes, the dinner was good, but I still don't like the way they serve it, — one course at a time. First the soup then the sausage, then the vegetable, then the potatoes etc. Nothing will ever beat Mrs. V's cooking, — ever.

Goodnight face Laite, & Junior face laite.

Love, Always Mildred

No. 340   June-2-'45

Dearest Face Faite:

    Received four more letters from you today and one from mother. I have now about eight of your letters to answer, so I'll have enough to keep me going for a few days. Talk about mail service, I certainly did alright this past week.

    From the way you talk on your last letters you don't seem to be getting much mail. I guess we each have our slow spells. But don't worry, you'll get a whole batch soon.

    I don't no how or where, but I got a nice cold these last two days. You no me, a cold is just like a major operation. But in this climate it's not to bad. I'll be okay in a couple of days. Outside of that, everything is okay.

— 11 —

So Elaine got someone to take my place to give her those horseback rides huh? Well, thats only temporaly, I'll be back soon and I'll take over that job.

How do you like my pencil once more? I think I'll rite this way all the time. I'd much rather write with a pencil but I also no it's not very polite. You don't mind do you?

I'll make this letter short for tonight but I promise to write longer tomorrow. So long until then face laite. Oh yes, what about those honey orders from my two girls? I don't get it.

Love Always Wildé

No.　　　　　　　　　　June-4-'45

Hello Face Laite:

I received that surprise package you sent me today, and it *was* a surprise. I never expected it to be a ring. It's very nice and it fits okay. The only finger I can wear it on is the third index, the same as the wedding ring. I don't no how long I can wear two rings on the same finger but I'll try it anyway. Thanks face laite, I'll try to do as much for you.

I've subscribed for the Yank magazine today and I'm having it sent direct to you. I'm sure you'll like to read it. You people can't get it at home, only servicemen. You should start receiving it in about 3 or 4 weeks, a copy every week for a year.

In reference to those guys who told you that Carl Cook was going home, you can tell them that they're all wet. It is his brother who has gone home on furlough from the west coast. Cook is still here working with me. He's been here quite a while tho and has a good chance of going home, but not for some time yet. As a matter of fact he has 70 points, I wish I had that many.

I don't think Conrad will be lucky enough to go home on furlough because he hasn't been over long enough. My guess is that he'll go from Europe direct to this theatre. But you never can tell tho. As for Lionel, my opinion is that he won't see much action, on account of his hearing. But again you never can tell. Jerald will sure be glad to get home for a while, but he'll soon be on his way over here too.

I haven't heard from Fern for a long time. I made out a money order to pay for the pictures she's going to have finished for me, but I'm waiting

— 111 —

until I hear from her before sending it. I have other pictures being developed here and they should be ready this week. I don't no how much they will cost but I'll bet it will be plenty. I'll send them as soon as I can.

Hope that big girl is doing alright. Have you been out walking with her lately? And how's her english vocabulary, has she picked up any new words? Ah me, I'd sure like to see you both. Let's hope that day isn't too far off.

Solong until tomorrow face laite,

Love Wilde

No. 343   June-5-'45

Dear Face Laite:

Haven't received any mail for a few days but I guess I can stand it for a few more. I still have some of your old ones to answer.

My day off today and I've spent it by writing and sleeping. I still have a little cold and the sleep did a world of good.

I was out on a little deal last night that wish I could tell you about. If I was sure it would pass the censor I'd tell you. Boy there are so damn many angles in this job, it's funny at times and at others not so funny. But I guess this time and story will have to keep like all the others.

Well, I guess by now Tousainte must be home enjoying the luxuries of life. I was going to write to him yesterday but didn't have the time.

-11-

But I must do so tonight.

From the efficiency rating you got at the yard, you sure made out alright. Chances for promotions in that department have always been slow tho. But please don't worry about losing that job. Even if you did quit working now you should stay home for the rest of the duration. It won't be so very far away you no, and you would get a good rest. How about it.

I intended to write a much longer letter but with a big head and writting so many other letters, I guess I'll cut it short right here.

So until tomorrow, solong face lite, take care of you both for me.

          Love Always
            Wilbie

No. 343   June 6-'45

Dear Face Laite:

    Hello honey, received a letter from you late yesterday and another one today. As it stands now, your letters are all up to date.

    On your previous letters you said that hadn't received any mail for a week, but on today's you finally got five. Don't you ever dare say that I'm not writting to you, because I always do. When I get tired of writting I'll let you no. I haven't lied to you yet so why should I start in now.

    Was glad to hear that Ernest is expanding. That's a good sign of business picking up, and I'm glad for him. He had it tough to begin with so whatever he has now he's earned.

    So Elaine is an outdoor girl huh? Glad to hear that because I want to take her hunting when I get back. How about that, okay?

As for having the kids watch over her out of doors, I wouldn't trust them to much because they're pretty wild themselves. Maybe they've changed I don't no, but take good care of that big girl, there's only one like her and I sure wouldn't want anything to happen to her. Gosh, I'd like to be there to play with her, I'd spoil her for sure.

My cold is all gone now, I guess a day's sleep and a little vicks cured it. It sure don't take long to get rid of a cold over here. Back home a cold used to last me three or four weeks. Maybe it's because the old blood has thinned out or this tropical climate that does it, but when I get a cold now, I can get rid of it in three or four days. (But—I'd still rather live in Berwick.)

I saw a picture of Durham College coeds today, in the Yank magazine. It also showed

-111-

part of the main street there. I recognized it right away, even before I read about it. Boy it sure looked good, even if there wouldn't have been any coeds in the picture.

I've been writing so damn much today that my fingers actually ach. You see, when I translate these french reports I have to write it all down by hand. And if you write all day something is found to ach. If I only could type I wouldn't have to write so much. Believe me when that girl grows up, she's going to learn how to type and do all my bookwork, — if I have any.

I'm enclosing a picture that was taken quite a while ago. There will be more coming in a few days. Hope you like it.

So long face laite, until tomorrow
Yours Always Wildé

No. 344   June 7 - '45

Hello Face Faite:

    I finally got around to answering your last letter I received. I had a small stack ahead of me but I finally caught up.

    So you think I'm kidding when I say that I enjoy reading your letters more every day? That's the gratitude I get for trying to express my feelings on paper huh? I can't tell you exactly how it feels to read your letters, believe it or not. I may have kidded you once about your letters, and I guess you haven't forgotten it, but whatever gratefullness I try to put down on paper now, I really mean. If you don't think I'm sincere I'll swap places with you, how about it?

    According to all you say about that big feed Elaine put away she certainly did justice to that food. No wonder she's bigger than most kids of her age. When I get back you'll have two gluttons

-11-

instead of one. The Roys seem to be treating you okay and I'm sure glad.

By now Tousainte must be home and enjoying all the good things of life. I'm anxious to hear from him, but don't expect to right away. If I was in his place I wouldn't bother to write either.

A bright idea struck me today. You no, there's a small daily paper here, printed in french of course. I thought if I sent it home to my mother by regular mail she'd be very happy. I've got to find out first if I can do this and if I can, I'd sure do it.

Solong for now face laite and take care of you both. -

Love Wildré

No. 345   June 9-'45

Dear Face Faite:

    Now that I'm caught up answering your letters and have nothing else to talk about, I'll tell you a few things that I haven't spoken about before.

    I was fortunate enough to visit a leper colony yesterday,— on business of course, because it's "Off Limits" to all personal. First, to get there one has to pass a causway then travel for several miles on a one-lane dirt road which is built along and around the sides of several hills, until finally, the colony looms into view quite suddenly, lying in a great green valley.

    Along the road I was fortunate to run into the nun with whom I was to do business with. (The colony is operated with and by Catholic nuns.) She was short and quite chubby, about fifty years old, and had a pleasant personality. She lead

—11—

me into a small den, which I gathered was to be the dispensary, and talked and transacted whatever business we had. Before entering, she had warned me not to touch anything as a precautionary measure. Because, as you no, leprosy is nothing to fool around with, and you can well imagine how careful I was not to touch,— anything.

After the matter of business was over with, she invited me to visit the sick wards, and I was just about to accept when a car full of visitors, (relatives of the sick) drove up. Knowing that she would be occupied with these people, I settled for a visit to the chapel only. Leaving her with the new visitors I sauntered up to the chapel by myself and what I saw inside left me awestruck and speechless. Of all the churches and chapels I've ever visited, this one was the most colorful and yet simple I've ever seen. I won't try to describe it because I no very well that I'll never do it justice.

- 111 -

After saying a little prayer and the little wish you told me about, you no, about entering a new church, I stood around a few minutes taking in the full view of such a big little community. There were some patients working in the gardens, others were standing in doorways or peeking thru windows at us. Upon approaching some of these people, one could see their twisted, distorted bones and features. Some just stared and stared at us, others just stared at nothing. These last were standing or sitting in the shade looking at nothing but the hills and the sky. I couldn't tell whether they were blind but even if they weren't, this desease is enough to turn anyone's mind. When one is affected, it's goodbye to the outside world for good. Just the prospect of such a thought is enough to make anyone's spin chill, can you imagine what it does to an affected person?

-IV-

As I was driving away from this forlorn colony in the valley, I couldn't help but have some feeling of sympathy and pity for these people. But above all, a deep feeling of charity, unselfishness and devotion for those nuns who sacrifice their lives to care for these people. Were I asked to do as much, I couldn't guarantee an answer.

The nun I referred to in the beginning was named Sister Elizabeth.

Wish I was more of a genious at writing, I would have made this a better story. But it gives you some idea of my visit to a leper colony.

Solong until tomorrow,

Love Wilbur

June 9 - '45

Dear Mr. & Mrs.:

Just a few lines to enclose along with the money order I promised to send in order to pay for those pictures. I was waiting for a letter from you before sending the money order, but if I wait much longer it won't be any good. I haven't heard from you for nearly three or four weeks now. I have a few pictures that were taken here all developed and I'm enclosing some so that you can get a glimpse of your dear in-law and also some of the surroundings.

Everything here is about the same, the same old grind every day. There are a few bits of choice news but can't tell you about it right now. Can't think of much to say right now, so until ~~it's~~ next time, So long and thanks.

Vildé

No. 346   June 10-'45

Hello Face Laite:

You and that big girl are still in your beauty sleep as I write this. But as for me, it's two oclock sunday afternoon. I've been to church and as I'm writting, thoughts of home are uppermost in my mind. They always are but more so on sunday. As time goes by and I see fellows all around me getting ready to go home, home gets to be more precious all the time. It seems that I just can't wait another minute to go back, but I somehow manage to sweat it out.

I met a Tousaint this morning at mass, he's a cousin of Laurent who lives in Salmon Falls. I no him well. We both recognized each other right away. He's been here four months and I didn't no about it. He's been over a long time and has 87 points, so he'll be going home soon. I believe you no him too, he used to go out with a girl from Somersworth I forgotten her name now, and she

– 11 –

married another guy while he's been away. I told him about Laurent being home, he hadn't heard. We didn't have much time to talk because he had to leave for his outfit. I didn't even get a chance to get his first name. But he knew that I had married Jeannette Breton. Seems like his old flame knew you well. I'll try to see him again before he leaves.

If you remember, a while ago I told you about a chaplin we had here who came from Brooklyn. We got word this week that he was killed on Okinawa. He was an allround good fellow and was liked by everyone here. We're having a solemn high mass for him this coming week.

I haven't received any mail for a few days now. When I don't get any news about you and that big girl time drags by all the slower.

I'm enclosing some pictures that I took last

-111-

last week. If you look in the back you'll see the names of the persons. The one of the french cops, the one named Gauthier is the the man who gives me a free feed once in awhile. Hope you like them.

Guess that's about all for now, so until tomorrow solong face laite,

Love Wilde

No. 347   June 12-'45

Hello Vase Faite:

    Received two letters yesterday, one each from Fern and Alice but known from you. Maybe I'll have better luck today.

    Fern tells me on her letter that your supposed to visit her sometime in July with Irene. She also says that she would like to have you stay a month, but maybe you wouldn't want to stay that long. I'm all in favor of you and Elaine to stay there that long, how about you. She wanted me to use my influence to make you stay but I don't see how. If I was home I could probably do something about it. But as it is now, all I can say is that I hope you will stay at least a whole month. How about it?

    You no, I've often thought about my homecoming. I often wondered how it would be. Well, this is the way I'd like to have it. When I get off that train in Dover, I'd like to have you and

-11-

Elaine waiting for me at the station all alone. No big crowds or anyone else there but just you two. You'll probably have to introduce me to Elaine because I certainly won't no her and she won't no me either. Then all three of us will probably ask questions all at once, that is, after I crack a few ribs. You'd better wear a steel corset and Elaine Also. All that and maybe other little things will happen. But that's the way I think of my homecoming. That's the way I want it, how about you?

I guess that's all for now face laites solong and take care of you both.

Love Always Willie

No. 348   June-13-'45

Dear Face Faite:

I received seven letters from you since yesterday and a few from the other folks.

Among those letters was the card and picture of you and Elaine. I was sure glad to get that picture, I hadn't had one of you for so long. You look more beautiful all the time, and that girl also. I've been looking at it all afternoon and I'm still looking. You both look swell in your new suits and I wouldn't have known about that material of which the suit is made, if you hadn't told me. You can't tell in a picture anyway. Your coat seems to be a little big but maybe it's the way the picture was taken. You two must look pretty snappy, both dressed in the same color cloth.

You seem to have gained a little weight.

—11—

Not that it doesn't become you, because as I said before you look more beautiful than ever.

And as for Elaine, she sure is growing up to be beautiful, — just like the old lady. She even poses like a little lady. And thanks for the card you sent me for Elaine. —I'd forgotten all about Father's day. Keep those pictures coming honey, I no it's hard to get films but do the best you can. How about it huh? Oh yes, about saving your money, that was a very good idea you had. Talk about frugal New Englanders, boy you've got them all beat. I can't miss if I have you handling the family pocketbook.

In reference to that confession business, I don't think I'll have to tell you when to go. —I don't see what you have to say anyway, you never do anything wrong.

So you also turn off the alarm clock huh?

-111-

Isn't it nice to turn that damn clock off and go back to sleep? Just you wait, some day soon you won't have to worry about that clock. He'll just throw it out the window, — for a short time anyway.

I guess I'll close for now face laite. I want to save some of those letters to answer in the coming days.

Solong for now, and thanks for the picture.

Love Always,
Wildre

NO. 349   JUNE 14, 1945.

HELLO FACE LAITE:

    Received another letter from you today and also one from mother, so I guess I have enough ahead now to keep me busy.

    So that big girl keeps looking for a fight with the boys huh? She'd better watch that temper or she'll get her nose flattened. And with a flat nose she can't be beautiful. I would'nt want her to become a tomboy just yet, i want to have that privilege of makeing her that way. At this rate she'll be teaching me.

    I see your still keeping yourself cooped up, that's bad. I wish you would go out more often. I don't no how many times I've told you this but still you don't do anything about it. I no it's hard and lonely to be alone but there's not much we can do about it, and the best thing to do is to keep yourself occupied one way or the other. Certainly staying at home won't help. So how about stepping out a little more often huh? We have'nt got very long to wait now and I would'nt want you to crack up on me at this stage.

    I've been showing your picture around to the fellows and they all wanted to no how you ever managed to fall for a guy like me. They said that you looked much too inteligent and beautiful to be my wife. Well, they're right about that but the fact stilll remains that you are my better half and I'm hanging right on to you. Just let some other yokel try and cut in and I'll show them.

    There is'nt anything new over here, every day is just another day. I'm keeping my fingers crossed about that point system. There will be some changes made next month on that and you never can tell when my turn will come up.

    Solong for now face laite, until tomorrow I remain the same

              ALWAYS   WILDRE'

No. 350

June, 16, 1945.

CHERE FACE LAITE:

    Received another swell letter from you late yesterday when I really was'nt expecting any. This last one took only six days getting here, so you see the mail service has been pretty good lately.

    In todays news I read where the 7th Army is staying in Germany as occupation troops. So if Conrad is in that outfit he won 't be home for a while yet. Jerald has a good chance of getting back tho. He should have guite a few points.

    In reference too those gifts I bought for you over here, they may cost a little money but thats' no sign that I won't get any more. Don't you worry about my finacial statues, I'll get along all right. After all I would'nt feel right if I was'nt broke trying to make you happy.

    You'd better take good care of yourself working in that baskelite. From what you tell me it is'nt very pleasant to handle that stuff. Don't want anything to happen to my face laite. Don't depend on the time off you have coming to go to Conn. Take a month off anyway. Thats' the least you can do for yourself.

    So, you been flirting with that setup man huh? You've got a nerve , after telling me to be good or else. Now it's my turn to tell you the same thing,———— OR ELSE. I have'nt lost faith in you yet but if this keeps up I don't no what I'll do. Seriously tho I no you would'nt do anything wrong because you would'nt no how, and you would'nt do it in the first place. So keep right on as you are and don't change in the least bit, I would'nt want to start getting used to any other ways you may accumulate because it took me too damn long to get used to you in the first place.

    I see you people are still getting plenty of cold and rain yet. If this keeps up you won't have any summer at all. Fromm the way you describe it the weather is about the same as we have over here, the only difference is we have it year round.

    According to my estimates, we now have $1406.25 in bonds. Thats figuring at the original value, but counting the interest it's much more than that. I forgot now what we have in the bank besides that but if you figure both totals together let me no what it is will you? We must have nearly enough to pay for that FARM We're going to get. You can't imagine how much I dream about that farm. Some of these days I'm going to draw a whole plan and send it to you for your approval, okay?

    I'm glad to hear that you don't think I've changed any. I guess your right when you say that we have our disgusted moods every once in awhile and we most always show it in our letters. We try to bear up under this kind of living but it being agaisnt our grain, we just have to break down sometimes. I firmly hope that it will not upset our lives too much anyway and that it will make us all the happier.

    Well, this turned out to be a long letter after all. It does'nt look it but a typewritten page like this ie equivelant too three or more handwritten pages. You can imagine how long it took me to write it. But for you it's worth it,————SEE.

    Solong face laite, until tomorrow,

                                    LOVE ALWAYS

                                        WILDRE'

No. 351   June-17-'45

Dearest Face Faite:

I received something today that I have never yet received since I've been in the Army. That something was in the form of 21 letters. Eight were from you alone and the others were from all the other people I usually correspond with. The reason for so much mail was because they all had been addressed to my old address, and they had to travel all the way to the Philippines and back here. So you see, that sort of makes up for the days I was without mail the first month I had changed address.

In Vern's letter she had enclosed a picture of you & Elaine with Marie and Conrad's wife and their offsprings. Elaine looks so small on that picture but you look the same as on the last picture you sent me. René also sent me a

— 11 —

picture of himself. It was taken in a studio I guess because its very well taken. He looks well and seems to have grown. He also has that matured look about him which no doubt he's acquired since being across.

I was sure surprised to hear that you visited your dear brother Hervey at his new, shiny home. Not that I have any objections, mind you, but I never expected it. My attitude towards him hasn't changed I guess. I never thought him any good and I still think the same. The cowardly deeds he has done in the past are not to be forgotten too soon. But I'm glad you've enjoyed your day in Biddeford. Go out as often as you can honey, it will do you both good.

Don't you ever say that any other girl is smarter than Elaine. Just because that little kid over here started to walk earlier than Elaine is no sign that she's smarter. You said your

—111—

self that Elaine has nice straight legs. She probably wouldn't have if she started to walk younger. Can you imagine what a beauty she will be at eighteen?

So you told old man Frenier a few things, well it's to bad about him. He never was very intelligent anyway. So I wouldn't waste too much time talking to him.

Well, I guess that's about all for tonight. Solong until tomorrow,

As Always
Wilbur

No. 352   June 18-'45

Dear Face-faite:

Got another nice letter from you today, and also one from Alice.

So you think my last letter to the Free Press was okay huh? Well it's about time you begin to notice some of my abilities. You didn't no you had a smart husband did you? Well, now that you no, you'd better treat me with respect,—see. Seriously tho, I could do much better with you as a subject, and I really think I do.

You were wondering whether I had received my ring. I've already told you about it I guess, and I'm still wearing it. Talking about anniversaries, ours is coming up soon, do you remember? (don't answer that). I don't no what to send you for this one. Maybe I'll send you a wooden cooking set so that when we start housekeeping again you won't burn the food again, like you did the

– 11 –

first time. But you weren't too bad tho, so I guess I'll take another chance with you. I no this next anniversary of ours is supposed to be wood, but I'm not in a very good position to send anything like that. But you can be sure to get something and this time I won't tell you. I'll get even with you for not telling me what you sent to me the last time.

You told me about Elaine trying to write me a letter but you didn't enclose it. I don't imagine I could have read it but anyway, the next time if you would send it I'd be glad to look at the sciffling. You also mentioned that she wakes up at night and wants to sleep in the big bed with you. You no, I've often thought about her doing that very thing. You can't tell me that dreams don't come true. Just wait until I get back, I'll spoil her for sure. You won't mind will you?

Solong for now face, laite.

Love Always, Willie.

A World War II Story: Dad's Letters Home

No. 353 June-19-45

Hello Pace Lute:

Just received another letter from you and also the note Elaine had enclosed. I think I'll keep that note just for the hell of it and show it to her when I get back. Or better still, show it to her when she graduates from high school.

According to my estimation we now have approximately $3,438 in bonds and in the bank account. I was surprised to have so much stored away. We have enough as it is to get that farm and pay cash for it. And I'm not forgetting that, had it not been for you we wouldn't have so much put away. You alone is responsible and once again, I don't no what I'd do if it wasn't you I had as a partner instead of some other spendthrift. All I can say is thanks and I'm lucky beyond expectation.

-11-

I wrote to René and Medee today besides too you. I sent two pictures to René because he had sent me his. I also sent the last one you sent me to him, but just to look at. Because that is the best one and the last one from you and I want to keep it. — I wanted him to get a good look at that big girl.

I hope your not working too hard at the shop. Take care of yourself because it won't be to long before I get back now, and I want to see you both in top shape.

Solong until tomorrow face laite.

Love Always Hilde

NO.   June 20, 1945.

DEAR FACE LAITE:
　　　　Received another letter from you today along with several others, and also the pictures I had sent to Fern to have finised for me. She had enclosed a short note telling me that she had sent you a set, hope you liked them.

　　　According too your letter you people have finally inherited some warm weather. What with you working on that glassite I'm getting worried about you. If it's as bad as you say it is I wish you would quite that job. Don't injure your health for anything, at least not for money. With the warm weather coming on it won't be very pleasant to work in that stuff. How about it huh?

　　　I'm glad to hear that you and Elaine had a good time at AL's place. I was thinking that maybe Marion must envy us for having such a nice big girl. I remember how she did'nt want to have any babies, she always had some excuse to give. You would'nt want to change places with her now I'll bet, neither would I. She can have her 4F Bernie and we'll keep our Elaine. And as usual, I gather you both put on the visiting feed bag. Boy, maybe I won't catch up with you both when I get back.

　　　Sorry to hear about Fat Liberty's grammy passing away, but maybe it was for the best. I don't think she was wanted anyway. I suppose Fat is always the same,----all ass and plenty of wind. Nevertheless, it will be good to get back and see him and all the other people that make up the big town of Berwick. Just think, it is already one year and three months that I've been across. These last months went by pretty fast, but now the longer I stay away the more I dream of home. If I have to stay here another 15 months I don't no how I'll be able to stand it. So you see face laite, you'd better take good care of yourself and that big girl for, if I do come back half batty I'll have somebody to guide.

　　　Alice tells me that Mr. Harrity died a few weeks ago and I was wondering who was taking over his affairs. So you might check up on that by saking Alice, she ought too no. Solong for now,
　　　　　　　　　Love always
　　　　　　　　　　　Wildre'

No. 355   June-21-'45

Dear Face Laite!

Got another letter from you today, it was a little old but am always glad to get them, no matter how old.

You no, did you ever notice that on every letter that I write to you, I always head it by saying "face laite", and you do also. Did you ever wonder why I don't change that and say something else instead? I've often wondered why you did'nt. I guess there's no explanation to give for that. Maybe it's because we started that when we first met. I don't recall which one of us said that first, but that phrase is stuck with us for good. I've often thought about that, as a matter of fact I think about it every time I write, and I never dare to change it. And I keep wondering if you will. It will always be "face laite" with me, how about you?

– 11 –

Well, I'm always in very good health. Outside of being soft around the muscles and quite lazy there's nothing wrong with the old frame. But the mind still longs for home always.

Our weather is a little cool at this time of the year, about 65°, but to me its seems like winter. What am I going to do when I get back to Maine? I guess I'll take my chances on that anytime they let me.

I hope your not working to hard at the shop. Take care of yourself and that big girl honey. Can't think of anything else to write, so solong until tomorrow.

Love
Wilde

No. 356 June-22-'45

Hello Face Faite:

Received two more letters from you today and three more from the other folks. The mail is sure coming in these last few days. I have so many to answer now that I don't no when I'll be able to catch up. And to make matters worse, we're kept busy as hell at the office. However, I'll do the best I can.

First of all, I gather from your latest letter that you also have plenty of mail and you seem to be bursting with news. In reference to those pictures you sent me, it wasn't my film nor my camera which took them, therefor choosers can't be beggars. But I'll mark them for you.

I was sure glad to hear that Laurent was almost home. I can imagine how Dula will be glad to see her old man. I wrote a letter to

Laurent last week in hopes that he would receive it on his arrival home. When you see him ask him about it. I wish it was I also that was in his shoes, but my turn will come in time. So lets wait a little longer huh and keep your chin up.

Was glad to hear that you were planning to go to Conn. around the 4th of July. I'd be much happier tho if you would stay for a month instead two weeks. The hell with that job I say.

I also got a surprise today. Do you remember when I sent you two addresses to keep for me when I transfered to this outfit? One of them was of Bruno Ciotti. Well, I got a letter from him today and guess where he is, — Okinawa. That's where the old outfit went when they left here and that's where I'd be if I would have stayed with them. I'm kind of sorry now that I've

-111-

had that transfer. I guess I miss the excitement we had then of moving all the time. And I'll bet they had plenty when they first got there. Oh well, I may get excitement before this show is over with yet. He didn't talk about anything in particular, except that they were a long time on the boat.

I guess it's time to sign off for now. I want to catch up on some of the other letters. Solong and take care.

    Love Always
     Wilbur

No. 357   June 23 - '45

Hello Face Faite:

Received two more of your perfumed letters today, telling me all about Laurents' home coming. It's funny I never noticed that before, but as soon as I opened the first letter, the smell struck me like a ton of brick. Did you do that accidently or on purpose? Anyway I like them that way for a change and thanks.

I did'nt quite get the point of your explanation about Laurents' furlough and rest. But you'll probably tell me more about him in your next letter. So his kid caught on to him okay huh? He hasin't been away very long you no and his kid was pretty big when he last saw him. While I'm still away and have been for a longer period. I don't no how much longer I'll be away but I have a feeling Elaine won't no me. But I'd bet she will in no time tho, I hope. And how about you, will you no me? Don't answer that, ha ha

-11-

Well, I'm glad to hear that you finally got some warm weather. But then again you had more rain to go with it. And with everything going wrong at the shop, I can just picture the expression on your face. Cheer up face laite, you won't be at that old job very long now. You'll be in your own home again soon, and you'll be able to stay in bed in the morning. I'll make my own breakfast and yours too just like old times. Oh yes, I'll have an extra one to prepare, mustn't forget that big girl. It's nice to dream about it for now anyway.

Well, I guess it's time to sign off for now. Until tomorrow, solong honey. Oh yes, about going hunting with Elaine & I, you'll have to ask her. I think I could stand you around.

Love Wildie

No. 358   June-25-45

Dear Face Laite:

Yesterday was the first day I didn't get any mail for quite some time. I'm not kicking, mind you because I still have a whole stack of letters to answer.

Well, I start working nights tonight, and for the next two weeks. I'll be changeing from night to day every two weeks. Of course I can't tell you why or what for but I wish I could. Then maybe it wouldn't be so difficult to write every day.

In reference to the ring you sent me, I'm still wearing it on the same finger. It doesn't bother me so I guess I won't send it back to you. That's the only finger it will fit and now that I've got it I might as well keep it.

I started sending the local french paper to my mother this week. Whenever I write to

—11—

her my letters are'nt very long, so with the paper she'll have enough to read to keep her going. It comes out five days a week. I'll send it in the regular mail. I'm sure she'll be glad to get it.

I don't no what's the matter, but I can't seem to think of anything to write today. You must get that way too sometimes, On some days you can write on and on, and on others you can't think of anything. Well today is one of the latter kind for me. So until tomorrow, solong and take care of you both.

Always Wilbre

No. 359   June 26-45

Dear FaceLaite:

I've just received two more letters from my better half, and I'm no sooner finished reading them, than I sit right and answer. How about that huh?

Your sudden heat wave does'nt seem to be agreeing with Elaine. I was bothered the same way when I first got over here. I overcome it by using Mennen's antiseptic powder at frequent intervals during the day, and also just before going to bed at night. Any good powder will do it, why don't you try that on Elaine. And as for her being afraid of the passing train at night, I don't no what could cure her of that. Maybe by going out with her as often as possible would help, but she'll probably get over it in time. At any rate, take good care of her and yourself.

René seems to be doing alright with his bank

—11—

account. It's a good thing that he had you start his account instead of his folks. I don't think it would grow as fast if they had it. He's doing a wise thing which he won't regret.

You'll find that Lionel's address will change again. I won't site to him now but wait until you send me his new A.P.O. number.

I'll be anxious to see those pictures of you and Elaine dressed in your sunday best. And I'm glad that you went to the beach, it must have been nice. There are plenty of beaches in the South Pacific, but they are far from being anything like back home. Won't it be nice to go to those places again and have some fried clams, lobster, popcorn or what have you. That's living the way life should be lived, or at least part of it.

So long until tomorrow face laite,

Love Wilbur

A World War II Story: Dad's Letters Home

No. 360   June 27-'45

Dear Vace Faite:

Got another letter from you yesterday and also one each from mother + of all people Conrad. Yours was only six days old, so you see we have pretty good mail service now. As for Conrad's letter, I was very much surprised both upon receiving it and reading it. I don't no who gave him my address but it was old as the hills, and addressed to my old outfit at A.P.O 708. My second surprise was his penmanship and grammar. Boy, he could stand a lot of schooling. It's a pity not to be more educated than that. Believe me, our Elaine will have an education if it's the last thing I do. Gosh, I'll bet she knows as much as he does right now.

Well, I see your both finally stepping out more often, it's about time. It will do you both a lot of good, so take advantage of all the chances you can get.

-11-

This four to twelve shift I'm working on is not bad, but gosh I get to much time to myself now and I don't no what to do. I get up never later than eight and then I have until four in the afternoon to hang around. I've never been so rested up in my life than since I've been on this job. And I'm so damn soft, my skin is just like a woman's. If I don't do some manual labor pretty soon I'll get sick. You no I'm not used to office work yet, and I guess I never will. And being on this job, doing almost nothing, only makes me more anxious to get going on our farm. You can't imagine how anxious I am. But no matter how anxious, I guess I'll have to wait until the army says "your free".

Solong honey, take care.

Faithfully Wilbr

No..   June 29, 1945

Dearest Face Laite:

      Just this minute received your letter of June 22, and here I am answering right back.How's that for being prompt. I was glad to get it too because i did'nt no what to write.

      That must have been quite a thunder storm you people had. There are'nt usually many storms like that in that section of the ~~xsutry~~ country.This place here is supposed to have storms like that but we did not have any this year. Maybe the world is changing or something.You people seem to have all the bad weather .

      So you took my picture to the shop and showed it around huh? If i would have known that I would have taken a glamour picture. But than you probably would'nt have shown it to anyone.You should no by now that when I turn on the charm I'm quite irrisistable to the women.ha ha.You see, I have'nt changed much,I still brag about myself.

      I'm glad to hear that you finally put on a little weight. I guess I had toleave you for a little while and that the reason why you gained a little.I think you could stand a little more too because you'll need a lot of resistance against those bear hugs when I get back.

      If you intend to be with Fern around the 15th of next month do you want me to send my letters there or keep on as I am? Last year I think they were sent to Berwick and Annette in turn sent them to you. Anyway let me no, I'll keep on writing as usual.

      For the last few days I've been doing a little bycicle riding for excercise.I usually go along the beach and watch the ships come in and out, and take in the scenery .At first I went just a little ways because I did'nt want to get stiff.But today I went about six miles and boy am I stiff.After being accustomed to manual labor all my life and than falling on a job like this, it sure gets a man soft. When I get back home it will take me six months to get hardened to real work again.

      Well,I just about runout of words again so I guess it's time to close another letter.Oh yes, I wrote to Mary yesterday and boy did I Give her a line about how beautiful and smart Elaine was.When she reads that she will sure burn up.Solong until tomorrow,

                      Love for you and you,

                            Wildre'

NO.362   June 30,1945

Hello Face Laite:

Received another letter from you today and also one from Annette.They were both a little older than what I usually get, but I was glad to get themm anyway.

Glad to hear that you received those colored pictures.I had to laugh to myself when I read how you tried to give me hell.I can just picture you trying to raise your blood pressure. It's no use you no, I'm to šar away for you to be giving me hell.But I will try to get more pictures for you,and this time I'll try to be amongst the scenery,--bodily.Okay?

You spoke of your mother šeing 52 years old on her last birthday.I thought she was much older.By the way, I don't hear about the old man very often.Is he still the same ,raiseing hell all the time or has he changed?The kids must be growing allthe time.I'm sure I won't no them when I get back.But than,most everything will be changed.Not you though,you'll stay the same always.

I'm enclosing an article which I found hanging around, and I thought pretty good.I don't no if you work around some of those Fšangers but this little story describes just about what they do.I no because I use to work with them.Take it to the shop and show it to the other girls,they'll get a great kick out of that.

Well, I guess that's about all for now,so until tomorrow solong and take care of you both for the old man.

AS EVER THE SAME
LOVE   WILDRE'

A World War II Story: Dad's Letters Home

No. 363 July 2, '45

Dear Face Saite:

Got another letter from you yesterday. You certainly sounded different on that letter than you did on the one I received the day before. First you give me hell, then everything is patched up when you receive a few more pictures. Oh well, I'm glad your not mad anymore, and see that you stay that way.

I see Elaine is taking after you, when it comes to money matters. Just think, she has all that money in the bank already, and I'll bet she asks everybody for 5 cents too. Just like a woman. She'll be glad when she's older, that you started that bank account for her. It will probably help her in many ways.

I was sorry to hear that you will stay only one week in Conn. I told you before to stay

—11—

at least a month, but I can't make you, so I guess it will be just one week. Hope you have a nice time. Just you wait until I get back.

You said that the first time you went to see Laurent & Lou, they were snoring. Are you sure of that? He was away a long time you no. Anyway you can't blame them much, can you. What would you do in the same circumstances? Don't answer that.

I went to a civilian mass yesterday just to break the routine. It seems good to hear a french sermon for a change. It takes me back to Berwick and more dreams. I can't wait to get back.

I guess thats all for now, so until tomorrow solong and take care,

Love Always Wilse

No. 364   July-3-'45

Dearest Face Faite:

    Hello honey, received another letter from you today and also one from Florida.

    On your letter, you said that Elaine was trying to read a book and that she acted just like me. The way you described it, I could almost picture her sitting in that rocker trying to read. What a gal we have there. If she's that interested in reading, then she must take after the old man. I still do a lot of reading and sometimes my eyes get sore now, then I have to lay off for a few days. Guess I'm getting old, or else I need glasses. But I hope not.

    Yes, René must have a lot to say as to where he's been. He's seen a lot. But remember the long letter I once wrote to you all about my trip across the states and another about the trip across? That one was longer than eight pages. I don't have

- 11 -

So much to talk about now, and so my letters are shorter. But whenever I do have something to talk about, I'll try to make it as interesting as possible.

Concerning those typewritten letters I manage to send you, it takes me quite a while to write one that way. I only write them that way when I have a lot of time on my hands. I'm no longer a schoolboy you no, and I don't believe I'll ever master the true art of typewriting. But when there's not much to do, it's a good past time and it does make you a little happier. Doesn't it?

Yes face laite, we will go to those Red Men suppers when we get together again. Everything we've missed before, we will make up for, that a promise. Remember when you used to get mad at me because I never wanted to go out. Well, that's going to change, believe me. I'll make up

-111-

to you everything we ever missed out on. And that also is a promise.

So the Tousaints are keeping themselves shut up in a shell huh? Well, I don't blame them much either. What would we do in the same position?

I finally got around to buying Annette a gift today. It isn't much, only a necklace. But coming from the South Pacific, it's a souvenir anyway. Hope she likes it. Will try to send it airmail tomorrow.

Time to sign off for again; solong until tomorrow.

Love Always Willie

JULY,6,1945.

Dear Mr.&Mrs:

Just received another letter from you along with a few from my girl and needless to say,was very glad..

According to your letter,mail has'nt been coming in so good lately. But over here we have been getting very good service.I've received some that were only six days old.Sure has changed in the last few weeks.

Speaking of shows of which you mentioned in your last letter,I sure would have liked to see one like that again.The last time I played in one was at Salmon Falls also.It was a minstrel given by the Red Men.You seem to be occupied as usual in your music.I never could sing a hell of a lot, but what I did no I don't believe I no any more.I don't feel happy enough to sing in the army therefor the old cords are pretty rusty.(that is among other things)

I also swa the picture 'Flicka' over here last week and I thought it was pretty good.You no,seeing a movie is about the only entertainment I've ever had since I've been overseas.Of course,I could get other past-times if I wanted to,butthat girl of mine would divorce me if she ever found out.(she said so)

Well,Igot you a souvenir of our charmante Nouvelle Caledonie at last, and I'm sending it to you via airmail.You should receive it within two days after you get this letter.I could'nt get you a wristband for your watch because I did'nt have your measurement.So I got hte next best thing.(Guess what)It's not put together very strongly but maybe you can have it fixed the way you want it.

Another holiday is almost gone and Idid'nt see it.Do you think that we'll ever get back in the groove again and recognize a holiday when we see one in the future peace?I tink we might,---but not for some time after the last shot is fired.I need not repeat how sick and tired I am,because there's a lot more like me.So I guess We'll grin and bear for a little while longer.

Solong until next time,and excuse the mistakes for I'm a poor amature.

AS EVER,
WILDRE'

No. 366   July-5-'45

Dear Face Laite:

    Another day, another letter to the face laite. It seems that nothing much is accomplished in a day unless I write you a few words. I somehow don't feel right if I skip a day. I guess I got into a big habit when I started this letter writing to you, and now I could'nt get out of it if I wanted too.

    Glad to hear you like your new job. Getting to be some class huh? Guess I'll let you earn the bread money when I get back. As an engraver you should make much more money than I could.

    Seems that the Tousaints are having quite a vacation huh? Well, cheer up honey, when our turn comes we'll really show them how to take a vacation. I've got so many plans now that if we only fulfill a small part of those, we'll be doing a lot. Just you wait & see.

—11—

Glad to hear that Elaine is getting to be an outdoor girl. I was just thinking, remember when she was small and you used to put her outside in her carriage? Her legs were all tan then. Now maybe she could get tan all over. When I think about those little incidents, it seems that I could almost reach out and touch. I just can't wait to get back, face laite.

Well, I guess there isn't much more to say for now. Take care of you both, and don't work too hard. Until tomorrow,

Love Always
Wilbur

No. 367   July, 8 - '45

Dear Face Laite:

Received two more letters from you today, — right on time too.

First of all, let me put you straight on one thing that you seemed to have misconstrued. That is, when I mentioned to you this batty business. I certainly did not mean that I would get off the train drunk, or that I was to become a drunkard. When I mentioned the word 'batty', I said that I might be that way if I had to spend another 15 months away from home. Batty was used to mean 'crazy'. See what I mean now? But never fear tho, I was just making conversation and didn't mean anything by it. Speaking of drinking tho, you don't seem to have changed your ideas. I don't think you ever will either. According to these frenchmen here, anyone who is a descendant of

- IV -

Bretony, France is tête tue. (is that spelled right). So if your parents come from Canada or rather Quebec, then they are descendants of Bretony, France, — and that makes you tête tue. Me to, because my parents come from Quebec also. How's that for telling you your fortune. Anything else you want to no, just ask me. Smart guy your husband.

So that's the way face laite was invented huh? Glad you reminded me how that name came about. And I'm still a good-looking husband too. How about that huh?

One of your letters I received was of nothing but Elaine. When I read a letter like that, it seems that I'm almost in the same room with you both. Just keep on writing like that and I'll ask for

-11-

nothing more from you as long as I'm over here. Those kind of letters are the best morale builders.

Yesterday, I and another fellow went about 70 miles up the island on business. It's certainly nice up that way. Sure wish you could be here to see the nice scenery. If I stay here a few more months, I'm going to try and get a pass and spend two or three days up that way. I'll tell you all about it if I do.

Guess it's time to close again. Until tomorrow take care of you both.

Love Wilbie

No. 368   July-10-'45

Dear Face Faite:

Just received another letter from you, the one of July 1 telling me all about the busy weekend you had with Fern and Bill.

According to that letter you and Elaine had a nice time. It's about time too, cause all work and no play is bad for anybody. I no you haven't had enough recreation, but I couldn't do anything about it from here. Even tho I've told you time and again to go out more often, you simply won't listen to me. Well, I may not be able to do anything now, but I'll sure fix that the very first chance I get.

Elaine seems to be still the main attraction where ever you go. With each month that passes by, I no that I'm missing a lot by not watching her grow into a big girl. But there's

-11-

nothing much I can do about that either. I've got a lot to catch up on, and it's a hard long wait believe me.

You should be receiving your Yank magazine by now. I just bought the new edition and thats what made me think about it. Lately, they've been printing pictures of streets of various cities in the states. In today's there was one of Boston and it sure looks nice.

By the way, how about some new pictures of you and that big girl. Haven't had one for a long time now, and I miss them. I want to keep up on you two to see that you don't change too much. So how about it huh.

Solong face laite and take care,

Always Wilbré

No. 369   July, 11-'45

Dear Face Laite:

Got another letter from you today and here's another one for you.

I'm sure glad to hear your finally enjoying yourself. If that's the only way you'll go out, I think I have Fern to come down more often. That is, until I get back only. How about that?

So I made you mad because I said that I was kind of sorry to miss the excitement I would have had with the old outfit? I can just picture you now,— being mad at me. Truthfully now, you wouldn't get mad at me would you? Remember how you used to try it, but you wouldn't stay that way very long? I guess it was my irresistable personality, or maybe my good looks that stopped you. ha. ha. Anyway, don't you worry face laite, I was only making conversation. I no very well when I'm well off, and I'll stick it out this way too. After

-11-

all, I don't want you to have gray hair. Not that it would make any difference to me to have you with gray hair, because you'll always be the same old face Laite to me. How's that, do I sound convincing enough? If not, I'll try to do better on my next letter. Okay?

So Elaine is getting to be like a real farmer huh? Well, just keep on taking her on the farm, and by the time I get back and we have our own, we won't have to hire any helper. At the rate she's growing now, she'll take the place of two men. I have great plans for that gal. Some day when I don't no what to write about, I'll tell you what I have in mind. Then you'll tell me if you agree. okay?

Time to sign off for now, solong until tomorrow,
   Love Always
    Hildie

No. 370   July 12, '45

Hello Face faite:

    This is the first day for quite a while that I haven't received any mail. But I still have one of your old ones, so that's something to talk about.

    On your letter, you spoke of the time we went to the Barn on the Mass. & New H. border. I remember that also. And I also remember that we had just bought our Oldsmobile. I had lost my keys in the nightclub and what luck we had to have been able to find them again. Remember that? Ah me, can't forget historic moments like that. On the contrary, I try to plan out our future big moments. At least I can dream about them.

    Concerning those perfumed letters, they don't smell anymore. I thought maybe you did that on purpose, but according to your letter, it was just

-11-

accidental on your part. It was nice while it lasted anyway.

So Elaine is putting up a kick because Fern sleeps in the same bed with you huh? You'd better start training her, or else get her a private room. But don't let a little thing like that worry you, she'll get over it.

Can't seem to get on my thinking cap tonight. There are plenty of things I could talk about on everyday happenings here, but just can't get around that censor. I sure could tell you a lot if it wasn't for that, because God knows there is plenty going on. Oh well, I'll save it all for the big day when, we'll be sitting in that nice cozy chair. Then you'll hear some hair raising stories. Or maybe I'll save them for Elaine as her bedtime stories.

Solong for now face laite.

Love Always, Wilbre

NO. 371   July 13, 1945.

DEAR FACE LAITE:

    To make up for yesterday's letterless day, I received four of them today,one each from you,Annette,Alice and Toussaint.Of course I don't have to tell you how glad I am to receive mail,especially one from you,so I'll skip all of that and start on something else.

    According to your letter Elaine is enjoying the good old summertime by playing in the sand pile,and getting herslf plenty dirty. I'm sorry that I can't picture her that way.She must have changed so much since I last saw her. The pictures that you send me are okay,but it is'nt like seeing a person in the flesh.Just think,she was only a baby and could'nt walk when I left,But now she's half as tall as I am.I just won't beleive she's our daughter when I see her again.I'll have to be convinced some way or another.

    That must be quite an album you have there.With all those pictures you have it should be almost full.And by the way,I was wondering if you still keep those old letters.If so You'll be needing a special store room pretty soon.

    The Toussaint family seem to be enjoying themselves immensely at a socalled Lake Ossippe in Maine.He said on his letter that it was situated between Bidderford and Limerick.He also said that they were staying there for three weeks and that they were having a very nice rest.Boy,don't I wish we were in a place like that.You can be sure that we'll do something like that or maybe even better.I've said that to many times to back down on my word.

    I'm back working days again.I sure got lazy on that night shift.In the morning Iused to get up when I felt like it,but now I have to get up in time to go to work at 0730 and I find it tough.Gosh,what am I really going to do when I have to go back to work.

    By the time you receive this letter Annette should have received her package.I hope she likes it.I did'nt no what to get her but finally decided on that necklace.

    Well,can't seem to find any more words to write so I guess it's time close once more.So until tomorrow,solong and take care of you both.

                      Love   Always

                              Wildre'

No. 373   July-20-'45

Dear Pace Faite!

It has been four days since I last wrote to you, the reason being that I went on a little trip. I don't no if I can name the places that I visited, so I'll skip the names for now.

A few days ago, I told you that I would try to get a three day pass and go visiting on this island,—well, I received that pass quite unexpectedly just two days after I told you. It was either taking it now or maybe never, so I took it. I don't no whether I can put down all what I saw and did in this letter, but here goes.

Accompanied by another fellow who works with me, we started in the early evening and drove until ten oclock where we stopped at a place we'll call X for now. We couldn't take in very much scenery on account of the darkness, but we saw this same part on the way back in the daytime. We had late supper at my freind's freind home and turned in for the night. The following morning, we started out for the opposite side of the island from where we were and didn't stop until ten thirty at another place called ex X. This place wasn't so big as the first but it was much prettier country. Talk about scenery, that was a painters paradise. There are rivers and mountain streams and anything else you can think of. There are wild oranges or tangerines, coffee plantations, cattle and other good things too numerous to mention. We visited a native village and the house of the chiftain, and also a beach nearby that was something to talk about. It wasn't very safe to go swimming there because of sharks, but it was nice to look at. Anyway, I didn't have my trunks along.

After staying at this second place all day

—111—

and night, we drove back to the first place, and proceeded up the island for another three hours. Once more we stopped, and this time we stayed at a hotel. But what a hotel. I didn't expect anything in the line of Hollywood style, and yet I was disappointed. The hotel was a one story affair, made of wood and cement. There was a bed (what a mattress) and a table and one candle in the room. In front was a three foot wide porch (rotten) and we had chickens ducks and other animals as bed companions all night long. We had a nice supper tho and that helped a little. This town was the most beautiful we visited tho, regardless of the sundown conditions. This was the furthest point we reached on the trip. The next morning we headed back to camp. We stopped at a few little places on the way back, the ones we had bypassed, and didn't get back until late at night on the last day of our pass. I was tired, but glad I had made the trip. Of course, this is

— IV —

just a brief outline of the trip. Instead of putting down everything in a letter and then have the censor cut it out, I'll save all of that until I can tell you personally. All in all, we traveled a distance of about 250 miles. It was very interesting and nice to see. I only wished you could have been with me. Everytime I'd see something nice, I'd say to myself, 'face Laite would be glad to see this'. Someday we'll make up for this lost time, just wait and see.

When I got back to camp, I had several letters from you and others waiting for me. Even tho I was tired and sleepy, I read all of yours before going to sleep. I had to do that. I guess I'll close for now, tomorrow I'll start answering your letters. Solong face Laite, and take care.

Love Always,
Willie

No. 374   July 21-'45

Hello Face Laite:

    Received three more letters from you today, along with a few others. While I was away for three days, I guess I received a letter from most ~~everybody~~ and now I have a lot to answer.

    So glad to read your letters written in Conn. You and Elaine seem to be having a very nice time and I'm sure glad to read about it. I won't try to comment on those letters, it's enough to say that I'm happy that your happy.

    So Elaine likes to walk huh? Remember the time you and I walked all one sunday afternoon and landed at your father's farm? I remember so well, that you were surprised that I had wanted to walk so far. That was before Elaine was born, but maybe she inherited that trait from you anyway. I used to like to walk, but since

I've been in the army, walking is no longer a hobby. I still like to walk tho, when I don't do much of it on duty. And as for singing, I don't no who she takes after but I'm glad she likes it. You no, ever since she was born, I always hoped she would like to sing so that we could give her the opportunities that we didn't have. I had a chance once, remember when I first told you about it? I never took it tho, and that's the reason that I'd sure like to have her become a great singer someday. Wouldn't it be kind of nice to sit by the radio and hear our great Elaine singing to the world? That's something to look forward too in any language. So lets get this old war over with in a hurry, so that we can get started together in giving her that push forward and up among the great. Okay? Solong until tomorrow honey.

Love Always — Wilbur.

A World War II Story: Dad's Letters Home

No. 375   July 22 -'45

Dearest Pace Laite:

    Well, today is sunday again over here and I just got back from mass.(6 oclock at night.) I went to communion again too, not bad huh? I've been going every two months lately.

    I'm just about getting over my trip up the island now. It had been so long that I had gone anywheres like that, that it sort of broke my routine of everyday existence. But I'm glad I went tho and I enjoyed it all very much. In the three days I was gone, I didn't get much sleep. I met a lot of people up there who knew me over here, and they were all so very nice to me. It cost me very little money too. As long as I could speak french to them that's all that I needed. I showed everybody my pictures of you and Elaine and naturally they all thought you both very nice, or in their language—mignion et

- 11 -

très chic. If you could only have been with me. Your probably wondering how and why I enjoyed myself so much. Well, you remember the time we went to Canada, it was about the same thing where I went. The only difference was that I was in uniform this time. But there was no soldiers up there tho, and I felt and acted like a civilian again. That's the big reason why I liked the trip, the only catch was that you were'nt there with me.

Now to start answering some of your letters.

So you too are planning something for our get-together huh? I'm referring to that barbecue place you stopped at on the way to Conn. Well, it sounds good and we'll sure go if you say so. (surprise?) Remember when you used to tell me that I never wanted to go anywhere that you wanted? Well, I've changed in that respect see! I'll do anything and go anything you say from now on.

Your in for a surprise huh?

Say, what is this about you having to ask Elaine what to do? In your letter you mentioned that you had to ask Elaine when to go swimming. Is she getting that bossy already? I haven't had the chance to spoil her yet, but I guess your doing a pretty good job of it yourself. So, when I get back, you'd better not give me hell if I spoil her a little more.

I'm enclosing some negatives of some pictures that were taken when I first came into this outfit. Rickson's wife had them all the time and she just sent them to him this week. You can have a set printed for yourself but send me back the negatives, because Rickson wants them back. And if you want to no what the pictures are I'll write on them if you send them to me. One of those negatives are of yours truly alone. Solong for now honey, antil tomorrow,

Devotedly, Willie

NO.376   July 23, 1945

HELLO FACE LAITE:
    Although I have'nt received any mail from you for a couple of days, I've been getting at least one letter anyway. Just now I got one letter each from Medee and Rene. I sure don't mind receiveing a lot of mail but I sure hate to answer them all. As it is now, I'll bet that I'm the champion letter-writer in the whole South Pacifie.

    Enclosed you will find some snapshots taken in New Zealand. Rickson went there on furlough and took a whole lot of pictures and gave me some. I did'nt inscibe anything in the back of them because I did'nt no what they were. But they are something to look at anyway, and will help fill that album of yours.

    Do you remember the last picture that you sent me? Well I sent it to Rene the last time I wrote him so that he could take a look at you and that big girl of ours, but I also told him to send it right back to me because that was the best picture of you two that I had. I got it back in his letter today but he said that he sure hated to send it back to me. I also think that it is the best picture that I have of you two and I want to hang onto it.

    As for Medee, it seems that somebody told him that he had the best looking girl now. I think it's Camille who told him that, but he would'nt tell me. Anyway I won't argue with him for now because I don't like to write that much. We'll settle that question when we both get back. So you see, you'd better take good care of that girl because with all the bragging I've been doing, she'd better be the best looking or else I won't be able to face those people. But I'm not really worried, if she's anything like you we can't go wrong bragging about her.

    Well, it's time to close once more, so until tomorrow, solong face laite.

                                    Devotedly Yours,
                                    Wildre'

NO.377   July 25, 1945

DEAREST FACE LAITE:

      Just received another letter from you a few minutes ago and needless to say, was very happy to hear from you. Your telling me all about your swell vacation in Conn. makes me all the more lonesome for home, but I am glad to hear that you both are having a nice time. I can just imagine you and Elaine sprawled out on the beach enjoying your relaxation. Last year I said that we would be together for this year, but here we are still in the same rut. To be on the safe side this year I won't comment on the years to come and in that way maybe we will be together a little sooner.

      Enclosed is a caption that I cut out of the Time magazine which I thought pretty good. I often think of myself being in the same predicament some day and I wonder if Elaine will react in the same manner. Such a meeting could be very embarrassing I guess but I hope not too much, for I sure want to no that big girl of ours a little better than I do now. With your help tho I'm sure things won't be too difficult.

      On the last letter that I received from Camille, he asked me if we wanted to sell our refrigerator, that he wanted to buy it. Of course I told him no. We paid a lot of money for our furniture and I'm sure you'll agree with me that we should hang on to it all. And besides, if we sold our furniture now, it would'nt be the same old life that we left to start buying new again. It will be hard enough as it is to take up where we left off. With the same familiar little homey things, such as our wedding furniture, it will help a great deal to put us on the right road. What do you think, agree or disagree?

      Well, I've spouted off about enough for one day so I guess it's time to close once more. Until tomorrow solong and take very good care of you both.

                                    ALWAYS YOURS,

                                    WILDRE'

No.378　　　　　　　　　　　　July 26,1945

Dearest Face Laite:

Received another letter from you today along with one each from Fern and Alice.The latter writes to me at least once a week,I can always expect at least one letter from her every week.I can't say that I do the same for her but I try anyway.

Was glad to hear that Annette had received her necklace and I hope she likes it.I have'nt heard from her since I sent it but should get word from her any day now.

On one of your letters,you mentioned that Pauline Rainy had a baby. I was surprised to hear that in fact I was not sure whether she was married or not. How about Millie,has she got one too oris she still single?

In reference to your being lazy while on vacation,well,all I can say is that that's what vacations are for.And besides that I don't agree with you when you say that your lazy.If that was the case we would'nt get along so well. If any one in the family is lazy I'm the one.

And the next time you go in that Fun House be careful that you don't get yourself wet again.That could be very embarrassing if it happened too often.

I still have a lot of letters to answer but gosh,I don't no when I'll ever answer them.My mail either comes in bunches or not at all.And when they come in bunches it's hard to answer them all at once.

There is'nt much change over here,it's the same old thing every day. Things are a lot more quiet now than when I first started to work here.

Well,I guess that's about all for now so until tomorrow,solong and take care of you both.

　　　　　　　　　　　　　　　Love Always,
　　　　　　　　　　　　　　　　Wildre'

No. 379   July-27-'45

Dear Face Faite:

    Received three more letters from you today and also one from Florida. On one of them you were telling me all about your trip to the beauty parlor with Elaine. That girl sure gets around lately. She seems to make friends with most anybody she meets up with. Quite a change in her since you started going out more often. And as for you, if Fern keeps giving you all those beauty treatments, I won't no my own wife when I get back. I'll have to start courting you all over again, and I sure don't want to do that all over again. Not that I wouldn't mind you, but I had such a hard time convincing you the first time that I mean to hang on to you now. Anyway, anything that Fern can do to beautify you is okay with me. But I doubt it tho, I don't no of any improvements that

-11-

could be made. Your tops with me, period.

As for Laurent, I've already written to him twice. On his last letter, he said that he would see you for sure the minute they got back from their vacation.

I'm anxious to get some of those pictures that you had taken in Conn. I haven't had any for quite a while now. Lately, I've been sending you a lot of them but now I don't no when I'll be able send any more.

Well, I guess that's about all for now, so until tomorrow, solong and take care of you both.

Love Always,
Wilfre

No. 380   July-29-'45

Dearest Face Laite!

Haven't received any mail for a couple of days now, that seems odd because I've been getting at least one every day.

Well, I went to a civilian mass this morning, just to break the old routine. To my surprise, it was a high mass, and the very same mass that we used to sing in Berwick. I still remembered most of it and I helped the choir along under my breath. Gosh, for a while I could close my eyes and pictured myself in Berwick. And then hearing a french sermon once more, it was just like home.

This afternoon, I saw the first football game New Caledonia ever held. It was an all army affair, with the M.P.s on one side and the Chair-borne Commandos (office workers) on the other.

—11—

That also brought me back to the good old fall days back home. There were cheering squads and even three acting coeds, just like the high-schools and colleges back home. The coeds were in the form of Red Cross workers. All in all, it was nice to see and I enjoyed it very much. I don't think you ever saw a football game, but when I get back that will be another must on our list. Oh yes, the M.P.'s won the game, 28 to 6.

By now, you and Elaine must be home again. I'll bet you hated to leave that place. By your letters I received while you were there, you both must have had a swell time. I'm sure glad for you, only hope you could have stayed longer. Let's hope that, next year, we'll all be together so that we can all take a longer and better vacation.

If you have to go back to work on that graveyard shift, I hope you don't take it. It's bad enough on that second shift, but if you have to walk to the shop beginning at midnight, I certainly don't approve. If that be the case, I'm asking you now not to work at all. I'd be so worried about you that I'd certainly wouldn't be much good to the army. So please, for my sake and Elaine's, don't take that shift. I'll be waiting anxiously for a reply to that, and also doing a little worrying on the side.

Solong for now, and take good care of you both.

Love Always

Wilor

NO.381　　　　　　　　　　　　July 30,1945

Hello Face Laite:
　　　　Not having received any mail again today,there is'nt much to talk about.So I guess I'll tell you some more about my trp up the island which I took last week.
　　　　In some places where we traveled thru made me recall a lot of the time we took that trip to Canada in 1940.There is'nt so much flat land over here as there was in Canada,but the scenery was about the same.In order to cross from one side of the island to the other there is only a one lane road and the curves in that road are something to remember.In spots,there is room for one car only to travel with one side of the road having a high cliff and the other having a drop of several hundred feet.As a matter of fact,most of the road is cut out of the side of a chain of hills all the way.It made one sort of dizzy to look down in one of these deep canyons for the first time.In these deep canyons there were some small native farms with fruits and gardens seeming to sprout right out of the ground.From the road where we were,all of these things looked like midgets or a bunch of ants darting to and fro.If we would have had more time we would have gone down there and and visited these places.And to give you an idea as to high we were,in some spots we actually drove thru clouds.One minute the sun was shining brightly and the nextthing we knew we would be in the fog.One stretch of low land I remember,there were a lot of cattle grazing just like we see back home in our open fields.There are a lot of cattle here on this island, much more than I expected to see.For water, these cattle drink out of several small streams which come down from the surrouding hills and mountains.It was nice to see these streams come tumbling down in a white foam from thesee high hills, and than come to rest peacefully in a small river below.If only you could have seen tese things,I thought about you often on that trip.I only hope that some day I'll be able to show you something like that,if not here at least somewhere back in the States.Solong for now face laite,
　　　　　　　　　　　　　　　Love,　　Wildre'

No. 382   July-31-'45

Dearest Pace Laite:

    Finally received a letter from you today. It was dated much earlier than the last one I got from you, so I guess it must have jumped ahead of the others.

    A few days ago, I wrote to you and asked that you shouldn't work on that graveyard shift. On today's letter you tell me that you've already started on that shift. I certainly did'nt like that bit of news. I don't want you to think that I'm trying to tell you what to do, or in other words trying to boss you around. On the contrary, I trust everything you do and your certainly old enough to no what to do. In asking you not to work on that shift, I only had your welfare in mind. That is, walking to work late at night, and most of all the extra physical hardship you'd have to undergo. It's bad enough for

-11-

a man to work that way but for a wife, and my wife at that, well, I just don't like it. God, why doesn't this ~~ole~~ war hurry up and get over. Anyway face facts, your the one who's going thru this and you must no what your doing. So, I won't talk about it anymore. All I ask is that you take good care of yourself, and don't be afraid to quite that job if you have too. You come first, to hell with the money.

Well, I see that your taking care of the business end of the family. The insurance on the furniture I mean. I'll bet that next year at this time, you won't have to pay another premium. (I hope)

I'm glad you both had a nice vacation with Fern. It's too bad you couldn't stay any longer. Maybe next year things will be different huh? Again, I hope.

It's been a long time since I told you anything about myself. Well, to sum it all up briefly there isn't much change. At present, I go to work at four in the afternoon and quite at midnight. I sleep as long as I want too in the morning. After writing a few letters and doing the necessary things to live, it's about time to go to work again. When I work days, I usually go to a show and write more letters at night, than it's time for bed again. So you see, the only excitement there is, is whatever I can sum up against at work. Outside of that, it's just a matter of marking time until we can both get back to the old life again. That is, a real home like we used to have, — remember?

So long until tomorrow face laite,

Devotedly Yours,
Wilbr

No. 383   Aug. 2- 45

Dearest Face Laite!

Received two letters from you yesterday. On one of them, you were telling me all about your trip home from Conn. It seems that you had a good time up till the last minute. It makes me happy just to read about it. About those two soldiers you met on the train, I hope you don't judge everyone like that. I haven't lied to you so far, so why should I start now? Believe me face laite, I've had a lot of chances to be that way but I can honestly say that I didn't take them. I've seen too much of that dirty work going on, and even if I hadn't I still would feel the same way about it. So don't you worry about this end of the bargain, it hasn't changed and never will. But just wait until I get my hands on the other end of that bargain. Have you bought that steel corset yet?

-11-

Sorry to hear about the Proups. Hope they get well soon. As for the runt and his girl friend, I see they are always in the same old rut. I'd sure like to see those two, just to see what they really do first hand.

So you still keep my letters huh? You must have a special room to keep them in. I certainly wouldn't have the patience to do the same, and besides it wouldn't be very practical in this business.

Well, I guess this is about all for now, can't find my thinking cap. Maybe it's because I was up all night. Solong until tomorrow faci laite.

Love Always,
Vilde

August 4, 1945

Dear Mr. & Mrs:

Received a v-mail from you a few days ago and today received another air mail from you again. So I guess it's time I should answer huh?

Jean and Elaine seem to have had a very nice vacation at your place and I'm sure glad to hear about it. She sent me some pictures today that were taken at your home, and they were all very good. Jean seems to have added on a little weight and I think it's very becoming too. As for Elaine, She's gotten so tall that I hardly recognized her and beautiful too. She sure will be tall girl if she keeps growing. Imagine me coming home and have a grown up girl besides a wife to greet me. I'm afraid I won't no how to act. Anyway I'm willing to find out,--anytime. And as for you, you don't seem to have changed much. A little rounder maybe but the same old mug always. By the way, congratulations on your new promotion. By the time I get back you'll probably have a job working on my hair line. They are sure getting thinner every day. Can you make hair grow too, or have'nt you taken up that course yet? On second thought maybe I'd like being bald headed, would'nt have to worry about it than. Bill does'nt seem to have changed much either,----outside of being a little tinner than usual. But having a woman full of vim and vitality such as you it's little wonder he's able to survive, let alone gain any weight. Maybe it would do him a lot of good to get away from all that temptation for a while. ha, ha. Seriously tho I hope he stays right where he is. One sure does'nt gain anything by being away from his loved ones, except maybe to appreciate home and all it stands for a lot more. You just don't no how it is until you get away from it, believe me.

Any pictures you may have I'll sure appreciate if you will send them to me. Especially of Jean and little Miss long-legs. Boy they sure are long. Outside of having the real persons handy pictures are the next best thing, and I never refuse either. Have to close for now, will try to write more next time.

As Ever   Wildre'

No. 384   Aug. 4 - '45

Dearest Face Laile:

Just received two swell letters from you and also the vacation photos which were taken in Conn. First of all, I want to say a few things about those pictures.

There wasn't enough of you in the first place, in fact there was only one good picture of you. That was the one with you, Fern and Elaine on bicycles. That outfit you had on is new isn't it? At least I don't remember seeing it. And I like that bare mid-drift too, you should get more outfits like that. You seem to have put on weight and it sure looks very becoming.

As for Elaine, I can't get over my surprise of her being so tall. She looks like a little Amazon. If she doesn't stop growing so fast, she'll be taller than you in another year. Imagine me coming home to two girls instead of one. I can't wait to get near enough

-11-

to touch you. All in all, the pictures were very nice and they brought me home for a few minutes. They are the next best thing to the real stuff, believe me. The only fault I can find is that I never get enough of them. So keep them coming as often as you can.

Irene didn't seem to have changed any, but Charlotte has tho. Gail is a nice kid but not when she's beside Elaine. Can't beat that gal. Fern seems a little stouter and she's getting to look more like the old man every day. In another few years, I think she'll look like a little round ball. Not you tho, you'll never change.

Was glad to hear that your getting along okay on that grave yard shift. As long as your not afraid and there's no danger, I

-111-

feel better. But don't forget, if you can't make out alright, don't hesitate to leave that job.

So the Tousaints finally came to see you huh? He sure had a nice long vacation. When he goes back to camp, he'll probably get a soft job because he hasn't got enough points for discharge. Well, when I get back I think it will be to stay,— as a civilian. It might take a little while yet, but when it does comes, we'll enjoy it all the more. Until then, take care of yourself and Miss Long-Legs.

     Love Always,
      Wilbre

No.385   Aug.5,1945

Dearest Face Laite:

It's sunday again over here and another day almost over once more.But most of all it's another day bringing us closer together and that's what counts the most.I went to a french civilian mass this morning again,it's gettinf to be a habit.But it seems so nice to get away from military surroundings that I think I'll keep on going as much as I can.This afternoon I went to another football game,the M.P. against a team called The Green Tide,and our team won again.It was much warmer than it was last sunday and as a result my face is red as a beet from standing the sun all afternoon.There must have been a crowd of about 10,000 or more,including civilians and servicemen.These people never saw a football game until last sunday,but they turn out to see it just the same even tho they don't understand all of the plays.

Rene seems to be saving quite a bit of money thru you.I'm glad for him, when he gets out he won't be broke like a lot of other fellows.And it's a good thing that your his banker,I'm sure he could'nt find a better one.I ought to Know.

I see that your always busy with some kind of sewing.And about that new coat that you need,you'd better buy one now cause if you wait for me,you'll probably wait until nextwinter.So the next time you send me some pictures I want to see a new coat along with you in it,---or else.Than when I get back I'll really show you how to buy cloths.But please don't be afraid to get yourself a few things in the meantime.After all,I don't want the neighbors/that/Pelletier does'nt want his wife to buy any cloths.
                                            to say

Well,I guess that's about all for now face laite,solong until tomorrow and take care of you both for me.

                                       Love Always,
                                         Wildre'

No. 386　　　　Aug. 6 - '45

Dear Face Lite:

Received another letter from you today. Was glad to hear that your doing okay on the new shift. You don't no what a relief that is to me. As long as you think it's alright that's good enough for me. Only take care of yourself.

With all those people Annette had in the house for a few days, you must have been pretty crowded. They didn't sleep in your bed too did they? Elaine must be all business with all those people around. She sure has changed, but that only shows how fast she must be growing. I have'nt quite gotten over my surprise of her being so tall. Boy, what a gal.

I've had something to tell you for a few months now, and I'm still anxious to

—11—

tell you too,—but I guess I won't just yet. I just thought that I'd mention it so that I could get you in a curious mood. Mean huh? I'll tell you soon, don't worry?

I've been receiving a few Chronicles since the past week. I hadn't had any for a long time. I haven't had a Free Press for three months now, but I don't mind too much. As long as the mail keeps coming as it is now, I'll be satisfied.

Can't think of much more to write, so I guess it's time to close. So long for now face Laite, take care of yourself and those little long legs.

Always,
Wilbe

No. 387   Aug. 8-'45

Hello Face Laite:

Received three letters from you today along with one each from Florida ad Butch.

From the last few letters I've been receiving from you, you seem to be enjoying your new shift. I don't no whether your telling me that so that I don't worry, but I hope your not. That's a bad shift, I no, because I worked on it too remember? Anyway, take care of yourself face laite.

I see you and Elaine had a busy sunday in So. Berwick going from place to place. Glad you had a nice time. And that Elaine is still wowing them too eh? No wonder she's so tall, if she packs away all the food you say she does, I expect to see a young giant when I get back. And Medée's girl can be cute but I'll bet not as beautiful as Elaine. How about that.

-11-

Well, according to the latest news reports, it won't be long now before the Japs give up. This new bomb that just came out two days ago will do the trick I guess. But we still don't no what the future holds for us, this may last a few months yet. There is some ray of hope for an early peace I'll admit, but it doesn't pay to expect to much in advance, — at least not in the army. I learned that the hard way. If the prediction I made a few months ago really comes true, I'll consider myself lucky. Let's hope for the best anyway face laite.

As for Lionel's new address, that's the same place I'd be at if I would have stayed with the engineers, I told you the place a while back, remember? Solong for now face laite,

Love Always, Wildor

No. 389   Aug. 10 - '45

Dearest Face Laite!

    Haven't received any mail for a few days now, as a result there's not much to talk about. But as you said before, a few lines is enough to satisfy you, so here they are.

    I just got back from the movie, I saw Salome. It wasn't so hot, only showed a lot of sex, and no story to the show. Imagine, I'm getting choosey about the shows now. Just goes to show that you can't please everybody. Maybe I'm getting sick of these islands and trying to take it out on the movies.

    Well, ever since the big news about Russia and that new bomb came out, there's all kinds of speculation going on among us. Even I have to admit that the coming months look rosier than they did. But I'm still keeping my fingers

- 11 -

crossed and trying not to be too optimistic. Gosh, I think,—oh well, I'll tell you some other time.

I just spied a lemon on the next bunk, and all of a sudden I felt like eating one. (Remember when we use to do that often? I'll bet your mouth is watering (because I'm eating it as I'm writing). Maybe the censor's is too.

Hope your not working too hard on that new shift. Take care of yourself and that big girl. Guess this is about the end of my few lines, so until tomorrow, solong face laite.

Love Always,
Willie

No. 390   Aug. 11 - '45

Dear Face Faite:

Received two letters from you today and was sure glad to get them.

Well, I guess you have heard the big news today, or rather yesterday your time. It isn't over with yet but I guess it won't be long now. There seems to be some question about what to do with the Jap. emperor; maybe there will be some answer to that by tomorrow.

I also received a letter from Butch and he told me that he was at the beach. They can have their beach but for me I prefer the lake. How about you? In all the time I've been over here I went swimming at the beach only once. And I live right next to it. So you see how much I go for salt water.

On one of your letters, you said that you were writing it under the dryer. Busy woman that wife of mine. I can just picture you writing in that

-11-

position. Pretty soon now, you won't have to write any more letters, but until then keep them coming tho. Speaking of positions, I'm writing this one while sitting out of doors. It's five oclock and I've just got back from work. I'm writting this early because I want to go and see a french movie tonight. I've never seen one yet and I'm curious to see what they are like. Will tell you about it tomorrow.

It's so quiet out here right now that I can almost think that I'm home. The weather is very nice, not a breeze around and yet the temperature is just right. I'm afraid that I'll freeze once I get back to God's country, but I don't care. Just let me get back. So long for now face laite. Take care of you both,

Love Always,
Wilde

No. 391   Aug. 12-'45

Dearest Face Faite:

It's sunday again over here, the first day of another week for me. As it is still saturday back home, you must be sound asleep about this time. And with all this sensational news that you've been hearing these past two days, I'll bet your dreaming of peace. Well, your not the only one. Although the final word is not official yet, I'm sweating it out along with millions of other guys. And yes, I too dream about it. I'd like to tell you something right now that you've probably been thinking about. Even tho the war should come to an end tomorrow, that does not mean that I'll be home in two months. Before getting your hopes too high, I want you to no that I'm liable to stay here any where from now till one year, or

−11−

even more before getting a chance to go back. Now, if we both think that same way, we won't be disappointed if that's the case. And in the meantime, if I do get to go back sooner, think what a surprise it will be. So you see face laite, don't get any false hopes, we don't no what to expect,— at least not I, as long as I stay in this uniform. But we can hope. Everything sure looks pretty good right now.

 Went to a french mass again this morning. Getting to be quite a habit with me now. Maybe I'm getting to learn how to be a civilian again.

 Well, I guess that's about all for now, solong until tomorrow face laite.

Always Yours,
Wilbré

No. 392   Aug. 14 - '45

Hello Face Faite:

    Just received three letters from you, and also one from Alice.

So Laurent is going to Lake Placid huh? Glad to hear that, because from what I hear, that's a nice place to be. Don't think it will be long now before he'll be able to get out entirely.

    You seem to be having all kinds of trouble trying to go to confession and communion. Well don't worry to much if you don't go. I can't see what you have to confess anyway. You couldn't do anything wrong even if you tried.

    I see your pulling some of my old tricks and shutting off the alarm huh? You'll have to admit that it's a good alibi and a nice way to get a night off. I haven't heard an alarm for the last two years now, and I'll bet it will be nice to listen to one again.

-11-

I see that your taking care of your molars regularly. But it seems that each time you see a dentist you have to have one filled. I have not been to a dentist for a year now, and I hate the thought of going. He'll surely find a half dozen cavities, and you no me when it comes to drilling. But I take better care of them now then when I was home, that is by washing them at least twice a day.

That must have been a nice picnic spot that you told me about. The one near Farmington. And it's not if I want too but rather if you want to that we'll go there when I get back. He'll make up for everything that we ever missed, wait and see.

Solong for now face laite, until tomorrow

Yours Always,
Wilbr

Aug. 16 - '45

Dearest Face Laite:

I don't no what your reactions were when you first heard of the big news, and as for me, well, my reactions were many and varied. When I first heard of the news I was in a boat crossing a bay on the way to a little island off the mainland. When I suddenly heard sirens, horns and ship's whistles blowing, I knew the end had finally come. I felt like shouting and laughing and about everything else, but I didn't. The first thing I really thought of doing was to offer some little prayer of thankfullness. Then I really got down to thinking and tried to imagine what it would be like when I got back. And for the first time since I've been across I think that my imagination that day brought me

-11-

nearer home than at any other time. Why, I was actually home on Bow St. sitting in my easy chair, with you and Elaine crawling all over me. I can't put down on paper all of my thoughts because I'm sure I couldn't express them as they appeared to me.

The civilians here as well as G.I.'s and everybody else went just about mad. In no time at all, there appeared makeshift parades all over town. Singing, dancing, shouting and everything else could be witnessed everywhere one could be. Everybody celebrated, — everybody except the M.P.'s. The only celebrating I did was take a few pictures around the town. At night, after working hours I thought maybe I could get into it, but no soap. By the time I was ready to join, everyone else was to far gone for me to enjoy any-

-111-

thing, so I was satisfied with having a few drinks and to bed early. I have a lot of celebrating to do, but not over here. I'm saving that for the big day when we'll really do a good job of it.

According to the news, I may get back sooner than I expected. Anyway I'm keeping my fingers crossed and firmly hope that I do. Days will get increasingly longer now, but we've stood it this long, surely we can take a little more. So, take extra good care of yourself and Miss Long-legs now, and before you no it we'll be back to living like people should live.

With love and gratitude to you and you,

Devotedly Yours,
Wilde

No. 395   Aug 17 --

Hello Face Faite:

Here it is, two days after the big announcement and there's more news to talk about right now than I care to discuss. First of all, that which concerns our going home is the most interesting, but I still say that it will be a few months before I can get overheated on the subject. So I guess we'll just forget that for a little while longer. When I do get some news on the matter, I'll be sure to let you no, — the very first.

Well, there was a lot of celebrating done a couple of days ago, but from this morning's news I gather there's still some fighting going on on quite a few fronts. It will be some time yet before all arms are laid down. We can only hope it won't be too long before this fact is realized.

-11-

We weren't so very busy during that big celebration, but since then I've been running around like a mad dog. Everything happens at once or not at all in this job.

I said at the beginning that there was a lot of news to talk about, but now I don't no how to talk about it. Maybe censorship will be lifted pretty soon and I'll be able to write with better sense. As it is now my style is cramped considerably.

Oh yes, you must have had two days off this week. The President announced that all government employees were to have this last Wed. and Thurs. Pretty lucky I think.

Solong for now. face laite, and take care,

Love Wilbur

No. 396   Aug. 18-'45

Dear Face Laite;

Received a whole batch of letters today, two from you and others too numerous to mention.

So Elaine is growing fast huh? Imagine her trying to tease you, and at this early age too. I'm not there to get you angry, so somebody has to take my place. What are you going to do when you have the two of us, you probably won't stand a chance huh? But don't worry too much, we'll take good care of you. Elaine may be a little spoiled now, but after all, she has a right to be, for she's the only one we have. So don't be too hard on her huh?

Glad to hear that you found a ride back from work. That must help a little. Take care of yourself face laite. According to your letters you seem to be getting plenty of sleep. Even Annette tells me that you seem to be getting along okay and I'm relieved to hear it.

Now that this show is finished Bill won't have to worry any more. He would not have passed his physical anyway. And as for Nel I believe I told you that that was where he was.

And as for Florida, she's still up to the same old tricks huh? Well, you can't teach an old dog new tricks. Lorette has been writing her letters to me lately and she's pretty good too. She has a nice line of chatter and it does make sense. In fact she's much better than her mother. In one of her letters, Florida told me that Lorette might not go back to that same school next Fall, because they did not have the money. But it seems that

-111-

she has plenty of money to spend on a summer long vacation. Wait until I write her the next time, I'll tell her a few more things.

Well, the celebrations are about over here, that is as far as we are concerned. But the French people are just starting a three day holiday tomorrow — three days after we did. These people are funny that way, always celebrating at the drop of a hat. As for us, we are now sweating out that boat that's to take us back once and for all. May take several months, so don't be too impatient. Solong for now face laite.

     Love Always,
     Wilde

No. 397   Aug. 19-'45

Dearest Face Saite:

    Another sunday, another beginning of another week bringing us nearer and nearer together. We can at least hope a little more for the big day now. As it was before, there wasn't much hope, but now things look a little more cheerful. Maybe in a couple of months we'll be able to say for sure just when we can expect that last boatride. Gosh, I can't wait. I'm getting more impatient every day. I never did listen to the news very much, but now I listen all the time. Talk about a sweat out job.

    Well, this is my forth letter today. I wrote to Penn, two of my old buddies at A.P.O. 331 and now you. That's a lot of letters to write for me in one day. Boy, I've certainly lost the knack for writing. There was a time when I wrote as many as eight several times a week.

-71-

If I stay over here much longer, I'll have a hard time too write to you. So you see, they'd better send me back soon.

I worked all day today, so I couldn't see the football game. But I heard it over the radio tho. And I managed to go to mass this morning, but not to the civilian mass.

I have two rolls of films to develope now, and when there ready I'll send them to you. I can't have any prints made over here anymore, so I guess you'll have to do it yourself. And if you want to no what they are, you could send them to me and I could mark them. But they won't be ready for a couple of weeks yet.

I guess that's all for now, so long until tomorrow face laite.

Love Always, Willie

A World War II Story: Dad's Letters Home

August 19,1945

Dear Mr.& Mrs:

Received your letter dated 7th Auguast yesterday and also your package which must have been dated six months ago.The latter must have traveled all over the South Pacific because it sure was in a bad shape when I got it.I managed to save the canned goods and the books but the cigaettes were not any good.However, thanks for everything,I was glad to receive them.

Well,now that the big show is over with you can feel more at ease now. That last deferment that Bill had will last along time now.He was lucky on that point but I don't think he would have been called anyway.

Well,how did you lucky civilians take the big news?I can imagine what a riot there must have been all over the States.Over here,Most everybody went wild for a whole day and a good part of the evening but the next day everything was back to normal. Today,four days after such breath-taking news,one would not no it had happened.over here.Naturaly it's a great relief but I'm still in the army and until THE day when I can call my life my own,time will just drag along .

In reference to the girl whom I am fortunate enough to call my partner, I know only too well the qualities she possesses that goes to make life happy and contented for one like me.I have never doubted nor worried about her truthfullness, nor will I ever.There is no need to linger on this subject,I accept all of this with humble thankfulness.

Now that this war is finally over you can look forward to seeing me along with Jean and Elaine on their next vacation in Conn.Of course I hope that I can get home sooner,but that's the least I can hope for at this time.

Solong for now,until another day,I remain

As Ever

Wildre'

No. 398   Aug. 21-'45

Hello Face Laite;

    Haven't received any mail for a few days now. It's been slowing up since the Jap surrender. Should be picking up soon.

    Well, I started to work nights again last night. This shift gives me lots of time to write my letters, and also plenty of time to sleep and loaf around. A typical day would be to, go to work at 4.30 until 12, in bed by 1230. Get up in the morning anytime I wish, but usually at 8 or 9. Then go for a walk or play ball to get a little exercise, dinner at 11.00 and read or write letters all afternoon until time to work again. I've been doing this now for almost a year. Of course everyday is not always the same, if it were, it would drive a man nuts. There's usually plenty of excitement at work, and a good thing too. Later on, if censorship is lifted, my daily letters will be

-11-

more interesting, maybe.

For the past two days I've been playing baseball after I get up in the forenoon, and boy am I stiff. Guess I'm getting old and don't no it.

My watch stopped on me again last night. I don't no whats the matter with it, but I'm sure it's nothing serious. The spring isn't broken because I wound it up to the limit, but it still won't go. I'll take it to a french jeweler tomorrow and see if he can't fix it without he soaking me too much. I'm so used to it now that I feel undressed without it.

A couple of nights ago I opened up a can of tuna fish that Fern had sent me in a package, and gosh was it good. It had been so long since I had tasted it. I tried to buy some in the french stores here but they didn't have any. All they have is sardines and salmon, and that we have at the mess hall.

It's little things like that that we miss most over here. That is, as far as eats are concerned. We can't complain too much tho because we have plenty of good things to eat, only, it isn't like home.

I'm anxious to get more pictures of you and Elaine again. The last batch you sent me, there was only one good one of you two. You tell me that I should send you more of mine, well, I'm telling you the same right now. How about that huh? And hows that big girl lately, still bossy as ever? Probably takes after the old man. But she'll have to change her ways, because he sure has changed in that respect. Am so anxious to see you both again. It won't be many more months now, so hang on to the fort face laite, I'll be back before you no it. Solong for now,

Love Always, Willie

No. 399 Agust 22,1945.

Dearest Face Laite:

No letters again today but here's the customary few words anyway. First of all, I don't remember whether the number of this letter is correct or not. You see, I usually take the last number down to work and when there is'nt much work, I type out your letter. Well, today I forgot to take the last number so I took a chance on my memory. Anyway, I'll straighten it out tomorrow.

Well, the news have'nt changed much in the last few days and I still don't no what's going to happen in regards to our return. I was thinking today what would happen to Andre and fellows like him. From the last letter I received from him I gathered that he was about ready to come across. But now that the war is over I figured he would probably get his discharge. He's certainly got more to worry about than we have. He told me that his wife was expecting that littel bird again sometime in October or November. With three kids on his hands his place is at home and not in the army. Anyway, I hope that everything turns out okay. By hte way, I wrote him a letter today and can't mail it because I lost his address.

I heard on the news broadcast that all goverment employees were going back on a 40 hour week. That must apply to you too I guess, so that will be alright huh? It will give you more time at home with that big girl and also more time for relaxation. You've been working too much to suit me.

Well, I guess that's about all for tonight, so until tomorrow solong and take good care of yourself.

Love Always,

Wildre'

No. 400   August 23, 1945.

Hello Face Laite:

Another day without any mail, and the old brain is straining to jot down these few words. I did receive a Chronicle tho and that was something. Lately those papers have'nt been coming in very good, but then I can't kick too much because they are free. Oh yes, about that number on yesterday's letter, it was correct,--much to my surprise.

We had a very nice dinner today and I'll bet you can't guess what we had. Fish, that's what it was and boy did it taste good. Some of the boys went fishing and came back with quite a haul. That was the first fish I had since leaving the States. I've been asked several times to go fishing with them, but oh no, not me. I get seasick every time. I'll do my fishing on a nice smooth lake,--when I get back.

There's all kinds of rumors floating around here as to when and how we'll be getting back. But as usual you can't believe those rumors. If you did you'd go crazy. But I like to listen to them anyway and they give us something to talk about.

By the time you receive this letter it will be time for another one of our anniversary. Just think, five years so soon that you took a chance on me. Are'nt you sorry now?(don't answer that) When I stop and think sometimes as to the hard time you gave me trying to win you over, Boy that was certainly a stuggle, but it was worth it. And I think I'd do it over again too. This will be our third that we will have to celebrate separately but our fourth will surely be different. Oh yes, you have a surprise in store for this one but I won't tell you now, because you may get this letter before the 31st. And you can't tease me now because I'm too far away. Well, I guess it's time to close once more, so until tomorrow solong and take care of you both.

                                    Yours Always,
                                    Wildre'

No. 401   August 24, 1945

Dearest Face Laite:

    Another day without any mail and I'm just about run out of words. If this keeps up I won't have anything to talk about, so I8d better get some mail soon.

    I got my watch back today and it's running swell again. It did'nt cost me anything to have it fixed so I can't lose much. The fellow said that it was a little dirty and that's all that was the matter with it.

    There's not much going on tonight so a few of us got ot talking about what it would be like to get back home again. One guy was saying that as soon as he would get his discharge he would hike home, in order to save his money; that he would need that money to have a good time with. I said that I certainly would not hike but would take the fastest transportation available; that I had wasted enough time already and that I would not waste another minute as long as I live. Then the conversation went further into detail as to what we would do after getting out etc. Gosh, I can't put down everything that we say because it would take to long. But I guess everything we say now won't all come true no matter how hard we'll try to make them come true. Personally, I've had so many ideas for the post war world that I'm all mixed up now. I don't think I really no what I, or rather we, will do. We'll just have to wait until that day comes along. The only fact that I'm sure of, is that we will have our farm no matter what. Anyway, this is one big sweatout. I can't wait for the final ending to this chapter in our way of life.

    Hope your not overworking yourself lately, and take good care of Miss Longlegs. It won't be long now that she will be meeting the old man. Salong for now, until tomorrow,

                Love Always,

                  Wildre'

A World War II Story: Dad's Letters Home

No. 402   August 25, 1945.

Dearest Face Laite:

       Just received four letters from you and I was sure glad. These were the first letters I got from you this week, and they were perfumed too. I was anxious to hear from you how you took the big news. Now that I've read your version I guess it was about the same every where. And it's a good thing that the Japs did give up because you would have lost a lot of sleep at the rate you were going. Oh well, it's over with now and all we have to do is wait.

       So Elaine gets your dander up because she eats those green apples huh? I would'nt say too much if I were you. Remember when you used to do the same and I got angry at you? Well, like daughter like mother, so take it easy on her. I no they're not good for her but don't punish her too much.

       So your curious and want to no what I got for you huh? Well, I guess I'll tell you. It's a ———, no, I think I'll wait another day before I tell you. ha ha.

       If Conrad has a chance to get home so soon he sure is lucky. I only hope he is'nt in a division that's going to police Japan. If he is'nt he has a good chance to get out of this army one the first.

       In reference to the shorts I mentioned on an earlier letter, it was'nt very hard to no the name "mid-drift" because it was stareing me right in the face. And I don't recall you ever haveing an outfit like that, if you did it was hidden some where in the attic. Anyway I still think it's a nice outfit and you should have more of them.

       Two of you letters smelled so nice that I hate to throw them away. If that's any sample of how the real thing smells like you'd better watch out. Solong for now, until tomorrow,

                      Love Always,
                      Wildre

No. 403   August 26, 1945

Hello Face Laite:

It's five oclock in the afternoon over here and I'm just statting my night's work. If your still on that midnight shift you also msut have just started your night's work. So I guess we're both in the same boat huh?

I went to the ten o'clock mass this morning and during mass there was a baptism ceremony going on in the vestry. After the baby was baptized they rang the church bells. The priest explained that the ringing of the bells meant a sign of joy because a new baby had been born. I never knew why the church bells used to ring at most any hour of the day, but now I do. This afternoon I went to another football game. I sat facing the sun all afternoon and right now my face is burning like a red hot stove. It was'nt so interesting to watch this afternoon. Maybe it's because the war is over and that all I can think about is going home. Oh yes, the M.P.s lost the game.

In case I did'nt mention it, I received a letter from Mary yesterday also. Can you imagine, she finally admits that they have never been able to get another man to take my place since I left. She also said that some day they would try to repay all that I've done for them. It's a little late to think about that now is'nt it?

Well, by the time you receive this letter you probably have that surprise I've been talking about. It won't be much of a surprise because you've already had the same thing on your last birthday. That was the best I could do for now, when I get back I'll make up for everything. That's a promise.

Well, I guess that's about all for now, solong until tomorrow face laite.

                                Love Always,
                                Wildre'

No. 404   Aug. 28-'45

Dearest Face Laite:

Hello honey, as I'm writing this letter you must be working in the early hours of the morning. Today is my day off and I have nothing better to do than write you a few lines of nothing. In other words I can't think of anything to write, so if the following seems strange to you, don't pay any attention to it.

There hasn't been very much work these past few days and as a result, I've caught up on sleep, reading and writing. And to top it off I haven't received any mail. So right now, I have nothing much to do except loaf around.

I was just thinking, the weather must be about the same at home as it is right here at this time. As a matter of fact, it could be warmer at home than it is here. If I remember right, it's pretty hot in August at home. Over here, we're in the spring of the year and it's not too cold or warm, just right to be going without any clothes on. As a matter of fact, people go swimming the year round, so you see, it's not too cold. When I work on the night shift, I have a good part of the day to get me a good tan, and that I have.

I'm so anxious to see that big girl again. Tell me, is she still as bossy as ever? Try to send me some more pictures of you both will you? It may take a few months before I can get back, and in the meantime I want to get acquainted with my family.

-111-

I no you haven't changed much but Elaine has, there's no doubt about it. Oh yes, one of the last pictures you sent me, the one you had taken dressed in that midriff outfit, you had a pair of arms that looked like a small wrestler. It must be the way the picture was taken or else they got that way from lifting Elaine. Anyway send me more of them if you can, I sure like to see them. Don't mind the wise cracks I may pass on them. I haven't changed much you no, still the same old sour puss, and I hope your still the same old face laite.

So long for now,

Love Always,
Wildre

No.405.   August 29, 1945.

Dearest Face Laite:

Hello honey, I have'nt received any of your letters for a week now, and I'm back again not knowing what to say. I guess all the ships and planes are further up north taking care of the occupation of Japan. When that's over with maybe the mail situation will be cleared up.

I did receive a letter each from Meddee and Rene tho today. Medee says that he has three battle stars to his credit, (15 points). I've been kidding him all along as to the soft job he had. But I guess the last laugh is on me because with those extra 15 points he probably has more than I have, and will get back sooner that I will. Talking about points, there's so many rumors going around here that they keep one's head in a whirl. Fortunately I don't take them too seriously, for if I did they'd have me in a straight-jacket. I like to listen to them but that's as far as I go. Rene also talks about going home in his letter, but fellows like him deserve a break. He's been over here 30 months now and most of that time was in combat. Although I'm a little jealous of all those points, I think fellows like him deserve the first chance of getting back,---- and they probably will. The first prediction I made about my return still holds as far as I'm concerned. If I get a break before that I'll be one lucky guy.

Well, what are you doing with all that extra time on your hands these days. From what I hear on the radio all government workers are back on a 40 hour week. that should apply to you also, so that must leave you with a whole Saturday and Sunday doing nothing but stepping out with that big girl and enjoying yourself. It won't be long before I'll be there to add my two cents worth. I get so anxious sometimes that it hurts. But I manage to stand it some how.
Solong for now and take care of you both,

                                        Love Always,
                                          Wildre'

No. 406   August 30-'45

Dearest Face Laite:

Finally received some mail from you today, five letters from you and one from Alice. Even tho the war is over, I still like to hear from you, in fact more so.

On one of your letters you stated that I didn't sound very encouraging about getting home soon. Well, I just don't want you to think that, just because the war is over doesn't mean I will be going back in a month or two. I simply don't want you to build up any false hopes. We may as well face this from the army point of view, and I certainly no how that is. It may take a few months to get back and then again it may take a long time. All we can do is wait. So lets not be anxious face laite, it doesn't pay. The first thing you no, I'll be back and getting you angry again.

I see you still have that small radio. Pretty high class to have a radio right in your bedroom. I didn't think Elaine could sing as loud that you couldn't hear the radio. That must be quite a voice she has. And she's still eating those green apples huh? I don't agree with you that by putting her to bed is good punishment for the petty things she does. I think a good slap on the back side will get better results. You don't have to wait for me to get back in order to carry that out, if I remember right you had a pretty good arm, so why not use it.

I was surprised to learn that Conrad is back already, and with two campaign stars, too. I don't see how he could have gotten two stars in the short time he was over. He wasn't there more than two months was he?

-111-

Oh well, that means 10 additional points anyway.

You no, I've started collecting some names and addresses of people I no over here. I'm putting them in my diary. By the way, I don't think that I'll be in the army long enough to fill that five year diary. At least I hope not.

I wonder what's going to happen to André now that the war is over. Alice sent me his latest address and he's in California now. I hope he doesn't come across now.

Well, I guess that's about all for now. So long until tomorrow,

Always Yours,
Wilde

A World War II Story: Dad's Letters Home

No. 407 Aug. 31 - '45
Anniversary #5

Dearest Face Faite;

Tho many miles separate us once more on this fifth anniversary, I can at least wish you a happy one. I hope you got the flowers okay and also the song I requested over the Portsmouth station. Unless I'm very much mistaken, we'll spend our next anniversary and all the others after that as they were meant to be spent, — together.

I received another letter from you and one from Camille late yesterday. But now I probably won't get another one for a week, at least that's the way they've been coming in.

You mentioned that my mail was not supposed to be censored anymore. Well, I can assure you that they are, but when they do stop reading our mail we'll be advised before you. I don't believe the censors like their job

-11-

very well and they will be only to glad to let us no the first ones.

You no, I weighed myself yesterday and was surprised to learn that there's 209 pounds of me. So you see, I'm not very slim. I haven't got the pot belly I had when I came in the army, but still the weight is all there. I've got a couple of pictures of me taken without a shirt on, and you'll see for yourself just what I mean. I only have the negatives so far but as soon as I have them developed, I'll send them to you. And by the way, how about some more of you and that big girl? Haven't had any for quite a while now.

It was sure glad to hear that you were done with the midnight shift. And that five days a week is alright too. Don't worry too much about that layoff. Even if you did stop working now until I get back, it would be okay with me.

-111-

It would give you a chance to get rested up. You could go on the farm when you wanted too, and maybe get some color in your cheeks. Anyway, don't worry about being without work, you have plenty of money to keep you until I get back, and don't be afraid to spend it.

I wonder what's going to happen to Bill and all those people in Conn. I wouldn't be surprised if they came back to the old home town.

Well, I guess it's time to sign off once more. Solong for now,

Love Always,
Willie

No. 408   September 2, 1945.

Dear Face Laite:

It's sunday over here and also V J day. I heard the official news at 1230 while you must have heard it at about 2130 last night. Right after the news we heard a victory command performance which orignated in Hollywood, and I guess all the stars participated because it was very long. All afternoon long there were all kinds of speeches and V J day was mentioned time and again. Now that it's finally official all we have to do is wait for our own special day, the day when we will start living again.

While all this was going on we had a little excitement of our own right in our tent. It had started to rain early this morning and continued until right thru the momentous ceremony. It was raining so hard and the wind was blowing so hard that the only safe place was right in our bunks. At least that was the driest place. We had the radio on full blast and yet we could hardly hear it, that's how much noise there was, caused by the wind and rain. For about an hour we thought sure that the tent was going to blow away and carry us with it. But it finally held together and the storm passed without to much damage. The odd part about it tho was that the storm lasted thru the ceremony and a few minutes later everything was quiet and calm once more. As if to say thateverything was at peace again, now live and let live that way.

Well, I got another letter from you late yesterday, much to my surprise because I had already received quite a few a few days earlier and did'nt expect any for another week. That's the way the mail has been coming in lately.

I did'nt no that the 23 Aug. was the date you had started working at the yard. But now that you mentioned it, this month seems to hold quite a few anniversaries for our small family huh? Keep up the good cheer face laite, we have pretty good assurances that you will not celebrate another August 23 by working at the yard.

That big girl sure is growing up fast. From what you tell me about her she's not a baby any more but really a big girl. Gosh, I'm anxious to get back. If I did'nt hold myself in check I think I'd get sick with anxiety. But a little while longer can't be too bad so I guess I'll stick it out .

Solong for now, until tomorrow

Love Always,

Wildre'

No. 409.   September 3, 1945.

Dearest Face Laite:

Here it is Monday again and I'm back working on days once more. Have'nt received any mail for a few days but I still have two more of your old ones, I should be able to dig up some gossip in those.

This noon, there was a short wave broadcast coming from San Francisco broadcasting your V J celebrating. We could'nt hear it very well and it was cut off a few minutes after it started. This was at 12 noon over here but at home it must have been about 6 o'clock at night, Sunday. The President spoke also and he stated that we would get back as fast as transportation was made available. I don't think we will have to wait too long, I'll be back before you no it.

I got a great kick out of reading that Elaine was acting just like a tom boy and tears her overalls while playing. What a gal she must be. And you have a nerve to talk about tom boys. I guess you acted like that many a time and you were much older than she is now. She has to take after somebody and I guess your elected this time. She may have some of my traits but she sure must have some of yours too. And that's not bad, that's good.

I have'nt heard from the Tousaints since I last wrote to them about a month ago. Well, they must be haveing a nice time and I don't blame them much for not writeing. I'd do the same if I were in their place. He probably will get his discharge now that the war is over, therefor he'll be a civilian before I will.

Have'nt heard from Rene for quite a while now. Would'nt be surprised if he got his orders to go home before he has a chance to answer.

Well, can't seem to think of anything more so I guess I'll close. Until tomorrow solong and take care.

Love Always,

Wildre'

No. 410   Sept. 4 - '45

Dearest Face Faite:

    Hello honey, no mail again today, but I did get a Chronicle which was dated April 27th. If we had to wait for the paper to get the latest news, we'd wait a long time huh. But we don't have too, so that's that.

    My friend Cook received the Portsmouth Periscope yesterday, and after reading a certain article in it I almost blew my top. This article was to the effect that, all persons who had been hired after March 15-1942 were not eligible to their old job after they got back from the war. Now, I'm not sure when I started to work there, but I am quite certain that Hervey started sometime after Mar. 15-'42. And yet he's considered as a permanent employee. His name is in the Periscope indicating this fact. I was wondering

-11-

if you look up and see just when I started to work there and let me no. Not that I give a damn about going back there, because I may not, but rather to see if Hervey is putting a fast one over on them.

Well, they've lowered the age limit for discharge from 38 to 35, and also the point system from 85 to 80. Before you no it, they will be down to my level, then I'll be on that ship at last. Once they get that ball rolling it won't take long. The one thing we shouldn't do is get over anxious. Our turn will come sooner that way.

Heard over the news that mail censureship will soon be over.

Solong for now,
As Ever Yours
Wildie

No. 411　　　　　　　　　　　September 6, 1945

Dearest Face Laite:

　　　　Hello honey, this is the start of a new era one might say, the reason, as of today the mail is no longer censured. I don't no if this will make any difference but it sure will help me to find something else to talk about besides the weather.

　　　　To begin with, I must confess that I did not write to you yesterday, and no other reason except that I simply could not think of a thing to say. Altho it's only morning right now I thought I'd start this letter now. I still may receive some letters today, I have'nt had any for a week tho. From now on I can tell you just what I do every day and in that way, maybe give you some idea what I do. Okay?

　　　　As I probably told you earlier this week, I'm working days now, and there is'nt so much going on in the day time as there is at night. Yesterday there was'nt a damn thing to do. I came to the office in the morning and hung around all day. When there's nothing to do like that I usually go and see the french cops and shoot the bull with them. My watch had been on the bum for some time and I had given it ot one of the cops to fix for me, and I got it back yesterday. But it still won't go, so I guess I'll send it to you. Nothing is broken in it, It just won't run that's all.

　　　　There was a dance at the area where I live last night. Of course I could have gone but I did'nt. I'm being continually asked to go to these dances but I never go. So you see what a good boy I am? You'd better be the same way too, or else. There's going to be a social affair on the 15th, that is, dance and party given by the french M.P.s and they invited me. It would'nt cost me a cent and I could get drunk and get a girl free too, but I won't go. So you see, that's the kind of temptation I've had ever since I've been here, and I never fell for it yet. I've seen so many other married men shack up (sleep with) girls over here that I'm sick of it. I've seen hundreds of married and single men get clapped up and yet they go back for more. That was part of my job, to investigate these clap cases and find the girls or women responsible. I must have picked up hundreds of these. Every time a new case comes up, I and a french inspecter have to go out and find these women. When a girl finds out that a soldier can speak french, she sets her cap for him and trys to make him. That's the way they are over here. Of course there are some nice girls too over here, but those nice girls don't act that way. I could go on and on tellin you of these things, but I no so many stories like that, that it would take me a long time to tell them all.

　　　　There have been so many stories going around lately about getting out of the army that it makes my head swimm. I can tell you now that I truthfully don't no when I'll be able to get back. Sometimes I think that I might get back before Xmas, and other times I don't no what to think. One officer who predicted the end of the war correctly said that we would get back before Thanksgiving. But that&s only a guess. The only thing we can do is wait and hope that we will get back soon.

There are not many troops left on this island now. Some with high points are leaving every month. In my section, there were only ten men in all, two have already gone home, and all the others have 74 points or more. they will be leaving here before me unless theres something new comes out bout married men like me. Counting the extra points I had since last May 12, I have 54 now, and that's not much. Oh well, we'll see what happens.

I must tell you what I did yesterday. Some time ago I received a letter from Mary. I opened it and read it and then put it aside to answer later. It was only yesterday that I noticed it was addressed to me but the letter was started with Dear Medee instead of Dear Wildre. When I first read it I thought it funny that Mary should say to me that, she was not afraid to tell me now that missed my help that I used to give her and that some day she would repay me for all I've done for her. She never said anything like that to me before because I no that she still carries a grudge against me for leaving the farm. That letter was meant for Medee and not for me evidently. When I got the full meaning of that letter in my head, I sat down and wrote her just what I thought of her, and I was going to tell you to keep away from her. After I had it all written I tore it up. I figured that I'd have nothing to do with her anymore. She has'nt changed a bit, still the same old crab with a long tongue.

I have just now received four letters from you and one each from Annette and Fern. I had to take time out of course to read them all. On one of those letters you gave me the news about your release from the yard. Don't you worry face laite, you don't have to work anymore if you don't want too, There's enough money saved up for you both to take it easy until I get back. This will give you a chance to go to Conn. and on the farm and do whatever you want. Take it easy and have a nice long vacation. How about it huh? That must have been quite a layoff they had at the yard. I might want to go back there for a while after I get back. Just to get started again, but I don't intend to stay there long. After figuring it out the other day, I think I started to work there In October of 1941, so that makes me eligible for my job back if I want it. But to make sure, why don't you look it up for me. I think you have a record of that some where in your chest.

Well, I guess I've said about enough for now, this turned out to be a long letter after all. It seems so good to say what you think for a change that I can't stop talking now. When I get back, you'll probably say that I'm an old maid because I talk too much. See what you have to put up with?

Solong honey and take good care of yourself for me.

Devotedly Yours,

Wildre'

P.S. Am getting to be pretty on this typewriter huh? Did I make to many mistakes?

No. 412   Sept. 7 - '45

Hello Face Saite!

Another day, another letter. Not much news but there's not a censure to cramp my style anymore.

Just got back from the show. I didn't stay till the finish, the damn machine was on the bum and it spoil' everything. Won't it be nice to go to a real movie where you won't have to wait between reels, and hear the sound. Lots of little things like that will be nice for a change. Just think, we've been missing all these little things, now you can imagine how much we've missed the big things, and all this time.

Well, now that I can tell you what I do every day, here's my first account of a normal workday. This morning another guy, (Hickman) and I had to go to Tantouta to investigate an auto accident and a theft. Of course, you don't no where Tantouta is because I've never been able to say these things before. It's about 35 miles from Nouméa, which is our base headquarters, and also the biggest town here. — I have a small map of the island and when I get back, I'll be able to show you just where all these places are. Anyway, the auto accident turned out to be phoney, and the theft was also. The frenchman who made the complaint claimed that some doggie had stolen his horse saddle. When we tried to find the frenchman in order to question him some more, we couldn't find him. So we said, to hell with him, we weren't going to run around all day just trying to find him. As it was, we got back at 2 o'clock this afternoon. And me not having had any breakfast or dinner either. Believe me my belly was quite empty. But that happens often on this job. One day a while back, I went all day without breakfast, dinner or supper, and didn't eat until late at night. That's not very good on your stumoch I no, but what can you do about it. Especially when we have to go up the island, the roads are so rough and these G.I. cars are so hard that it's a day's work just to ride a few miles. But hell, I'm not complaining, not by any means. When I was with the engineers, I had it much tougher than that. This job is a snap as compared to the engineers.

You've heard of Danny Kaye the comedian huh, well, he's just come on the radio. Everyone hates that bird because he's always singing and saying the same thing. So, we just turn off the radio.

Well, there wasn't much news but I managed to write three pages. Not bad huh? Your not mad are you? ha. ha.

Solong honey, until tomorrow

Love Always, Wildre.

No. 413 Sept. 9-'45

Dearest Face Faite:

Hello honey, it's sunday afternoon over here. I just had dinner and having nothing else to do, I thought of writting my letter now. Later on this afternoon I'm going to see my first Rugby game. Some New Zealand troops are going to play. In case I have'nt told you before, we don't work on Sunday any more, nor Saturday afternoon either. And besides that we have a day off during the week. That's what its supposed to be, but in the case of me, when I work days, I have to work Sat. afternoon. And when I work nights, I have to work 6 days a week. That's because I'm an interpreter. Anyway, you can see that we're taking it pretty easy now.

I did'nt write to you yesterday because they don't mail the letters on Sunday any more. There wasn't much to write about anyway. There wasn't a thing

-11-

that happened. In the afternoon I was all alone at the office and I didn't do anything but read and listen to the radio. Sometimes, I get so sick of reading and doing nothing that I don't no where to put myself.

This morning I went to the 10 oclock mass at the Cathedral and came back to camp right after. We had a pretty good chicken dinner and I filled myself up plenty. Very often, I go without breakfast and when it comes time for dinner, I'm pretty hungry. But I don't seem to reduce very much even tho I go without meals often. I don't work very hard either.

It's very nice out today. Cook is outside trying to get a tan so he show his folks how hot it is out here. He expects to go home pretty soon. Rumors are still flying around pretty thick but you can't believe anything just yet. When I get some good news I'll let you no as fast as I can.

I should get some pictures this week, and

-111-

if I do, I'll send them to you right away.

You must have received your flowers by now, and I'm anxious to hear from you to see if you liked them.

I suppose that big girl is still up to her tricks as usual huh? Gosh, I can hardly wait to see her. If you think she's spoiled now, wait until I get back.

Well, I guess that's about all for now. So until tomorrow, solong face laite.

Yours Always,
Wildré

No. 414   Sept. 11-45

Dearest Face Laite:

    Received three letters at last, one from you, Alice and mother. Yours was dated the 30th. I was anxious to get one of the 31st to see if you got the flowers alright.

    Today is my day off again. I'm so rested up now that I really don't no what to do with myself. I got up at 9 oclock this mooring, took a warm shower and washed my shoes and then it was time for dinner. After dinner I laid down on my bunk and fell asleep. I did'nt wake up until 3 oclock, and here I am writing this letter. That's my day so far. Tonight I'll go to see a movie — if the machine does'nt break down, and then probably write to Alice and then it will be time to sleep again. That's hard work huh? ha ha

-11-

Seriously tho, I'm sick and tired of this job and this easy life. I guess I just wasn't cut out for such easy work. I'm anxious to get back to hard work again.

I and another guy went to Dumbéa yesterday afternoon, to investigate a robbery in a Q.M. Laundry. This had been the 5th time it had been robbed, and this time was no different from the last four times. We no who's responsible, but just can't catch him. The thief is an 18 year old frenchman by the name of Gaston L'ijou. He's an escaped prisoner from the french jail. He lives all all alone in the woods and steals food, guns and everything else to live on, from American camps. This last time, a guard at this camp stopped L'ijou and while he was searching him for weapons, L'ijou flashed a gun and fired at him and got away again. This kid is dangerous now and will shoot to break away. I might get a chance at him yet.

We have some of the queerest incidents happening here sometimes. Yesterday, a french woman complained that her little girl was cut on the leg by some glass which was laying in the road. A G.I. truck came by and ran over the glass causing it to fly to the sidewalk and cut the little girl. Of course, the reason for the complaint was that the woman could probably collect damages from the army. I could tell you of hundreds of little deals like that. When the American troops first got here, the government paid the french plenty of money for damages like that. But since then, we've learned plenty and it's not so easy to collect now.

I mailed my watch to you yesterday to have fixed again. I had given it to a frenchman here but he couldn't fix it. There isn't anything broken in it, at least he said the wasn't, but it still won't run. I sent it airmail so you should get it soon.

I heard a nice juicy rumor yesterday. It's only a rumor tho and should be taken as such. I heard that this island would be cleaned of G.I.'s before Jan. 1st. If that's true that would mean that I would be home by that time. But don't be too hopeful, it's only a rumor. When I get the real dope I'll tell you so.

Solong honey, and take care of you both for me.

          Love Always,
          Wilbré

No. 415   September 12, 1945

Dear Face Laite:

Although this day is not yet over I thought of writing my letter right away. I'm at the office right now and there is'nt anything to do. I've been hanging around all day. This morning I wrote to Alice and I was saving your letter till tonight but I might as well write it now.

I just received the pictures I told you about a feww days ago this afternoon and I'm encloseing them with this letter. I wrote in back of them just what they werw about. When I get back I'll explain them more in detail. You'll notice on mine that IIm not very slim, also just as good looking as usual too. ha ha.

I went to a movie last night and I think it was one of the best movies I've seen since I been over seas. The name of it was "Junior Miss", It was a typical every day affair, in fact almost natural. There was'nt one word in it mentioned about military life, just an ordinary family living an ordinary life. If you have'nt seen it I wish you would. It would take your mind off other things for a feww minutes and I'm sure you will like it. If it ever comes to our local theatre when I get back I'll go back to see it a second time. I was thinking, Elaine should be old enough now to take to the movies is'nt she?

I heard a nice juicy rumor yesterday, but of course it's only a rumor. This island is supposed to be cleaned out of Americans by Jan.1st. If that's true I should be home Before Elaine's next birthday. But again I repeat, that's only a rumor. When the truth comes along I'll tell you aboutit for sure.

I have'nt received any mail for a couple of days now. This morning I was anxious to see if I had a letter from you but no soap. When I don't do anything to keep me busy I especially like to get some mail. It gives me more to talk about. And besides I wanted to no whether you received those flowers. Maybe tomorrow I'll get some.

Well, I can't think of anything else to say so I guess it's time to close. Until tomorrow, solong and take care of you both for me.

                                        Love Always,

                                        Wildre'

No. 417 Sept. 14 - '45.

Dearest Face Laite:

No mail today, had two letters yesterday and that's all I had this week. We've been getting mail once a week lately and that's all. Hope this changes soon. No news yet about going home. Still a lot of rumors going around and that's all.

Well, I went to the dentist this morning and had my tooth filled. This is the third time that this tooth has been filled. The next time the filling falls out I'll have to have it pulled, the hole is getting bigger all the time. Oh yes, he found another cavity too, so I'll have to go back next week to have that one filled.

I spent most of the morning at the dentist and didn't do much work, but this afternoon I no sooner got back to the office, than I got

-11-

a call to go out, and it turned out to be quite a case. It seems that one frenchman saw a navy truck stop in back of his neighbor's house and two sailors delivered some G.I. merchandise in another frenchman's house. The frenchman who saw this reported it to us. These people are very jealous of one another and if they can cut the other guys neck, they'll do it every time. Anyway, I and another guy traced these two sailors by the number of their truck. We questioned them separately and when their stories were put together, they didn't jive. So we brought them both to the station for more questioning. One of them finally confessed and said that he had given the frenchman an auto battery and other stuff. But the best part of the story is that the frenchman who got these articles was none other than a civilian police man. Boy oh boy, what a scandal this is going to be.

-111-

These civilians are not supposed to buy or accept any G.I. articles whatsoever. When they are caught with the stuff, they are punished by law, and so is the serviceman. Well, that gave me a busy afternoon. Of course that's not all the story but that's the highlight of it. Oh yes, just as I was about ready to go to camp, a lady came in the station and complained about a negro soldier threatening her and her farmaids. (She owns a farm.) She said that he kept asking her for zig zig (that means fuck) for ten dollars, and other things. I said, okay I'll go see you at 6 oclock to get your statement. I told her that to get rid of her because I wanted to go to camp. I sent the other interpreter when he came to work. You see, I'm so used to this job now, that I can get out of a lot of work. You be surprised to hear some of

-IV-

these stories sometimes. If you were with me to listen to them I'm sure you'd like that. Sometimes its very interesting, but other times it's not so funny. This kind of job is alright for somebody who likes to pry into other peoples' affairs, but I'm sick of it right now. I could go on and on telling you about these people, — what they do, how they act, and what my job has been with these people since I've been here. I'm not kidding one bit when I say I could write a book about all this. I've enough stories now to keep me talking for weeks. See what your up against when I get back? By the way, my letters have been longer lately huh? What do you think of them now?

So long until tomorrow face laite.

Love Always
Wilder

No.   September 15, 1945.

Dear Face Laite:

        Helloe honey, no letters again today but that&s nothing new, It's saturday afternoon over here and I've nothing else to do except write letters. I did'nt work this morning because I had to work this afternoon. I got up at 8 o'clock, had a shower and than laid on my sack the rest of the morning reading. What a life. I'm so damn sick of laying on my sack that I don't no what position to get in. I might as well be discharged as doing this job now, I don't do a damn thing.

        Well, hows that big girl getting along lately? Is she still learning new tricks every day. Gosh she must be pretty big now. The other day when you sent me those pictures to write behind them for you, I thought sure that they were pictures of you and her. It's been a long time since I got some pictures from you so how about sending me some new ones. After all, I want to get acquainted as much as possible with you both before I see you. I can't wait to see how this meeting is going to take place. I'm sure it's going to be a lot different from what I been imagineing all along. There's still not much news as to my possible discharge but when I get some news, I'll let you no as fast as I can. Okay?

        Tomorrow afternoon I'm going to see the last football game being played over here. It's a championship game between the M?P.s and another team from Dumbea. After that's over I don't no what I'll do for excitement. If I don't get out of here pretty soon I'll go nuts,from doing nothing.

        The town is dead over here now. There's hardly any more servicemen. Right now there are 87 bars in this town and they are not doing much business. One time these bars used to do a landslide business when there was a lot of servicemen. They sell the drinks for 50 cents a shot so you can see that it does'nt take long to get rid of your pay. But I never spent my pay that way. If I want to get drunk all I have to do is walk into a bar and order what I want and it would never cost me a cent. These frenchmen treat the M.P.s pretty good that way. When the troops first landed here there was only 3 or 4 bars in town but as soon as they saw that there was good money in it, everybody opened one. I could go on talking about the bars alone for along time, but that's something else that can wait until I get back.

        Well, I guess that's all for now, until tomorrow solong and take care of you both.

                                            Always Yours,

                                            Wildre'

No. 418 + 419   Sept. 17 - '45

Dearest Face Laite:

  I forgot to put down the number on yesterday's letter, so I put it down on this one, see the top. Received two letters from you today and one each from Annette, Everett and Ciotti from Okinawa. It was about time too.

  About that name plate you had made for us, that's getting pretty ritzy huh? What are you going to do with it, keep it for our farm? Not a bad idea.

  And about my letters not being censured any more, I'm waiting to see how you like them now. For one thing, they are longer.

  I see Elaine is still learning more and more every day. I hope she does'nt grow up too fast, for I'd like to take in some of that pleasure myself. Annette says that she sings pretty good to. So she likes daddy better than the old lady huh? Just wait until I get back, you won't stand a chance.

That's quite a bit of money you have coming at the yard. What are you going to do with all your money anyway? I could suggest that you take a long vacation, but you wouldn't listen to me. I'll make you pay for that when I get back, wait and see.

Well, I didn't do anything yesterday but go to mass and saw the football game in the afternoon. The M.U.'s won 14 to 6. Last night I went to the movies and as usual the projector broke down. Won't it be nice to go to a real movie and see it all the way thru without a breakdown. I'm telling you face laite, I'd appreciate everything once I get out of here. As a civilian, one just takes anything

-111-

for granted. When you miss these things for a long time, only then do you realize what they are.

I start working nights today for two weeks again. Time goes by pretty slow working nights. I work from 4 to 12 and always get up at about 8 oclock. Then I have all day to do nothing. That gets sickening after a while. I'm so rested up that I even lose my appetite sometimes. Oh well, it can't be long now, so I guess I can sweat it out for a little while longer.

I guess thats about all for now, solong until tomorrow and take care of you both for me.

Love Always,
Hilde

A World War II Story: Dad's Letters Home

No. 420   Sept. 18 - '45

Dear Face Laite!

    I just got back from the show and here I am with another letter for you. As long as I'm working nights, I'll have to change my plans in writing to you if I want to tell you of my day's happening. I'll have to tell you these things on the following day.

    Well, last night when I went to work, there were two french people waiting for me at the station. One frenchman had been caught driving an American vehicle and I had to take a statement from him. A french woman wanted to no how she could change some American silver money into bills. But the juiciest bit of gossip was about a frenchmen who came in the station, and all excited, ready to murder some guy. Well, after I finally got the story out of him, this was it. It seems that some American soldier was going out with his wife and he wanted us to ship this soldier off

-11-

the island, or else he was going to kill him. After handling these frenchman for a year now, this was nothing new. This happens very often. Well, anyway, I took this frenchman to see the Provost Marshal and after telling him the whole story, the P.M. said that he would take care of the matter. What he will do, is to simply tell the soldier to stay away from that woman, — or else. He will, don't worry.

This case of stealing a wife from another frenchman was'nt very serious. I have seen cases where the man was left with two or three small kids after his wife had run off with some soldier. But usually the wife went back to the husband, because the P.M., when he first heard about it, soon took care of the soldier. But then again, the soldier is not always to blame.

-111-

Do you wonder now why I'm such a good boy and don't mix with these french women? Believe me honey, I've had chances, but I never took them. I saw, and still see every day what misery and unhappiness this all brings about. I've missed you and Elaine a lot since I've been in the army, but even more so since I've been at this job. Maybe it's because I have to work around these civilians all the time. At any rate, there's one thing you can be sure of, and that is, I have not gone astray. I've never doubted you for a minute and I want you to feel the same.

So long until tomorrow,

Yours Always,

Wilbur

No. 421   Sept. 19-'45

Dearest Face Faite:

    It's only one o'clock in the afternoon right now. I wasn't going to write until tonight but having nothing better to do, I decided to write now. And besides, I have a bit of good news. Unfortunately, this good news does'nt affect me,—not just yet, but in time it will. There's an order that came out this morning saying that all men with 80 points will leave the island by Oct. 25. Of course, I haven't got 80 points, but it shows that the army is waking up, and my turn will come sooner. By letting these men go, it gives one some lift in spirit and we can at least look forward to final separation.

    Well, now that you have no more job, I hope your taking it easy. You must be having

-11-

some nice weather this time of the year. I no if I was in your place, I'd enjoy this time off to the fullest. That big girl would like to go walking in that kind of weather. And I'm not worrying one bit about supporting my two girls. Just let me get back.

There's nothing that happened so far today, because I haven't gone to work yet. So I'll tell you about it tomorrow, tonight's work I mean. As I sit here writing this letter, I see a ship coming into the harbor. That means somebody will be going home in a few days. There was one that went out this morning too.

Solong until tomorrow,

Love Always
Hildé

No. 422.   Sept. 20, 1945.

Dearest Face Laite:

            Did'nt receive any letters from you today again but here's my few words anyway.

            Well, last night there was'nt a damn thing doing. The only thing I did was to go out with a french cop and picked up a french woman who was drunk and was found in an American camp. The French celebrated another holiday also yesterday, it was the 4th anniversary of this colony's annexation to the Degaulle movement. In other words, it was four years ago yesterday that this island decided to go over to the side of Degaulle. These frenchmen have a holiday every other day so it's nothing new. I never saw so many holidays in my life. It seems every little excuse they have, there's a holiday to celebrate.

            This afternoon, I went to the dentist and had another tooth filled. This time I had another dentist to work on me and boy, he was just like a horse doctor. When he got thru drilling, after about a half hour, my jaw was so sore that I could hardly move it. So help me God, if I ever have another tooth to fill I'm going to have it pulled out. Right now, I have about every other tooth filled and I certainly don't want to have any more filled that way. I'm okay now for a while tho. Every one is filled and I don't have to worry for the next six months anyway.

            Well, according to that new order that came out yesterday, there are a lot of fellows leaving pretty soon. Oh yes, Carl Cook got his orders today, so he should be leaving in the next few days. I heard a rumor today, saying that I and the other fellows that were staying here were going to get a better rateing. I don't no how true this is, but anyway I certainly don't want a rateing, just let me go home. There were 400 replacements that came in yesterday. I would'nt be surprised if we got a few in our section. There's a chance that Andre would be in that new bunch that just came in, but I hope not. Fellows like him should be home with their family.

            Well, I had a lot to talk about when I first started this letter, but now it seems that I've run out of words. So I guess I'll close until tomorrow. Solong and take good care of you both for me, it won't be long now.

                                        Devotedly Yours,

                                        Wildre'

No. 423					September 21, 1945.

Dearest Face Laite:

        I finally received some mail today, four letters from you, one each from Laurant, Florida, Alice and mother. I was all caught up on writing but now I'll have to start all over again. I'm getting damn sick of writing and one of these days I'm going to stop altogether, except to you of course.

        Well, to begin with I was sure surprised to hears that you were working so soon. I see my advice did'nt do much good again. Just you wait until I get back. At least you took one week off, and that's some thing.

        Elaine is still the center of all attraction huh? Even Laurent spoke of her. He said that she takes after the Pelletiers but she looks like the Bretons. How about that, you never told me that before. Anyway, she's all ours and from what I no of her I would'nt swap for any one else.

        Well, last night there was'nt a damn thing to do at the office. Only one man was brought into the station and he was found on the beach. Somebody beat him up but he was too drunk to no who did it. There was 400 new replacements that came in two days ago and he was one of them. He'll learn to take care of himself if he stays here long enough. Today I got up at eight oclock this morning, went outside in the sun for a couple of hours and read. After dinner I laid down on my bunk and fell asleep and did'nt wake up till four oclock. By that time it was almost time for supper and then came to work at five. What a life. Now I won't be able to sleep tonight.

        There was some good news on the radio today. According to the news x the points will be lowered to 70 by Oct. 1st and to 60 by Nov. 1st. That by late winter all men with two years service would be discharged. Well, I'll have 60 points to my credit by Dec. 12 so I may get to go home sometime after that date. If there are enough ships I may get home before Elaine's birthday. But that's a big IF. Boy I'm really sweating it out now. Oh yes, Carl Cook got his orders today to go home on furlough. He has 78 points so by the time he gets home the points will be lowered and he'll probably get his discharge. It's about time too because he's been over here for three years now. Most every body in my section will be going home on this new ruling. I'll be the last one here because I'm the youngest one in poinTs. Oh well we'll see in a couple of months how things turn out.

        Well, I guess that's about all for one day, so until tomorrow solong and take good care of you both, cause it won't be long now.

                Love Always,

                    Wildre'

No. 424   Sept. 22 - '45

Dearest Face Laite:

It's saturday afternoon over here and here's another letter for you. There was supposed to have been some mail this morning but we got there too late. The post office closed at 12 noon and won't open until Monday morning now. So if I have some mail I won't get it until then.

Well, nothing happened last night at the office. I wrote two letters and played cribbage, that was my night's work. After I got to bed last night I could'nt sleep to save my soul. I tossed and rolled all night long. That's what I get for sleeping in the afternoon and not working.

After I got up this morning, I went to see a frenchman who lives near the camp. He had asked me last night to come over and show him how to operate a hand fire extinguisher.

-11-

Although he had bought it at a french store, it was made in the states and the directions on it were written in english. After I showed him how it operated he wanted to give me something the worse way. I didn't want anything but his wife gave me nine eggs and three tomatoes. I can eat the tomatoes but I don't no what I'll do with the eggs. If I was home I could drink them with beer (for my pencil) but it won't do me any good over here. ha. ha. Just wait until I get back, your going to catch hell, for a few weeks anyway. It's been a long time now, maybe you'll have to teach me all over again, or vica versa.

There isn't much more to talk about, so until tomorrow solong honey.
     Love Always,
     Wilbre'

A World War II Story: Dad's Letters Home

No.425   September 23, 1945

Dearset Face Laite:

I received an unexpected letter from you today. We don't usually get any mail on sunday on accountof the post office being closed. But one of the fellows went to the post office and brought back the mail anyway.

I see your making a new outfit for Elaine for this winter. I did'nt no you were a seamstress and could do things like that. I guess I was'nt married to you long enough to find out all your good qualities. Butuwhen I get back I'm going to look into this. And she's just as glad as you are to get my letters huh? Boy that must be some girl we have there, and I'm more anxious every day to get back and see just what she is.

Well, there was'nt anything doing last night again. Oh yes, about eleven oclock a frenchman came in and complained that two sailors had broken the windshield of his car. They were locked up pending investigation. This had occured at the french dance which was being held at the Hotelle de Ville.(that the french town hall). This dance lasted until three oclock in the morning, and Tonight when I came to work they were still dancing. That the way these french are over here. When they have a dance or celebration it usually lasts all night or a couple of days, and they have them often too. The American servicemen have a saying about these holidays, the frenchmen will celebrate at the drop of a hat, and I guess it's true. As there was nothing to do at the office last night, I took a ride around the dance to see what it was all about. It seemed funny to see the women dressed up in long evening dresses. They looked as tho they were out of place. Before the troops came here most of the women walked around the streets in thier bare feet, that's how poor they were.But since the troops landed here most of these people made beaucoup money. The Americans are always flush and they spend their money freely. To give you an idea as to how much they used to earn, before the war they earned about 15 dollars a month, now most of them work for the Americans and make any where from 25 dollars to 40 dollars a week. They have so much money that some of them buy any old beat up automobile for 500 dollars up to 5000 dollars. You no, when I sold our car we got 550 dollars and it was a 1940 model. Well, for the same car over here the french pay about 4000 dollars. Getting back to those bare feet again, even now there are a lot of french who still walk around in their bare feet. And some of those people have a lot of money too. I guess they can't get out of the habit. I could talk on and on about this place. As I said before, I'll bet I could write a book about the past year that I've been here. But not now huh? I'm too damn sick of writing.

I did'nt go to mass today. This morning I got up too late to go so I was going tonight at six. But as it so happened I had to go to Dumbea to pick up a french soldier who had trespassed on American property and I got back too late. One of these days I won't have to put up with this shit and I'll be able to attend mass when I want too. Well, solong for now and take dare of you both for me.

Always Yours,

Wildre'

No. 426　　Sept. 25 - '45

Hello Face Faite:

Haven't received any letters for three days now. It's a good thing our mail is not censured anymore or else I'd be at a loss to write. I've known many a day like that in the past.

Well, nothing happened at the office last night. Hung around all night long. Gosh the time goes by slow that way.

Today was my day off, and all I did was to lay around in the sun and read. Boy am I sick of doing nothing. Even tho I didn't work today, there is a piece of news to tell you about. The fellows who work days were just coming out of the office to come to camp, when they got a call that some frenchman had been run over by a truck. Well, it turned out that a navy truck ran

-11-

over an old man and killed him. He was 84 yrs. old. He didn't have any relatives or anything, in other words he was something like a bum. You no, in the old days, when this island was first settled, there were a lot of long term prisoners transported from France to over here. They were used for hard labor, building roads and buildings etc. The old man that was run over was one of those old prisoners. After these prisoners had served their terms, many of them went back to France, but a lot of them stayed here. There are not many of those old men left, and what there is, they are pretty old, such as this old fellow who was run over. There are a lot of stories like that I could tell you about, but not now huh?

Well, I hope your not working too

-4-

hard at your new job. Take good care of yourself and that big girl, it won't be long now before I get back.

I've been anxious to hear from you since censuring was stopped, to see if you found any difference in my letters. Have they improved?

I'm enclosing a few pictures that Rickson took in the office where I work. I wasn't around that day so I was not included. However, I may get some more later on.

Well, I guess that's enough for one night. So, until tomorrow solong honey,

Yours Always
Wildé

No. 427   September 26, 1945

Dearest Face Laite:

        Hello honey, another day without mail and I sure hope to get some tomorrow. I did'nt do much of anything today. This morning I stood formation at headquarters when the general presented the bronze star to one of the fellows who work in the office. I don't see any reason why he should get decorated for sitting on his ass all day, but he did. It was jordon who got the medal, I sent you a picture of him in yesterday's letter. Anyway, we had our pictures taken and if I can get one I'll send it to you.

        This afternoon I laid down on my bunk and read all afternoon. After dinner this noon I wanted to go bicycle riding but it had to rain. I was so damn sick of doing nothing that I wanted to do something just to get some exercise. Gosh the time goes by slow that way, I mean when you don't do anything.

        You no, I wanted to tell you the other day about a ship that came in the harbor. As it was coming in every body ran to the beach tp see if it was a troop ship. That's what happens every time one comes in now. Everybody is so anxious to get home that that is all you hear talking about; when will the ships come in; how many points have you got; do you expect to stay very long now? I've heard so damn many stories that I'm sick and tired of listening to any more. But don't get me wrong, for when there is a new story that comes out I'm the first one to listen in. I want to go home as bad if not worse than the next guy. Oh well, I still sayn that all we can do is wait and sweat it out.

        I'm encloseing a folder that I had bought some time ago. I've been wanting to send it to you but when our mail was censured I could'nt send it. It shows some of the scenes we have around this place, but don't take the pictures at their full value because they were printed to attract tourists. Every thing does'nt look quite like that over here I assure you. One of these days, and if it does'nt cost too much, I'd like to take you over here and show you all over this island. I'm sure you'd like that because there are many things you've never seen before. But before we do that I think it would be better to see the U.S. first huh? What do you think?

        Well honey, I can't think of anything else to say, so I guess it's time to close. Oh yes, today is the 4th anniversary of the corps of Military Police. All the MPs on the island are having some dance tonight, but your goddam husband is not going,-- as usual. Solong face laite,

                              Devotedly Yours Always,

                                  Wildre'

No. 428   September 27, 1945

Dearest Face Laite:

Hello honey, another day almost over and another day bringing us nearer together. Oh yes, another day without mail too.

There was'nt much that happened last night, only a fight which occured in a bar between two soldiers and a frenchman. That was settled pretty quick. This morning I went out in the sun all forenoon and read. I got quite a tan now. After dinner I went bicycle riding along the back beach road for a little excercise. I went about five or six miles in all and I felt much better too. Boy I certainly need that excercise, I'm so soft and flabby that I look just like a fat old woman.

Tonight there was only one incident that happened. There was a sailor who walked right into a french home, took out his cock and tried to sell the idea to the woman of the house and her kanaka maid. The woman finally managed to get him out of the house but he came back with his buddy and tried to enter again. When the lady closed the door on them one of them kicked the door and broke it. The MPs and SPs finally arrested them and locked them up. I had to go back to the house and get a statement from the lady. She was'nt too mad, in fact she got a kick out of telling me what the sailor had done. She said that she did'nt care for herself because she was married. But There was a girl in a room dressing up and if the sailor had gone in there he probably would have attacked her. This girl was about twenty years old, and not Bad either. In fact she was very pretty. The lady did'nt want to make it too tough on the sailor, so she told me to leave out the part where the sailor had taken out his cock. Boy, we meet up with all kinds of cases in this job. This is what I've been doing for the past year, and I've met up with some lulues.

Well, Ive just come back from the french police station. I go there often at night when there's not anything to do. We were talking about the difference there is between my french and theirs. There's quite a difference in case you don't no. When I first got here I had a hell of a time to get used to their slang. I still can't speak it very well but I can understand it pretty well. But I had to learn how to speak the correct french tho, that's the only way I could make them understand me. Wait until you hear me speak french, you won't no your own husband.

Tere's not much more to say so I guess I'll close once more. Take good care of you both for me honey.

                                        Love Always,

                                        Wildre'

No. 429	Sept. 28 - '45

Dearest Face Laite:

Finally received four letters from you and one from Butch and it was about time too.

I see you received my first letters that were not censured, but you didn't say whether there was any difference in them or not. If you can't notice the difference I think I'll make them short like they used to be.

So your back on the same old job at the shoe shop huh? I can remember when we first got married that you used to come home all tired out, and yet you took that same job. Even if it is for only four weeks, you'll still be working in the shoe shop after that. I wish you would stay home. I'd feel much better. You've been working hard all your life, do you want to

-11-

keep on that way and become an old woman before your time? I realize your intentions, trying to help me and save all the money you can, but your health comes first, to hell with the money. Anyway, you have more than enough to keep you and Elaine until I get back. I'm not there to sit you down now, but just wait till I get back, you'll sit down and like it,— see. And you'd better be in good condition too. There, how's that for giving you hell huh?

From the way you talk on your letter, Elaine must be able to talk pretty good. Boy, she must be quite a girl. I'm so anxious to get back and see her for myself, and you too of course. In fact even more so. I haven't felt the soft flesh of a woman for so long that I think I'll go wild when I do. If I don't look out, I'm afraid I'll break you in two the first time I get my hands on you. So you'd better watch out. Oh yes have you bought that steel corset yet? Talking about seeing you, I think I can make a guess now as to when I may go home. I think that I will probably leave here some time between the last part of December and the last part of January. There's a lot of talk about closing down this island by Jan. 1st. If that is true I should be home for Elaine's birthday. Anyway, I'll be able to tell you better in another month or two.

According to what you told me on your letter I started to work at the Yard in Oct. of 1941. Then my job will be waiting for me. I'm glad of that because I think it is a good idea to go back there until we get straightened out. Everything will be high the first year or two and a good job will come in handy.

-14-

As for dear Hervey, I have no pity for him. He's only good enough for him to get laid off. He'd better not come around me for anything because I don't want to have anything to do with him.

You no, I've been thinking what we'll have to buy when we go housekeeping again. First of all, We've got to buy you a lot of cloths, including a nice fur coat. You'll have more cloths than what you had when you got married,—that's a promise. Then we'll have to get a new stove, either gas or electric. Maybe a new washing machine too, because you used it at the Roy's and it's probably all shot. A new radio, rugs and a lot of other things I can't think of right now. Oh yes, we'll need a car to take you and that big girl riding. Believe me honey, I'm going to make you live for a change. You've worked enough in this life.

Solong for now honey, take care always,
Love Always,
Your Old Man.

No.430   September 29, 1945

Dear Face Laite:

Hello honey, I received another letter from you today and also one from Florida. When I got your letter it was so thin from the outside that I thought there was nothing it. But there was tho, two small pages to be exact. I'm not complaining mind you, but I have to find some fault. You no how I used to be I guess, I used to find a lot of fault. But I'm not so bad now, I've learned how to be a liite more patient.

I see you don't get your mail very regular eihher lately. I write every day tho, in fact even more so now that the mail is not censured. I guess it's the mail service, I usually get mail about once a week, so we're both even.

You mentioned the shoe shop again in your last letter. You said you were tired and the week was long. I gave you hell on yesterday's letter so I won't start all over again now. But I hope you quite that job now, as I said before I can't make you stop working because I'm not there to stop you. But I wish you would quite now. It won't be so very long now before I'll be coming home, and even tho you do work around the house you still won't work as hard as if you were in the shop. Just think, you could stay in bed in the morning as long as you wanted too, go out when you wanted too, and do other things too for the next three or four months. I don't think you will have to wait any longer then that for me to get home, at least not over six months. So how about it huh? Will you stay home? Oh yes, it's going to be cold in another month or so, and you'll have to get in the morning when it's cold to go to work. Let me no what you think of my idea.

I can just imagine that you will hang on to me when I get back. But baby hang on all you want too, I'll be doing the same to you. Do you see what your in for too when I get back? How's Elaine getting along with her blocks, has she built that house yet? You might have her start building our new house

Well, there is'nt much more to talk about. Everything is pretty quiet tonight and was last night too. So I guess I'll close for now. Solong until tomorrow honey, and take good care of you both.

                                        Love Always,

                                        Wildre'

No. 431   October 1, 1945

Dearest Face Laite:

Haven't received mail for three days now, but that's nothing unusual for we're still receiving our mail only once a week.

I hope your not working too hard at the shop. I'm anxious to hear from you about that idea I had for you to stop working. I hope you take that bit of advice, I'll feel much better. And Elaine must be the same as usual, learning more every day I'll bet. Gosh, I'm anxious to get home and see you two. It seems that the time just drags by lately. We should no something definite in a couple of months, about going home I mean.

Well, I'm back working on days again., starting this morning. And it feels good too. Last night there was three vehicles stolen and that kept us a little busy for a while. They were all recovered within a short time, but we had to take statements and that took some time. There was a fight also between two soldiers and some frenchmen. One of the soldiers had a cut over his haed and had to be taken to the hospital. The frenchman hit him over the haed with an auto crank. this morning a french girl came to the station and asked us to call up some sailor for her. She said that this sailor's girl was ready to have a baby and she wanted to let him no about it. The girl is chinese. I later found out that the sailor did not want to marry the girl and did not want ot have anything to do with the baby. And nobody can force him to marry her either. That's the way it is around here, if a serviceman goes out with a girl and puts her in a family way, nothing can be done about it. Some girls actually want to have babies by the Americans and they ask any support in return either. Some fellows even live and sleep with their girls every day and night. In the morning they go back to camp and at night they go back. Nice work if you can get it. But I got along without it so far, so I guess I'll stick with the cute little shit. And you'd better be prepared too when I get back. You can imagine me watching this kind of stuff going on for the past year and not tasting it. Boy are you going to catch hell. ha ha.

Oh yes, this morning there was another accident between a navy jeep and a french truck. But it wasn't very serious tho. Well, I can't seam to think of anything else to say so I guess I'll close. Solong honey and take good care of you both for me.

Love Always,

Wildre'

No. 432 Oct. 2-'45

Hello Dace Laite:

No mail again today, but I should get some in a day or so.

I just got back from the movie and it was very good. The name of it was "Kiss & Tell," with Shirly Temple. I never cared much for her, but in this picture she was pretty good. It was comical all the way and typified the average family. Be sure to see it. Oh yes, the machine didn't break down either.

Well, this is the month that the 80 point men are going to leave the island. Gosh, everybody is all on edge, that is the 80 point men. There are still a lot of rumors about folding up this island by Jan. 1st. Boy I hope they are true, because if it is, that means I'll be on my way home by that time too. Anyway, even if that isn't true, I think that I'd leave here by

-11-

Jan. anyway. Time drags by so damn slow. But it's really only three months away.

You no, those pictures that I have of you and Elaine, I guess I've shown them to most everybody in New Caledonia. It's funny how it happens sometimes too. This afternoon I went shopping for some souvenirs, (I'm buying a little each month to take back with me) and while talking with the girl who was waiting on me, the subject came up about the different climates. The girl said that she would like to see snow because she had never seen any before. I took out my pictures and showed them to her, and she was surprised to learn that I was married and had a daughter. I had my ring on but she hadn't noticed it. Of course she thought that I had a very nice wife and baby. She said Elaine looked like you and I said she was crazy, because she looked like me. First who does that girl

– 111 –

look like anyway. If I remember right, everybody used to say that she looked like me, but according to the pictures I have, everybody I show them to say that she looks like you. How about telling me yourself who she looks like. I hope she resembles me a little bit. Oh well, either way she can't go wrong, especially with me being the old man.

There isn't much more to say, so I guess it's time to close once more. Hope your not working too hard, and I hope you take my advice to stop working. Take care of you both for me.

Yours Always,
Wilbur

No. 433   Oct. 3-'45

Dearest Face Faite:

Hello honey, I have a bit more encouraging news for you, — and me too. On this island at least, the orders have been changed about the discharge system. Those who have 80 points were supposed to be released from their outfits to go to the Personal Center by Oct. 25, and those with 70 points by Nov. 1st, those with 60 points by Dec. 1st. Well, that's all changed now. Those with 80 P. will report by Oct. 15 — those with 70 will report by Nov. 1st and those with 60 P. by Nov. 25. Boy, according to that I will be next in line. If everything goes along as it should, I'll probably be on my way before Xmas, or at least not long after that. Now this is getting to be exciting and I don't mean perhaps.

—11—

Keep your fingers crossed face Caite, I'm doing it you can be sure of that. Boy, are the next few months going to drag by.

Well, so much for that. Now, from now on you'll have to address my envelopes to sergent instead of corporal. I just got news today that, as of Oct. 1st, I was made T/4 or sergent to you. That means an extra 12 bucks a month now. It will come in handy to buy some more things for you before I leave here. But outside of that I don't care for the rating, I just want to go home.

Well, there wasn't much happened today. Only a negro soldier who was accused by some Tonkinese to have stolen a pen from his kid. After investigating, we found that The Tonkinese was lying. The kid had stolen the pen from the soldier. If we had not investigated the soldier would have been court marshaled and probably gotten six months in the stockade. (prison) Many times this happens, the soldier being falsely accused I mean, and many times we save them from prison. But unfortunately, many times the soldier is guilty too.

Well, I guess that's about all for now. So long and take care of you both for me.

Love Always,
Wilbre

No. 434 Oct. 4 - '45

Dearest Face Faite:

At last I received mail from you today, three from you and one from Alice. And best of all I got some pictures of you and Elaine. Its seems that you're changed since the last time you sent pictures. But anyway, I think your getting prettier all the time. Nobody believes me when I tell them your one year younger than I am. They say you look like a kid. Wish they'd say that about me, but they don't. In fact my hair is getting thin and the boys keep reminding me about it. So you see, you won't have to worry about getting new cloths to impress me. I'm the one who will have to hang on to you. As for Elaine, she does'nt seem to have changed much on those pictures. She seems to be growing taller now instead of fat. But she's still the best there is for my money. The Kays haven't changed much either. And that's quite a shop that Ernest has. He must be doing pretty well.

In one of your letters, you didn't sound to be too happy. What's the matter honey? Is there something you haven't told me? Don't you hold anything back on me. I haven't done so sofar and I wouldn't want you to do it either. Or maybe I'm mistaken and you really had a blue moment. Cheer up face Laite, it won't be long now before I'll be home to take good care of you. I realize these past two years have taken their toll on you, and I'm sure lucky to have you as a partner. I'm not forgetting anything you've done, and when I get back I'll show you that I haven't either. It won't be long now, maybe not more than three months from now, I'll be home for good.

—111—

Well, there was a little excitement today. An army car which was driven by an M.P., ran over a small boy of 7 years old. Luckily the kid was not seriously hurt. As far as I no, he only had a long cut on his head and maybe a few other bruises. Maybe tomorrow I'll get more information on his condition. You no, when anything like that happens, I and another fellow usually jump in a jeep and take off, with red light on and siren blowing. All the cars move off the road to make room for us. Just like in the big cities when police cars go rushing to a scene. It's quite exciting.

This afternoon, I had to go see the Procuror, he's just like a district attorney in the states. I had to see him about some order we needed in order to pick up some confiscated tires. (the last word means saisé in french) You can imagine me

-IV-

going to see a big shot like that. Boy, I have to use my best french in order to talk with people like that, and I have to do a lot of thinking to do that. Anyway, I get along alright. Sometimes I have to go see even judges, and once I was complimented by one of those judges on my french. So I guess I must be doing alright. Smart man you have there. ha. ha.

Well, I had some sergent stripes sewed on today, cost me .25¢ for each shirt. That's where most of my money goes, paying for things like that. Oh well, this won't last long now.

Solong for now honey, take care,

Yours Always

Wilde

No. 435   Oct. 5 - '45

Hello Face Saite:

I didn't get any letter today, but I still have yours to comment on, so here goes a few lines for the record.

I'm glad to hear that you and that big girl are always well. I wouldn't anything to happen to you now that I'm almost home. See that you stay that way too, — or else.

Your first week's pay wasn't bad at all at the shop. But I still wish that you would quit now, so that you could rest up before I get back. And even if you do keep on working, I'm glad at least that you quit buying bonds.

Boy, won't it be nice to get back home again and sit in that old easy chair, and have you either sitting on the footstool or crawling all over me. Remember when you used to do that? Only now, I'll have two of you to take, but

- 11 -

honey you can crawl all you like. If I ever say anything just sock me or something.

So you noticed that my letters are a little different huh? That's nothing, if the mail had not been censured when I first came to work on this job, you would have had some nice juicy gossip. Things are very different now, there's only a small percentage of the servicemen here and therefor there isn't so much trouble. Take like today for instance, there was nothing at all that happened. All I did was sit around the office all day long.

I'm glad you liked those last pictures I sent you. So now you believe me when I say I've gained weight huh? That's what I get for taking an office job. Can't seem to think of much more, so I guess I'll make this short. Solong until tomorrow

Love Always,
Hilde

P.S. Did you notice the envelope. Rickson + I changed wives for tonight.

No. 436   Oct. 7-'45

Dearest Jace Laite:

Hello honey, today is sunday over here. It's five thirty at night and I just got back from supper. This afternoon Kickson and I went for a ride to Dumfea and Paita. We didn't have nothing to do and it gets so damn lonely hanging around the tent. There wasn't much to see up that way that we hadn't seen before. I've been up that way so many times. But we did go into the church at Paita. I used to see that going by often and I always wanted to see the inside. It was just as I expected, very old but nice to see. It was hand built and painted, and for lights there was lamps hanging from the ceiling. I wish you could have seen it, I'm sure you would like that.

I didn't write to you yesterday because as I said before, we can't mail anything and

—11—

don't receive mail on sunday. There was nothing that happened anyway. It's been very quiet for the past two days.

You no, those pictures you sent me last week, I couldn't recognize two kids on the horse with Elaine and Richard. I knew Richard, but only after looking at him over and over again. Gosh, those kids have grown. So how about telling me who the two other kids are.

I guess I'll have to make this letter short because I can't think of anything more. So until tomorrow, solong face laite and take good care of you both. It won't be long now.

Yours Always,
Hildre.

No. 437   8 October 1945

Dearest Face Laite:

Received two letters from you this morning and also one from Fern. I was very glad too because My disposition was very low and grouchy. But after reading your letter I felt much better. See what a moral maker you are?

You also sounded much better on the letters I got this morning than you did on the last ones that I got. Yes, you can bet your pants that I will be more than glad to get back and earn the living. You've done it longer then I wanted you too already. By the way, have you stopped working at the shop yet? I don't suppose you have but there's no harm in asking anyway. Just you wait until I get back, I'll fix you.

Sorry to hear that your mother was sick again. Is the old man still as bad as he use to be? From what you said on your letter I gathered as much.

As for Cook, he hasn't left yet. He and a lot of others are waiting for transportation. There hasn't been a boat in here for some time now. But according to the orders that came out he should leave soon.

So there making a lot of change in Berwick huh? I don't doubt but even if they didn't tear down those buildings I'd find it changed anyway. The first few months that I was over here, I could picture in my mind what it was like back home. But now I don't have the slightest idea how anything must look like. Even you seem to have changed on the last pictures that you sent me. You can imagine what Elaine will look like to me, and all the other kids too. Honey, you don't no how much I want to get back, a person in the States does'nt realize what he has until he's thousands of miles away from it all.

Well, altough tjis is only in the afternoon, I thought of writing to you right away while there was nothing else to do. It's still the same, we have nothing to do and if there is it's not much. This morning I had to go out with the french sanitary inspector to pick up a couple of native girls because they had the clapp. We've been having a lot of venereal reports lately, there was six saturday and three more today. But they are all on native or Javanese girls. It's very seldom that we pick up any white girls.

Fern says that they may have to come back to live in Berwick, or at least change places on account of Bill's legs. I had a hunch this would happen a long time ago. Oh well, ces la vie n'est pas? Solong until tomorrow honey and take care of you both for me.

Yours Always,

Mildre'

A World War II Story: Dad's Letters Home

No. 438   Oct. 9 - '45

Hello Dear Faite:

Received two letters today but they were not from you. One was from Annette and the other from Everett.

Today was my day off again, every Tuesday is. I don't no why I should get a day off because I don't do anything anyway. But as long as they want to give anything to me I'm going to take it. I've been lying around all day. This afternoon they were having a movie in the area so I went. There's going to be another one tonight and I'll see that one too. Gosh I'm sick of the same old routine every day. Last night after work I and two other guys decided to stay in town for supper for a change. We went to a place called Hotelle Central. It cost us two dollars apiece and

—11—

didn't get our belly full. Every place is the same, prices are high and you don't get anything. We had soup, a little chicken, cauliflower and bread, all for two dollars. Boy what a gyp. I'll be glad to get home and get some of your cooking again.

There's no news about my leaving here yet. By next monday there's suppose to be a lot of men going to the personal center. When they go there the next step is to board the boat. When my turn comes I'll let you no so you can stop writing to me. That will be <u>the</u> day. Maybe in a couple of months my turn will come.

Can't think of anything else so I guess I'll close. Solong until tomorrow honey,

Love Always,
Wilde

No. 439 Oct. 10 - 45

Dear Face Faite:

Another day that's bringing us closer together and boy are they getting long. Now that reunion is near time goes by so slow. This morning everything was so quiet in town that it was pitiful. And it almost drives me crazy hanging around like that. I still think that by Dec. or Jan. I should be on my way home. Of course there are still a lot of rumors and stories going around, and a lot of them are very discouraging to hear. But I still stick to my opinion of being home by Elaine's birthday. In two more months we should no for sure.

Well, although there was not much doing this morning, this afternoon I went out with another guy to investigate a robbery. It seems that a soldier had about $270 on him and some sailor stole it from him while he was drunk.

-11-

The soldier hired a room at a hotel and invited the sailor to his room. While they were both there the sailor fed the soldier plenty of whiskey and got him drunk, then stole his money. We went to hotel to question the chamber maid and she told us everything. She didn't actually see the theft but she knew enough to indicate that the sailor was guilty. About the other guy who was with me, I must tell you about him. His name is Jordon and he's what they call the provost sergent, or the chief under the provost sergent, I think, and all of us who work with him think that he's batty as hell. If you would see him you'd say the same. Anyway, whenever anything happens he's always got to butt his nose into it. I sometimes have to go out with him to act as interpreter, and when I do I get in a fight with him. He's always insulting somebody, and when you insult one of these frenchman, well, you can't get anything out of them. Anyway, this afternoon we were

-111-

at the hotel questioning the maid and he insulted her. Boy was I mad, and I got into another argument with him. And besides that I had to do some tall explaining to the girl. These frenchmen don't speak english but they understand it. But he thinks that they are all ignorant and that he can say what he wants to in english and get away with it. He's positively nuts that's all. He reads all those crazy detective stories and thinks he's Dick Tracy. Oh well, I haven't much longer to put up with him. Boy will I be glad to get out of this army.

I guess that's all for now, take care honey,

Yours Always,
Wildré

A World War II Story: Dad's Letters Home

NO. 440   October 12, 1945

Dearest Face Laite:

Have'nt received any mail for a few days now, but that' nothing new. Probably won't get any before next week now.

Well, I did'nt write to you yesterday nor to any one else for that matter. And I had a pretty good reason too. Yesterday morning I had to go to the dispensary to get a shot in the arm. A typhoid shot. It didn' hurt then but by last night my arm was so sore and I had quite a fever that I went to bed right after it was dark I've had plenty of shots before but this last one was the worse yet. And I never was sick like that before either. They say it's because of the climate that we get sick that way. After being here so long your blood changes and it's a different life altogether. I wasn't the only one that was sick, there were a lot of others. I was still pretty stiff this morning but I feel a lot better now. I hope I don't get any more like that.

Despite my being sick yesterday, there was plenty of work. It would happen that way. I could have forgotten about it and I should have too, but I went ahead anyway. A frenchman came into the station and complained that an American soldier had given a jeep motor to another frenchman and that something should be done about it. Well, I started out on that deal and was out all day running down different angles. I even went without supper and had to eat a couple of hamburgs down town. It turned out to be true alright that the soldier had loaned the frenchman the motor but not give it to him. On a deal like that There's so many things to do, go here, go there and especially when there's a frenchman involved. Gosh what a job. Anyway I believe the soldier, he didn't seem to be a thief nor would he give away anything like that. But It looks bad for him. I hope he don't get jail, it's too near time to go home. And besides all that, I had another deal to take care of too. Remember a few days ago I told you about a soldier trying to take out a Javanese girl of 13 years, well, yesterday the same people complained that the same soldier was still going there and was trespassing into the house late at night. Well, Hickman and I went out to find the soldier and brought him to the station. The provost marsahl gave him a warning that he should not go back there anymore. The next time he would go there he was going to get a jail sentence. I don't think he'll go back there. That damn Jordon, if it was up to him all the soldiers we bring in would go to jail. Instead of giving the soldier a break he wants to lock them up all the time. Boy that guy is crazy.

Well, Hickman got his orders today, he's supposed to repott to the personal center next Tuesday. That crazy Jordon was supposed to go too but his orders didn't come out. It seems we can't get rid of him. There's a lot of soldiers will be leaving either next week or the next. By the first of December there will be only I and another interpreter left here. But I'm hoping that by the end of Dec. I'll be on my way too. Well, until then keep your chin up face laite, and take care of you both for me.

                                           Love Always,
                                           Wildre'

No. 441   October 13, 1945.

Dearest Face Laite:

        It's saturday noon over here while in Berwick it's only friday night. It must be about 11 oclock last night and you must be sleeping like an angel. I didn't work this morning but I have too this afternoon. You see, we work only five and a half days a week now, but seeing that I work on the night shift two weeks and the day shift two weeks, my hours are all fouled up. I'll be going on the night shift beginning monday.

        Hickman was releived of duty today. That means that he won't have to report to work no more. Next tuesday he will go to the personal center and wait for a boat to take him back. Cook hasn't got his call yet but he should pretty soon. The 208 MP Co. gave a dance last night, they called it their farewell dance but it wasn't really. There are a lot of them leaving the same time as Hickman, almost half the company. Of course I didn't go but I kept a program of invitation and I'm encloseing it in this letter to show you. I suppose I could have gone if only to have free beer, but I haven't gone to any of them so far so why should I spoil my record. And besides that, I don't believe you would approve. I wouldn't want you to do that and I'm sure you don't want me too either. That' waht I call haveing mutual trust in one another. When I decide to go to a dance I'll have my face laite right along with me.

        You no honey, there's a lot of funny things that happen here. Take all these fellows that are going home for instance. Hickman got acquainted with a girl about four months ago and he's fell head over heels for her. She can speak pretty good english and she's a good girl too I guess, but I think he's trying to get her in the States in order to marry her. He lives in Texas and I no these Texans well enough to no that they will not get along together. Anyway he's single and he can do what he wants too. But there are some married soldiers who have steady girls and they also are leaving. I don't no if the girls no the soldiers are married but I see them parading the streets every day. Some even have babies by these married soldiers and they no that they are married too. I just can't figure them out. I no that if I went out with these girls my conscience with bother me for the rest of my life. But it don't seem to bother some of these fellows. I guess I see to damn much of this going on every day and that's why I don't step out of line. But even if I didn't see all of this I don't believe I'd do anything like that anyway. Oh well, let them do what they want, I no that I'm doing right and I no you are too and that's all that counts.

        Well, how's my two girls getting along? That may be a silly question to ask but I haven't received any mail for almost a week now, and when that happens it seems to me that it's more like a year. That's why I keep saying the same thing. Gosh I'm anxious to get back home, you don't no how much.

        I guess that's all for now. I didn't work this morning and I don't think anything will happen this afternoon so there's nothing to tell you in that line. Solong until tomorrow honey and take care of you both.

                                      Yours Always,

                                      Wildre'

VOUS ETES CORDIALLEMENT INVITES A ASSISTER A UNE SOIRE DANSANTE A L'OCCASION DU BAL DONNE POUR LES MEMBRES DE LA 208 M.P.CO. QUI SONT EN INSTANCE DE DEPART. CETTE DANCE AURA LIEU AU CLUB EDGEWATER, ANSE VATA.

LE 12 OCTOBRE 1945

28 ORCHESTRE DU SERVICE SPECIAL

SA DANCE COMMENCERA A HUIT HEURES ET FINERA A ONZE HEUR

UNE AUTO PASSERA VOUS PRENDRE VERS 19 HEURES SI VOUS LE DESIREZ.

RAFRAICHISSEMENTS

YOU ARE CORDIALLY INVITED TO ATTEND A FAREWELL DANCE GIVEN FOR THE MEMBERS OF THE 208th MILITARY POLICE CO. TO BE HELD AT THE CLUB EDGEWATER, ANSE VATA.

12 OCTOBER 1945

28th SPECIAL SERVICE ORCHESTRA

DANCING FROM 2000 TO 2300

TRANSPORTATION WILL BE PROVIDED FOR ALL GUESTS.

REFRESHMENTS WILL BE SERVED

A World War II Story: Dad's Letters Home

No. 442   Oct. 14 - 45

Dearest Face Faite!

    Sunday afternoon, and it's as exciting as a sunday afternoon ever was over here. This morning I got up early to go to the eight thirty civilian mass, just for a change. After mass, I came right back to camp and tried to think what to do today. Had dinner and afterwards I still didn't no what to do with myself. I laid down on my bunk and having nothing better to do, fell asleep. I just woke up a few minutes ago, and now it's four oclock. The day is almost gone but nothing much has been accomplished, in excitement or otherwise.

    Another ship went out today, headed for the States. When they go that way I see them all pass, from where I live. You can't imagine how much these fellows sweat out

- 11 -

these ships. Nothing is discussed more and more, ships and more ships. When will they come in.

Tomorrow I start working nights again. The next two weeks are going to be long.

I'm enclosing four pictures, three of which were taken of the office. You can see my boss too, in one of them. The one on which the group of M.P.'s are, was taken in Sept. You can see me in the rear marked X. This was on the day that crazy Jordon received a bronze medal from the general. This picture is of the guard detachment fellows, and I live with them. They are the ones who keep the prison stockade.

Guess that's all for now, take care,

love
Wildie

No. 443   October 15, 1945.

Dear Face Laite:

There was supposed to have been a lot of mail today but I still didn't get any. Maybe tomorrow tho I'll get beaucoup.

Well, this is my first night again. I got up early this morning because I couldn't sleep at all. So I had to hang around all day twiddleing my thumbs. After dinner I had a mind to go down town but after thinking it over I couldn't think of anything to do there, so I stayed in camp and read all afternoon.

When I came down to work tonight the town seemed to have a lot of swabbies roaming the streets. There was a cruiser that came in this morning and I guess they came off from that. Anyway it wasn't long before thinhs began to get lively. I started to write out my report of investigation on that motor deal that I told you about last week, and I was interupted several times before it was done. First of all I got a call to go to a bar where some sailors were causing trouble. After I got there the barmaid told me that four sailors had entered the bar and seeing that they were to drunk to serve them, she refused to give them anything, So they got mad and started to throw the chairs around and glasses too. She called the S.P.s and they took them away. They didn' hit the barmaid but they did break a couple of chairs.

Then the french MPs called me and said that another sailor had stolen one of their trucks. Luckily they found the sailor and truck right away and he was brought to the station.

Just before I came to work two french civilians stole an Army truck and they also were caught. There's never a dull moment when those swabbies come into town. It seems that just because they stop here for a few days, they think that they can do what ever they want. But they usually get caught tho.

You no, after trying to figure out just how I stood on this point business, I've come to the conclusion that if the points are defrosted in Dec., I'll be elligeble to go home then. I have 54 now and by the 2 Dec. I'll have 60. And then I figure that by Jan. 1st I'll be on my way home. How's that huh? I hope I'm right. And if I am I'll certainly be home for Elaine's birthday. Boy oh boy, I can't wait to see..

Well, honey, I can't think of anything else so I guess I'll close. I hope your taking good care of yourself and that big girl. Solong until tomorrow.

                                          Yours Always,

                                          Mildre'

No.444 October 17, 1945

Chere Face Laite:

Still haven't received any mail yet and I'm getting more impatient every day. It's been over a week now since I got the last one.

Well, to begin with there is alittle more news on going home, but of course not about me yet. Thereis another ship that came in yesterday and two more are expected in in the next few days. This morning they put out a call for all overage men, 35 or over, to report to the personal center. Also Cook got his call to report the 19, that's two days from now. That personal center is full right now but they will be leaving within the next few days. All the men with 70 points or over have to report by Nov. 1st, then come the 60 point men and probably me along with them. Things look mighty good now, and I can hardly wait. You no, I was thinking the other day that I forgot your telephone number. So if you want me to call you the first thing when I get back, you'd better send me you number soon.ha ha.

Well I'm going to move again, not to the States but to another camp here. You see, they are breaking up a lot of camps and moving to others. I think that by next week I'll be moving to another camp called Camp Goettge. That's right in the same area where the personal center is tho, so I won't have far to go when my turn comes. It's a much better place, it's right near the beach and everything else. I haven't been swimming once since I've been over here, but I think that when I move to the new place I'll try it once more. On the Guadalcanal the water was so warm that it wasn't much fun, but over here it may be different. I've never worn that pair of trunks that you bought me yet, so this is a good time to try them.

Tere still isn't much work. I'm still hanging around doing nothing but writing letters and reading. Oh yesn and sunning myself too. You ought to see the tan I've got now. They just brought in two sailors who stole an army jeep and they are in my office taking a statement from one of them. The town is full of crazy swabbies just off these ships and they try to get away with everything. I had to go to the Central Hotel a little while ago because two other sailors tried to steal a frenchman's car. That's all that happen so fartonight.

Well, I guess that's about all for now. Hope you and that big girl are in top shape, it won't be long now honey. Solong until tomorrow,

Yours Always,
Wildre'

No. 445　　　　　　　　　　　　　October 18, 1945.

Dearest Face Laite:

Finally received one letter from you today and that wasn't very long. It was dated Oct. 11 and I haven't yet received all the other ones from Sept. 29 to this one. A plane just came in this afternoon and they probably haven't had time to sort out all the mail. I expect to get a lot tomorrow tho. On the letter I got today you talked only about Elaine, but that's good. You also said that on that day you had not worked very much. I'm glad to hear that at least. I take it then that you haven't stopped working yet. And as for Elaine taking after me, well, it's still a little early yet to say that. Maybe she does stretch out like the old man but I hope she Doesn't take after me in everything. Wait until I get back there and then you'll see two of us stretched out in the sun.

Well, according to the radio today, the points are going to be lowered to 50 some time in December. Now we are pretty sure that I'll be back for Elaine's birthday. That's the best news that I've heard so far and this time it concerns me for a change. I'll go one better than that, I say that they might lower the points even before that. Of course that my guess, and what makes me say that is, now that the ships have started to come this way there will be more stopping here and as long as there is some space, they will load on anybody, points or no points. I hope I'm right. I guessed pretty good so far, my luck might hold put.

Rickson was released today and he's supposed to report at the denter tomorrow. That leaves only four of us left in the section but I think they will get some replacements soon.

There's nothing that happened so far tonight. I just got to work and as there was nothing else to do, I thought about writing your letter now. The night is still young tho and there are plenty of swabbies in town.

As usual today, I hung around all day long sunning myself and reading. Boy what a life this is. When I get back it will take me at least six months to get used to work. I'm so soft and fat now that' it's pitifull. But I'm not worried to much about that fat, the boat trip home will make me loose all of it. Espesially if the boat is crowded. When we came over they gave us on two meals a day and then we had to wait in line for hours. You can imagine how it will be on the way back with so many troops to handle.

Well, I guess that's about all for now. Solong until tomorrow and take care of that big girl and yourself.

　　　　　　　　　　　　　　　Yours Always,

　　　　　　　　　　　　　　　Mildre'

A World War II Story: Dad's Letters Home

No. 446　　　　　　　　　　　　　　　October 19, 1945.

Dearest Face Laite:

　　My hopes of receiving a lot of letters today were quite shattered, for I didn't get one letter. I was so disappointed that I didn't no whether to write to you or not. I've completely run out of words and there's nothing about my work to talk about, but I decided to give it a try anyway. So if this sounds dull to you I hope you won't mind.

　　I told you yesterday that Cook and Rickson were supposed to report to the personal center todayb but the plans were changed again and now they will report there tomorrow. Since I heard that news on the radio yesterday about the lowering of points sometime in December, I'm watching every bit of news that comes out on it. I'm in great hopes of taking that boat at the same time as the fellows who have 60 points. And that should be some time in December, just two months away. Our local radio station and the paper said today that there will be 4 ships in here within the next ten days, to load troops and take them back home. There's bout 2700 troops in all on this shipment. I'm doing alot of sweating right now and I'll admit that I'm a little nervous too. When I stop to think that I'm going home soon I don't no what to think. I get all nervous inside and no matter what I try to think I simply don't no what I'm going to do when I do get back. It's hard to explain, this feeling I mean, something like getting married or having a baby or something like that. Maybe I'm too anxious but I hope I don't get disappointed.

　　I'll be moving to my new camp next week. My address won't change tho so you can send my letters to the same address.

　　There's nothing that happened so far tonight. But this afternoon just before I came to work there was some trouble at the Pink House. I don't think I've told you about that place yet. They call it the Pink House but it's really a whoar house. There are three or four girls working there and it costs 5 dollars for five minutes. Some days there is a line outside a mile long waiting to get in. I went there a couple of times, but only on business of course and I never did see who the girls were working there. Every once in a while there's some trouble, either some sailor or soldier who isn't satisfied and wants his money back. Today it was three sailors. I don't no what the trouble was tho, but I'll bet he claims he got robbed too or something like that.

　　Well, I guess that's all for now. Here's hopeing you and that big girl are okay. Take care of you both for me, it won't be long now.

　　　　　　　　　　　　　　　　Yours Always,

　　　　　　　　　　　　　　　　Wildre'

No.447   October 20, 1945.

Dearest Face Laite:

Hello honey, no mail again today but I have some good news anyway. It was announced today that the points will be lowered below 60 even before Dec, 1st. That means good news for me, gosh I can hardly wait. They probably won't be lowered before next month tho. You no, I may get home for Xmas even, you never can tell.

Well seeing that I didn't get any mail from you there isn't much to talk about except my work, so here goes. Last night I had no sooner got thru writing your letter than everything happened at once, or so it seems. We got a call that an accident had just occured so we dashed out there right away. When we got to the scene we found an army small truck lying on it's side and in the ocean. It was only in a few feet of water. Another MP jeep was already there and they had helped the soldier to get out of the water. It turned out that this soldier had stolen the truck and was speeding down the street when the MPs saw him. They took off after him and after shasing him a ways, they saw him Zig Zag afew times and then run off the road into the water. Luckily the soldier wasn't hurt very bad. All he had was a cut over his nose but he was bleeding a lot. He was lucky he didn't get killed. Well, after taking care of that deal, I was just coming back to the station when they told me that a french woman was selling her ass at a camp nearby. I went to get a french policeman and with another jeep we all went to this place. I went with the French police commissioner and we all separated. We finally found the woman in the bushes and as we approached, about 15 soldiers all scattered. We got the woman tho and she readily admitted that she was laying for 5 dollars each soldier. She was taken to the french police station and locked up. On our way to the station, I was riding with the officer of the day, when an army truck almost ran over us. He took all the road and went right thru a Stop Sign. So we turned right around and chased him. We caught him right away almost, and told the driver to get out of the truck. We then took him to the french police station so that we could call up our station. This fellow was dressed like an American sailor but he seemed to dumb as hell. Anyway, when I took him in the french station I told him to sit down and all of a sudden he started to speak french. I almost fell over. I thought sure he was a sailor but it turned out that he was a french civilian. All in all I had a busy night. So far tonight there isn't anything that's happen and I don't want anything either.

I took Cook and Rickson to the personal center this morning and you should see how crowded that place is. They will all be leaving in the next few days tho and I sure wish I was with them. Oh well my turn will come pretty soon. Solong until tomorrow honey and take care always.

                                    Love Always,
                                    Wildre'

A World War II Story: Dad's Letters Home

No. 448   October 21, 1945.

Chere Face Laite:

       Hello honey. I don't no what there is to write about but I'll give it a try anyway. I've received only one letter in the past two weeks and it makes it pretty hard to carry a sensible conversation.

       Well, this morning I went to the ten oclock mass at the Cathedral and afterwards went to the personal center. Just as I got there they were calling out the passenger list for the first boat to arrive. And what a list. There are 1300 men to go on the first one alone. They will be loading tomorrow and will leave the next morning. There are four more boats due in within the week. That's good news for me too because the quicker the boats come in, the quicker my turn will come. I expect they will lower the points about the 15 of Nov. and I should get my call soon after that. I may be home for Xmas yet. Only time will tell but I can't wait to find out.

       Well, after I had written your letter last night, I got a call to go to the Pink House again. When I got there it turned out that the trouble wasn't there but at a house directly in back. This house is OFF LIMITS and there was two sailors in there and the woman wouldn't open the door to let them out. I had to go get a french cop and he made her open the door. We got the two sailors and brought them to the station. Can you imagine this woman, she is 48 years old and has two small kids. She's nothing but an old whoar. We use to ahve a lot of trouble at this house and that why they put it OFF LIMITS. Oh well, that's all that happened last night. I don't think that there will be much trouble tonight because all the bars are closed. Today was election day over here for the french.

       The officer of the day just brought in a french girl and a New Zealand soldier. The soldier did not commit anything serious. The only thing he did was to give this girl a ride in his truck and just because he didn't have the right trip ticket the officer brought him in. My sidekick gave the girl a ride home because she didn't have norride. There's always some chicken shit officer like that doing some mean think. I'd never do anything like that. Talking about this french girl, I no her pretty well. She, used to work in a bar in town. Don't get me wrong now because a while back I used to take care of all these bars. Delivering signs and taking care of the trouble they used to have. Anyway I found out that this girl went to a dance one night and two sailors took her out and attacked her. The result is that she is in a family way now and is living in the country. She never did report the matter to anyone, but one of her girl friends told me this. Just goes to show you what chances girls take by going to dances alone.

       I guess that about all the gossip for now. Hope you and that big girl are still okay. It won't be long now face laite.

                                   Love Always,
                                   Wildre'

No. 449   October 22, 1945

Dearest Face Laite:

        Finally received some mail today and it was about time too. There three from you, and one each from mother, Alice, Florida. In one of your letters there was two more pictures, the one of Conrad and family, and the other one of the kids on the horse. If you hadn't told me that it was Grace and Lorette I wouldn't have known them. Lorette has grown to be quite a girl. When I get back you'd better watch me so that I won't flirt with your kid sisters. And I still don't no who those two other kids are on top of the horse with Elaine. And I'm sure glad to hear that Elaine takes good care of my picture. I wonder if she'll recognize me when I get back. God you don't no how anxious I am of getting back there. And when you tell me things like that I get all the more lonesome. and as for Rene being in Japan I wasn't surprised to hear it. But he must have enough points for discharge now, so I don't think he will stay there very long. On today's paper it said that the fellows with 60 points will be one month ahead of scheduel in getting back. I don't expect the points to drop tp 50 before next month but I'm anxious to find out. They may announce that any day now.

        Alice tells me that Andre is at APO 72 now and that is in the Phillippines. The last time she told me that Keddee had 71 points, and if that's true he should be on his way home any day now. I'm sorry for Andre tho, he could apply for a dependency discharge but he probably don't no that. The next time I write him I'll tell him about it.

        If there's to many mistakes in this letter don't mind too much. For the past two nights I've had so much work that my head is dizzy. Right after I wrote your letter last night everything happened at once. There was an accident in Dumbea, and that's about 15 miles from here and then there was a rape case just before that. I won't bother to explain now, I don't believe I could go into all the details. I and the other guy working with me just got thru writing up about fifty pages of reports and it's now one oclock in the morning. But I had to write to my face laite just the same. See how true I am. You'd better have something good for me when I get back. After going true all this you'd better, or else.

        Well I guess I'll cut this letter short and will try to have more gossip for you tomorrow. Good night honey and take care of you both.

        All My Love,

        Your Old Man Mildre'

No. 451. Oct. 23-'45

Dearest Face Laite:

Hello honey, I thought I might get some more mail today, but no such luck.

Well, the first boat load left the island today headed for the States. There was about one thousand soldiers, some nurses and a few married french women. I saw the boat go by in the bay at noon and it was nice to see. At the dock there was a band to see them off. They were one bunch of happy guys let me tell you.

There were stories around today saying that the 60 point men will be called within the next few days. After them the points should be lowered, and I hope down to 50. I went to headquarters this afternoon and they were already listing the 50 point men. I listen to every bit of news, I'm so anxious. And that makes the time go by all the slower. Oh yes, Cook and Rickson will leave

-11-

the island the 25th, so they will be home for Thanksgiving. I'm hoping to be home for Xmas.

I was told today that I'll have to work nights from now on all the time. There's only two of us left that can do any investigating, crazy Jordon and myself. The others are all new fellows and are green as hell. Therefor, when something happens one of us has to be there.

I found out something today that is enough to make any American go crazy. Let me start at the beginning first. Crazy Jordon got a tip from some body today, telling him of some black-market activities going on, on a little island near here. It's called Ille Nou. The navy had a base there. Anyway, Jordon went there and with the gendarme of the island they went around every home. Of all the equipement and household

-111-

furniture they found, it would amount up to nearly a half million dollars, or maybe even more. There was refrigerators brand new, plush furniture, motors, tools and many other things to numerous to mention. And all this was found in the french homes or in warehouses that the navy left unguarded. When the navy left the island, they left all that stuff behind. Then all the frenchmen had to do was break in the doors and take the stuff away. Nobody was there to stop them. There was even some brand new washing machines not yet uncrated.

Just <u>think</u> of this, I said it amounted to half million dollars, but I'm sure it's much more than that. And yet,-we,- you and I,- and a lot of other people who scrape our pennies to buy bonds in order to help the war effort, that's what we get in return. You remember a while

-IV-

back, when I was asking you to cash all our bonds? Well, that was the reason I wanted you too. I couldn't tell you then because of the censures. They would not let that go by. I was seeing all this waste all the time, that's what got me so mad. I won't try to put all I no down on a letter, it's just too long to write about. But I can tell you some stories that would make your hair stand up straight. You simply wouldn't believe me. But for our sake honey, don't buy another bond until I get back. We won the war, but I don't understand how we did it sometimes. I'm too disgusted to write any more, so I guess I'd better close. So long until tomorrow, and take care of you both.

Yours Always,
Wilbr.

No. 451   October 24, 1945.

Dearest Face Laite:

No mail again today, that's only two days tho since I last received tree from you. Probably won't get any more now for two more weeks.

Well, according to todays paper there will be three more ships in here between the first and second of November. I look forward to having the points lowered around the first and if they do, I might get on one of those three boats. That's only my guess but I hope I'm right. Anyway, if I don't take one of those it will be soon afterwards. Don't bank too much on what I say because I may be all wrong. On those three ships there are supposed to be 4000 men loaded to go home. There's only about 10,000 men left on this island and with 4000 men to load there won't be many left here.

Well, there isn't much to talk about so far today. I just came to work and for the first time this week we're all caught up on work. Yesterday was my day off and I didn't do anything but hang around camp all day. In the afternoon I went to the personel center and saw Cook and Rickson. Cook said that he will go to see you when he gets home. But I will be back almost as fast as he will. At least that's what I think. He should leave any day this week.

I was just thinking about that big girl of ours. On your letter this week you said that she still kisses my picture every night. It makes me feel pretty good to read that. I keep wondering if she will no me by my picture when I get back. I can't wait to get on that boat.

Well, I can't think of much more to say so I guess I'll make this short. I want to write to Alice too tonight. Solong until tonorrow honey and take care of you both for me. It won't be long now.

Yours Always,

Mildre'

No. 452   October 25, 1945.

Dearest Face Laite:

Hello honey, don't let the red letter get you. Just for a change I thought a letter written in red would brighten up things a little.

Well, I got two more letters today, one from you and one from Marstella of the old outfit. I'm still about a dozen letters short from you but they'll come with the time. You were telling me about the trip you and Elaine took to the farm. That must be some girl we have there. She's getting smarter all the time. I can't wait to get home and show her a few tricks. And if you think you miss me more and more on account of the change in time, just picture me sweating out this point business.

I brought another fellow from our section to the personel section today. It was King, I think I've mentioned him to you before. He's one of the interpreters. And there are a lot of others that went with him too. All the 65 point men went there today. The 60 point men will go sometime next week and then I think it will drop down to 50. At least I hope so.

Rickson will board the boat tonight at seven oclock but Cook won't go until Monday now. Anyway he will be home before Thanksgiving and he will see you.

Starting tonight I'm going to write to everybody and tell them not to write to me any more. My turn isn't so very far away now and they'll only be writing for nothing because I won't answer them. But not you tho, you keep on writing until I tell you to stop. I hope by next week or ten days I'll be telling you the same thing. And if you see any of the others tell them for me not to write any more.

There's only three of us left in the section now. I think they will make me go on days next week. The plans have been changed again. Everything is happening so fast that everybody is going around like a scared cat.

Well I guess that's about all for tonight. So until tomorrow solong honey and take care of you both, for it won't be long now.

                                   Your Flameing Love,
                                   Wildre'

No. 453.   Oct. 26-'45

Dearest Face Laite:

    Finally got four letters from you today and also one from Medee. Yours were all dated in the first week of October, and I had already received some with an earlier date. It's only one o'clock in the afternoon at present, so I may get some more later.

    I gather from your letters that Elaine takes up a lot of your time by sewing for her. Well, that's as good as another for keeping busy. She also seems to draw the same amount of attraction as usual. She probably speaks better than I do by now. That must be quite a girl we have there. I can't wait to get back.

    Sorry to hear about Gagnon's wife. It's pretty tough and that will cost him a lot of money. Hope she gets well quick.

    One of the reasons why I keep asking you

to stop working, is because of things like that. Gagnon's wife for instance. I don't want you to run yourself down and become a victim of the same as she. It's alright to keep busy but there's a limit too. So if you insist on working, be sure to take good care of yourself. I gave you hell many times since I've been away, but I won't mention it anymore now. It won't be long before I get back and take over the reins. And you'd better be in good shape too. — Or else. Speaking of going home, there's no more news so far. Discharge points for the Marines have been lowered to 50, so the army should come around the first of November.

    I'm glad to hear that Elaine looks like both of us and not just me. She'll have to go some tho if she wants to pass my good looks. ha ha. (haven't changed much have I?)

-111-

I'm enclosing two snapshots of your beautiful fat ass husband, which were taken in my office. You can see how dark my face is, but that's only a tan. They don't show my pot-belly to advantage tho. And it's a good thing they don't, you might be afraid of me. For the past few weeks that's been my favorite position. Especially when there's nothing to do except read or shoot the bull. It's on that desk that I type all your letters.

Well, I guess that's about all for now. Solong until tomorrow,

With Love Always,
Wilbr

A World War II Story: Dad's Letters Home

No. 454   Oct. 27-'45

Hello Face Faite:

I've got some good news for you today. After you receive this letter, I'd advise you not to write to me anymore. How's that for good news huh? I'll keep writing to you as usual tho, because I'm not leaving just yet. But if you write to me I may not get them. I expect to leave here sometime between now and the 15th of Nov., and if not then, it will be soon after. Anyway, it's a pretty sure thing that I'll be home for Xmas and even before. I'll be there even before Elaine' birthday. Gosh, I'm so full of hope that I hardly no how to put it down on paper. So until I get further news on the subject I'll try to stop talking about it.

There's another boat that just came in

-11-

this noon. It will be leaving tomorrow I guess and Cook will be on it I'm pretty sure. Talk about the rumors that's going around here, there's a new one every five minutes.

There's plenty of crime going on right now, but to hell with it all as far as I'm concerned. All I'm interested in is going home.

Got another letter from you yesterday too.

Well, I guess I'll make this short because I'm too excited to do any more writing. Until tomorrow, solong honey.

With Love,
Wilbe

No. 455   Oct. 29-'45

Dearest Face Faite:

  Hello honey, haven't received any mail for a few days now. The mail situation is not any better.

  On yesterday's letter I sounded very optimistic, but today I don't feel so much so. The troops were moving off so fast that I thought sure I would be on my way before Nov. 15. But now I'm not so sure. There was a lot of troops that came in here from Guadalcanal yesterday. I don't no if they will stay here or go home. Anyway they'll take up just so much more room. Of course that's just my idea, and I may be all wrong. Anyway, just thinking about staying here for a couple of extra weeks isn't so good. Maybe I built up to many hopes. But at any rate, I'm quite certain

-11-

of leaving some where around the first of December at the latest. And I still say that I'll be home for Xmas. The only trouble with me is that I'm too anxious.

Well, there isn't much news from here. There are still plenty of crimes, but I don't feel like talking about them anymore. I've lost what little interest I had in the work. When there's a case comes up now, I try to keep as far away as I can. I don't feel like doing anything but go home.

I had a day off today, or rather I should say night off. I hung around all day. I got up early this morning because I couldn't sleep. I was up at six oclock. I had breakfast, the first time in two weeks. When I work nights I never usually get up to eat. After that I took a shower and washed a few things. This afternoon I stayed out in the sun and read a whole book. I do so much reading sometimes that I get sick of it. But then there's nothing else to do. Tonight I went to the movies and as usual the machine had to break down. Boy do I get mad. I'll sure be glad to get back and see a movie in comfort again. I just got back a few minutes ago. It's only eight thirty now and I'm sleepy at all. I just don't no what to do with myself. I guess I'll go to bed and read some more.

    Cook and King boarded the boat and left this morning. They should be home by the 10 of Nov.

    I guess that's all for now, solong until tomorrow. It won't be long now. Don't loose patience like I do, I'll make it yet. Take care,

        Love Always, Wilbre

No. 456   Oct. 31-'45

Dearest Face Faite:

Received a letter from you late yesterday and also one from Camille. I brought them down to the office last night in order to answer them, but once there I forgot that I didn't have any envelopes. And I forgot to take them back to camp too, but I'm writing anyway. Yours was the first letter I got which was addressed to Sgt. Pelletier.

Well, I still haven't got any news about lowering the points yet. You can be sure I'm doing a lot of sweating too. Maybe I was too hopefull last week, I don't no. But at the rate they were calling these fellows gave me quite an optimistic view. Right now I don't no what to think. All I can do and say is wait. All the sixty point ~~point~~ men are on orders now and they will be called in

-11-

the next couple of days. But after that — I'm keeping my fingers crossed.

I'm not working too hard now. All the accidents and petty things are handled by the officer of the day and patrol cars. It's about time too. They never did anything but sit on their ass and ride around town. I don't have anything to do with that now except when there's some french involved. There was a big accident last night and the officer didn't no what to do. He had to call on me for advice. I helped him out a little but he did all the work. To hell with them, they are supposed to no, that's why they have those bars. Oh yes, I wasn't supposed to work last night. They gave me two nights off for staying on the night shift. I stayed in

-111-

camp the first night, but the next day I was so sick and tired of doing nothing that I went to work. You haven't any idea what it is to stay here doing nothing but read or lay on your bunk. And besides that wait for the damn points to come down.

Well, I guess that's about all for now. Take good care of yourself and that big girl.

Yours Always,
Wilde

No. 457 Nov. 1-'45

Dearest Face Saite;

I still haven't got any letters yet but I've got a bit of good news anyway.

Of course we hear a lot of rumors still, but today I heard a good one even tho I don't no if it's true or not. There was supposed to have been three ships come in here before the 15, but I heard today that there were more than that coming in. And besides that orders have been cut with all those with 50 or more points, and they've already started on lower point men. Cuting the orders means that your elligible to be called anytime. Sometimes it takes two or three days and sometimes weeks. But that's a good sign anyway. Anyway, I'll be home in plenty of time for Xmas, that

-11-

I'm pretty sure of. It's this damn waiting that gets me. I'm so anxious for them to call me that I can hardly think to write. So don't mind my letters if they sound crazy.

The M.P. Co. that I work with got a new interpreter today. That's good news too, because I was afraid they would hold me back if they couldn't find anybody. He's a new fellow just came over. He comes from Maine but I don't no just where. Tomorrow is his first day to work so I'll find out everything about him.

I sat at a typewriter all day today. I started on days this morning. There's so many translations to do that I had to do something. All the clerks are gone so I do whatever I can on the typewriter. I'm pretty slow, but

-//-

—) surprise myself every day in my improvement. Smart husband you got there.

If you haven't sent my watch yet, I hope you won't send it. I think I'll be home before it gets here.

If you remember that diary you sent me last Xmas, well, I stopped writing in it. My mind can't think of anything but going home. Hope you and that big girl are okay. It won't be long honey. Solong and take care,

Love Always,
Wilde

No. 458   Nov. 3- 45

Dearest Face Saite:

Haven't as yet received any mail and it's sure a long wait between letters. I hope at least your getting my letters better than that.

Well, there isn't much news to add to the last letter. That is, as far as going home is concerned. Another boat came in today and about one thousand men left from here on it. It was supposed to have taken only six hundred, but at the last minute they put on four hundred more. The sixty point men have all been called but couldn't report to the personel center because it was filled up. With this bunch leaving they should be there early next week. After they go I'm keeping my fingers crossed as to whether they will call all the men from 50 points up. If they call

-11-

from 55 points up, that means I'll have to sweat it out for another week or two. We haven't had any hint as yet, as to what they intend to do. There are several boats due in here, according to rumor anyway. Gosh it's hell to wait. It wouldn't be so bad if I knew what was coming, but all we can do is guess. And that's not easy on the nerves. Oh yes, there's supposed to be a boat coming in next week, and it will take 1500 men. I hope that's true. The more they take, the better for me.

We got that new interpreter today. He speaks very good french, much better than I do. His name is Daigle, and comes from Fort Kent, Maine. That's way up near the Canadian border. He's only a kid, about 19 I guess, but he'll get along alright.

There's still the usual amount of work at the office. Right now I'm doing plenty of translations. There's enough reports ahead of me to keep me busy for a week. But with the new man now we'll soon catch up, I hope.

- Nov. 5 -

Not being able to mail this letter today, I decided to keep right on today on the same letter. I forgot my pen at the office so don't mind the pencil.

I was seeing a good movie tonight when I suddenly got a call to go downtown right away. The Major wanted me but I couldn't figure out what he wanted. I soon found out tho. It seems that some french soldiers started a fight with some negro soldiers and it turned out to be a riot. About 600

— IV —

people, soldiers and civilians came to the station and they wanted to storm the jail to take out the prisoners. That's not a pretty sight to behold, nor a very nice situation to be in. We had to call out all the French police and M.P.'s to quiet them down, and even the fire department. Things finally quieted down. Here it is ten o'clock and I just got back, and I missed a good show too. Oh well, just another day gone by. No news yet about my turn on that boat. Maybe tomorrow.

    Solong honey and take care of you and you for me.

               Yours Always,
                Hildré

No. 459   Nov. 5 - 45

Dear Face Faite:

I received so many letters today that I don't where to begin answering. From you alone I received nine, and four more from other people. It took me almost half an hour to read them all.

First of all, I want to tell you a bit of good news I heard about today. Major Jeters was talking to another guy today, and I overheard him say that the next boat will be in on the 11th and there are'nt enough 60 point men to fill it. So that means that they'll have to lower the points. Maybe they will, down to 55, and me with only 54. But he also said that after this boat, there will be one every week coming in here. He should no what he's talking about so I'm banking on his

-11-

say so. And I still say that I'll be home for Xmas. Earlier last week I heard some bad news but I don't no who started that story so I won't repeat it. The Major's word is good enough for me.

Now to start answering your letters. I wont be able to answer them all in this one, so I'll take one at a time. — I got a laugh reading how surprised you were to get a letter from Rickson. I did the same for him, so his wife must have surprised too. I like to keep you in suspense, and I can just picture your face as you were reading it. I'm going to keep you that way often when I get back, so you'd better be prepared.

And you seemed to make fun of your sergent, but I read right thru you. Your just a bit proud of your face late, I like you anyway. ha ha.

-111-

Say, I thought I was going to spoil that big girl. Now you tell me that you paint her nails. If that's not spoiling her I don't no what is. I hope you leave something for me to spoil. I can't wait to get my hands on you both. Boy, that must be quite a girl. In Alice's letter which I received today, she says that she wants to meet me at the train with you and Elaine when I get back. But don't you dare bring anyone with you except Elaine. As a matter of fact, I won't tell anyone I'm coming except you. Moments like that belong to us and nobody else.

As for all that money I'm making, it's $14 more a month, or $64 in all. I won't go into how it all goes right now, but I will when I get back. You'd be surprised and so am I as to where it all goes.

-IV-

By the time you get this letter, you'll probably have received the one I told not to write to me any more. After I heard that bad news last week I almost wrote you to keep on writing, but now I'm glad I didn't. It would only be useless to write to me any more because I wouldn't be here to get them. And after I'll get in the States I'll be home inside a few days. I heard that they fly troops from the west coast now when they land. If I'm that lucky, I'd be home within 48 hours after landing at Frisco. I can't get home fast enough to suit me.

Well, I guess I'll close for now. I'll keep writing until I leave here. I hope the number of my letters won't go past 475, that's fifteen days from now. So long honey, love,

Wilbur

No. 460   Nov. 6 - 45

Dearest Face Laite;

It's needless to say that I didn't get any letters today, but after what I got yesterday I shouldn't kick too much.

First of all, my news. And it's more good news too. Instead of telling you all about it, I'm enclosing a clipping which I cut out from our daily paper. It tells you the dates and ships that are due in here soon. I expect to make either the one of Nov. 27 or Dec. 5. But if I don't I'm sure of making one of the last two at least. I don't no if the following makes any difference or not, but today there was a staff meeting, that means a meeting of all commanding officers. I think that something was said about lowering the points. They'll have to whether they want to or not. No ship is supposed to leave here unless it's full, and there aren't enough 60 point men to fill them.

-11-

If you think your excited about these points, think of me. That's all I talk about and the least bit of gossip I hear about it, I take it all in whether it's true or not. And your the one who had better watch out when I get back and not me. I don't doubt for a minute that there are men being discharged before they're supposed to. It was the same way for the draft. But don't worry honey, my turn will come, I hope soon too.

Don't you worry about me buying you to many things. I'll buy you anything I want see. I don't think I'll ever be able to give you what you ought to have, but I'll make a good try at it.

I see Elaine had a cold again. I wanted to tell you before, couldn't you take her to the doctor so he could inject anti-cold syrum. I hear that helps a lot to keep colds away. I no that if we didn't have those shots for fever, dysentery, cholera or other deseases over hear, there would

— 111 —

be a lot of us sick or even dead. I never realized what help they were until I took them. Thats a smart girl we have there and we'd better take good care of her. With all the promise she shows so far, and if she keeps it up we're going to give her all the education she needs. I don't care if I have to work day and night. Education is nothing to laugh at and something everyone needs. I keep telling Alice to send her kids to high school, but no, she can't stand being without the few dollars they earn. Well, we'll be different with our kids.

 Well, I guess I'll close now before I preach you a sermon. Solong honey and take care. I'm counting the days now.

Love Always,
Wilbur

No. 461   Nov. 7 - '45

Dearest Face Laite:

    Here I am answering some of your letters again. I still have some left. There's nothing new to report on the home bound trip. Everything is as the same as it was yesterday. Something had better happen soon or I'll blow my top. This waiting is almost unbearable. Your on edge all the time waiting for some news about dropping those points. They haven't made any ruling yet as to the 50 pointers, but they will have to pretty soon.

    About that safty box you and Florida took at the bank, it's a good idea alright. You can put all your valuables there and it doesn't cost too much.

    Sorry to hear about Michaud passing away. I can imagine all his relatives flocking down

-11-

to collect his dough. My mother tells me that a Theoret girl died in So. Berwick too, she was the oldest one in the family. There will be a lot of changes when I get back.

I see your still trying to look for another job. I don't blame you for trying to get out of the shoe shop, but I still wish you would stay home until I get back. But I'll fix you when I do get there.

There's still plenty of work here, in fact I'm working more now than I ever did. But it helps pass the time away. I guess that's all for now. I've done too much paper work today and can't think any more.

So long honey and take care,
Yours Always,
Willie

No. 462   Nov. 8 - '45

Hello Jase Faite:

    Was surprised to get a letter from you today. I didn't expect any for another week.

    There's nothing new to report today. I heard on the news today that all the men already in the States could get discharged if they had 50 points or more. Well, we haven't heard anything new on that point over here yet. Maybe we'll hear something new in the next week.

    Glad to hear you like Elaine's new carriage. I'll bet she'll like it too. I hope get home soon enough to give it to her too. So if we both hope hard enough I might be there.

    Yes, that's quite a job I have here. You don't no the half of it. If I wrote you everything I did, I'd be writing all the time.

-11-

If you want excitement this is the job you want. But not me, give me that farm and a face late like you, that's all I want.

You no, I was thinking the other day. According to all the news the housing situation is not too good. Can we still get a good rent in Berwick or nearby? Of course you can't tell me now because you stopped writing. But if we won't buy a farm for a year or so, we'll have to find a rent. Oh well, we'll worry about that when I get back. We've done alright so far and we'll continue.

Guess that's all for now, solong and take care honey.

Love Always,
Wildie

No. 463   Nov. 9-'45

Hello Face Faite:

Received one letter today but it wasn't from you, it was from Jean. She had some good news on it for me, and for you too. It was something she had told me about some time ago. She said you were crazy about that something, so I wrote her back and told her to get it for you. I don't no if she's already sent it to you or keeping it for Xmas, so I'm not taking any chances by telling you now. If you haven't already got it you'll be in suspense until Xmas. Boy I can just picture you now. ha. ha. If I get back for Xmas I'll give it to you myself. I didn't expect to buy you anything, but

-11-

after she mentioned that, well that was a good chance for me to keep you in suspense. I wouldn't be able to do it if I were home but as long as I'm here I can. Are you curious? ha ha.

Well, there isn't any news about my boat yet. They announced yesterday that the boat that was supposed to come in Sunday was sent to Australia instead, to pick up some G.I. wives. If that don't get me sore nothing else does. But anyway, there's one coming in Monday and that will take most of the 60 point men. I'm still pretty sure of getting home for Xmas just the same. They haven't made any announcement yet but I expect one in the next few days. This waiting is hard on your nerves, mine anyway.

— 111 —

Oh yes, I got a letter from Toussaint the other day and he said that he would be discharged the first of Nov. So I guess he must be home by now. Don't worry honey, my turn is near now, so don't get too cranky about Elaine. If you'd stay home and rest it would help. But your still the boss as long as the other half gets there. Anyway, you'd better get all the rest you can now cause you'll sure need it.

Guess that's enough for now, solong and take care of you both,

Love Always,
Wilde

P.S. Better tell Fern not to write me anymore also all the others you see.

No. 464 Nov. 10-45

Dearest Face Faite:

Received another batch of letters today and three of them were from you. They were all old tho but was glad to get them anyway. Oh yes, one of yours smelled perfume too. Boy what a nice smell that is. It smells just like you and that's good. Pretty soon now, I'll be getting the real thing and it's sure hell waiting.

Well, according to the news today they are going to send another ship here instead of the one they sent to Australia. It's an escort carrier and should carry about 1000 men. It will be here about the 15 or 20th of this month. So things look bright again and I still say I will be in your hair for Xmas.

—11—

There's still plenty of work here and I'm sure anxious to get out of here. Today a frenchman shot and killed a native here. I don't know any details, I just heard about it. But it just goes to show you there's always something happening.

From what you say on your letters, mail has been pretty slow for you too. Well, I'm still writing to you as usual. If I don't get out of here by the end of this month I won't be getting any mail at all. I've already told most everyone not to write any more. But I'm pretty sure of leaving so that's that.

Nov. 11—

It's sunday night now and I just got back from the show. Today was dead as usual. After getting back from mass this morning I came to dinner and then took

—111—

a ride all by myself in the woods. On my way up and back all I could see was civilians and servicemen riding their girls. I was so mad at myself that I cut my ride short and came back to camp. As sure as God made little apples, we're going to make up for all this time lost. I get so damn lonesome lately that I get mad. I'll never let you out of my sight again. If I ever get out of this army they'll never get me again, that's sure. Oh well, if I keep talking this way I'll have you worried. There's nothing wrong with me really, just want to see my face late that's all. And in another month or so I will too. So long honey and take care of you both for me.

Yours Always,
Wildie

A World War II Story: Dad's Letters Home

No. 465   Nov. 12-'45

Dearest Face Faite:

Didn't get any mail today, most everything was closed down. I worked this morning but not this afternoon. I'm so damn restless when there's nothing to do that I don't no where to put myself. Didn't hear any more news today, but I did hear a lot of bad rumors. I won't repeat those because I get almost sick when I hear them myself. My morale goes up and down according to the news and rumors I hear. But I'm not losing hope yet.

That phone number that you gave me does not seem to be the same. I thought it was 154 but I guess you must no. Anyway, I'll call the number you gave me the first chance

-11-

I get after landing on U.S.A. And as for your not remembering my voice, well if you don't I'll sure remember yours, — I hope.

I don't no how it's going to be like getting back together again, but I'm sure it will be better than a honeymoon. We won't have to work very hard for our pleasure, and you won't be afraid either. Remember Hampton Beach? ha, ha. We ought to go back and try that same cabin. We'll do a lot of things when we get together again, wait and see.

Well, I guess that's all for now, solong honey and take care for me.

Love Always,
Wilbur

No. 466   Nov. 14 - '45

Dearest Face Laite:

    Haven't received any mail for several days now and it's sure to get along without it.

    Well, I haven't heard any news on us 50 pointers yet, they haven't announced a damn word about it yet. Yet they announced over the radio that they are discharging men with 50 points. If they don't do or say something about us in the next couple of days, I think I'll blow my top. I'm almost sick just waiting right this minute. There's a ship which left this morning with about 1500 men, but there are still about 500 more 60 pointers waiting for transportation. There's supposed to be another one in here in the next few

-11-

days. But these are beginning to give us a line of shit lately and we can't believe anything they tell us. Either they get us some ships in here soon or there might be trouble. Everybody is quite fed up. First they announce that a ship is due in here on such a date and then they tell us it's been canceled. I'm so worked up over the matter that I can't seem to write about anything. There's still plenty of work and this is getting to be a mad house. Most of the new men who are taking over are young kids fresh from the States, and that's just what they are, <u>kids</u>. I'll be glad to get out of this place, soon. Solong and take care,

Love Always,
Wilbur

No. 467 Nov. 17-'45

Dearest Pace Laite!

Received three more letters from you yesterday and also a couple of others. Before I go any further, I want to tell you again not to write me any more. If your still writing to me as of this date, I'll never receive them until I get home. I like letters alright but there's no need to write me for nothing. It makes a lot of work for the guys who stay behind too, they have to address them over again and send them right back. So if you haven't stopped writing yet, please do so at once. I'll keep writing to you until I leave here. (don't mind the splotch of water — I don't want to write this page over again)

Now for my news. As a matter of fact it still isn't encouraging. I still haven't got any new yet. It seems like the general here is waiting for orders from higher up to give the word on us 50 pointers. At least that's my opinion. They are getting ready for us anyway, because today I had to go to the supply room and give my size for winter clothing. My guess is that when we do get out of here it will be done fast. But I'm ready anytime they are.

Glad to hear that Laurent is free again and I don't think I'll be far behind him.

Went to a french supper last night, the same place that I usually go. The little girl is growing fast, I hardly recognized her.

Well, guess I'll make this one short too. Tell you more when I have better news.
Solong and take care,
Love Always,
Wilbre

A World War II Story: Dad's Letters Home

No. 468   Nov. 17-45

Dearest Face Faite:

Tho. my morale and hopes are at their lowest point right now, I thought I'd write a lines anyway.

You probably heard the news as well as I did but in case you didn't here's what it amounts too. It was announced that the points have been lowered to 55 and also those with 4 years service are elligible for discharge Dec. 1. When I heard that I could have done something bad. A feeling of, to hell with everything, came over me and the bitterness I already had for this damn army went up higher than before, if that' possible. This was the greatest disappointment I have ever witnessed so far and I showed it in more ways than one. I guess I was too sure they would lower them down to 50. Now, I'm almost sure I won't be home for Xmas, and

-11-

from now on I won't hope or state anything until I get in the Personel center. I'm sick and tired of watching and waiting for my turn. They are bound to make the little man suffer and they are sure making a job of it. I am not the only one in that position, there are many more like me. Anyway don't wait for me at Xmas, I don't no when I'll be back and I'm not guessing any more. I only hope at least that I'll make it for Elaine's birthday.

This is saturday night now and I think I'll go to a french movie. I've got to have something to do to keep sane. Can't mail this until Monday so I'll finish it tomorrow.

-111-

Nov. 18.

It's sunday night now and here I am finishing your letter. Altho I still haven't got much hope left, 24 hours has calmed me somewhat. I was so mad and felt so helpless yesterday that it wasn't funny. You can forget what I said at the beginning of this letter. I guess there's too much to hope for to forget and give up so easily. I'll still go on hoping and watching for every bit of news I can find. There's still hope that I'll be home for Xmas altho chances are very slim. Anyway, don't lose faith and I promise I won't either.

Another ship went out today and now that leaves only about 200 men at the personel center. Something should turn up this coming week.

Guess I'll close for now, solong and take care of you both for me. Yours Always, Willie

No. 469   November 20, 1945.

Dearest Face Laite:

  Haven't received any mail for several days now so I should get some soon. I&m always in very good health and the spirit is always the same. I just took an influenza shot this afternoon and by tonight I expect to feel it. They are giving it to everybody over here and almost everybody is sick afterwards too. But it will save a lot of sickness for the fellows who go back to the States, and for the ones who stay here too. I've got a little cold right now and maybe that shot will fix me up.

  Well, the latest news is still not encouraging for me yet. I heard from a very good authority this morning that the 55 point men won't be leaving here before December 1. In that case I won't be going before some time in December and it looks very much like I won't be home for Xmas. Of course there always something that may change this but I'm not hoping anymore to get home for Xmas. It seems very improbable now. However, I do expect to get back before Elaine's birthday, and this time I'm almost sure. Don't write me any more letters anyway because you never can tell what may happen. This damn army is still as crazy as ever.

  Well, I went out last night and had supper at a restaurent in town. There was seven of us fellows together and we had a very good supper. In fact it was the best meal that I ever had over here or since I left home. It cost us two dollars apiece but it was worth it. We had soup, specially prepared fish, peas, tomatoes with mayonaise, lettuce, french fried potatoes, roast chicken, and for dessert we had a very nice cake which tasted almost like ice cream because it was so tender. We had all we could eat and there was some left over. That's the kind of feed I want to give you and that big girl when I get back. Gosh, honey I can't wait to get statted again. Altho I keep saying that I seem to hang on anyway.

  It has been a long time since I wrote you a typewritten letter huh? But I've been kept pretty busy lately and didn't have the time to type one out. Today I finally got caught up and it's only three oclock in the afternoon. I thought of writing this letter now because by tonight I may be a little stiff and have some fever from that shot, and I won't feel much like writing. It's starting to work on me already.

  I'm enclosing two snapshots that were given to me today, I wrote in the back just what they were. I think you already have one of the big batiment.

  Solong face laite and take good care of you and you.

       Yours Always,

       Wildre'

No. 470　　　　Nov. 21-'45

Dearest Face Laite:

It's the day before Thanksgiving over here and tomorrow we'll have a day off. I told you on yesterday's letter that I expected to be sick last night on account of that shot and cold I had, well I was. By seven oclock last night I was as sick as I've ever been in my whole life. I didn't sleep but two hours all night long. I never spent such a long night and I was glad for daylight to come along. I worked just the same this morning and to make it worse it was warm all day. I feel better tonight and I hope I can get some sleep too.

Well, there's no news about my turn coming up yet. The 55 point men are supposed to leave around the end of this month. Then I guess it will be my turn, I hope.

Andre should be getting back soon too, because of that new ruling of men with three kids

-11-

will go with the 55 point men.

I bought a Xmas card for Elaine today and one for you too of course. I tried to get one written in french but no soap. I'm still writing to you as usual, but I've stopped writing to the others. I can't write like I used too and besides I think I've done my share.

Summer is really here to stay now. It's been very warm today and also tonight. When I leave here it will be midsummer and back home will be mid winter. So you'd better have a lot of loving ready for me, I'll need it to keep me warm.

Solong honey, and take care for me,

Yours Always,
Willie

No. 471   Nov. 23 - '45

Dearest Face Laite:

    Finally received three letters from you last night and one more today. After reading your letters I thought of the disappointment that you must be in for when you hear I won't be home for Xmas. I no I shouldn't have lead you to believe that I would be home by then, but the news were so good at that time that I would have bet anything I was right. Anyway, don't feel too bad honey, I will get home and soon too. As a matter of fact, I learned something definite about my turn yesterday. I got acquainted with a fellow by the name of Welsh who works in headquarters, and now whenever I hear some news it's not rumors it's the truth. You see he has the same number of points as I have and

- 11 -

he comes from Lawrence, Mass. So he'll be going back with me to the same separation center at Devens. Anyway, he told me yesterday that the 55 point men will be leaving around the end of this month, and the 50 point men will leave around the end of Dec. or the first of Jan. That's no bull because he sees all the orders that come to the General from Washington. So now when I tell you something it will be true. That's the setup at present, and of course they can always surprise us by sending us back sooner. Now we can look forward to something at least, and it looks like I'll be back for Elaine's birthday too. — I hope this makes you feel better, I no it did me.

Well, to give you an idea when and how I'll come back here it is. Before I leave here I'll write you a _last_ letter and tell you what date I'll leave and arrive in the States, and also what boat so you can hear it in the news. I'll probably land in San Francisco and probably fly from there to the East Coast. They are doing that now. I'll try to phone you from Frisco but if I can't, I'll do so when I get to Devens and tell you just when to expect me. If I can't phone I'll send you a wire. How's that, okay? Gosh, I'm sorry I had to disappoint you about being home for Xmas, but the next time will be true. I no I didn't feel so hot either when I learned that bad news. Cheer up honey, another month won't make much difference, I'll be home before you no it.

I must tell you about something that happened today. Some guy started a rumor that they were giving us 6 more points so that the 50 point men could get home for Xmas. Ever since last week I swore that I'd never listen to another rumor, but this one sounded so good that I did believe it. Then I thought I'd better check up and find out if it was true. After checking down the line from one man to the other, I found out that it started from a fellow who always talks to much. He's always starting stories like that. Right away I knew it was false so I decided to scare him once and for all. I made out an arrest report against him and signed the Provost Marshall's name to it. Then I put it on the Bulletin Board in the Company and all the fellows read it. Some body told the guy who started the rumor and when he read it he was sure scared stiff. He has 57 points himself and right away he comes to see me and asked what was the idea.

-V-

I told him that he had started that rumor and for that I would help put him in jail for six months. Boy, was he scared. He didn't hardly eat any supper and we couldn't get a word out of him, and he usually talks all the time. After supper I took pity on him and told him it was just a joke. But I warned him that the next time it would really stick. You should have seen his face when I told him it was a joke, he was not laughing much and he looked pretty silly. I don't think he'll start another rumor over here. This point business is not funny to us any more, we've been waiting too long to play that way.

Well, I hope this letter makes you feel happier honey. Take care of you and that big girl,

Love Always
Wilbur

No. 472   Nov. 24 - '45

Dearest Mae Faite:

It's Saturday night over here and it's raining like hell. I just got back from the show and found that my tent was leaking all over my cloths. Oh well, I haven't much longer to wait now.

I forgot to mail your letter this morning so you'll probably get it the same time as this one. I can't mail this one until monday so I'll finish it tomorrow.

Well, there isn't any news to add to yesterday's letter, except that there's a ship coming in tomorrow and it will take the rest of the 60 point men. Now that I no I have to wait until the end of Dec. or the first of Jan. for my turn, its not so bad. We can look forward to something.

I was just wondering if you were curious about that Xmas present I mentioned a while back. I don't no if Fern already told you but as

long as I won't be home for Xmas I think I'll tell you about it. Remember the last time you went to Conn. and saw those nice ear rings? Well, Fern told me about that, so I told her to buy them for you. I told her to give them to you right away but I think she'll keep them until Xmas. Anyway, she told me on her last letter that she bought them for you, and so you'll have your ear rings for Xmas. How's that, okay? When I get back I'll buy you something better than that. This is only a sample. Of course I expect something in return too.
I guess I'll close for now, until tomorrow solong and goodnight honey.

Nov. 25.-

It's sunday night right now and it's still raining. I didn't do much today. This morning I went to the ten oclock mass and after dinner I went down town for a while. It's the same old routine all the time. I get so restless sometimes that I don't no what to do with myself.

My cold is still hanging on but it's much better. This rainy weather doesn't help much.

We have a new interpreter who just came in last night. He also comes from Maine, Lewiston to be exact. He's married and has a boy about the same age as Elaine. His name is Bernier and he seems to be a pretty good guy.

Well, I can't find much more to say so I guess I'll close. Solong honey and take care.

Love Always,
Wilder

No. 473   Nov. 26-'45

Dearest Face Faite:

Hello honey, another day just about finished which makes it another day bringing us nearer together. I haven't got any more news as to my turn yet, but one thing is still pretty sure that I won't leave here before sometime in Jan., maybe around the first. It isn't so bad waiting now, because I'm quite sure that's the time I'll be leaving. As it was before I didn't no where I stood and I sure made some wild guesses. And I was disappointed too, but I should have known better to hope for so much. Of course there's always the chance that the army will surprise us and suddenly decide to send us home. It won't be no surprise to me tho, I think I no the

-11-

army by now. Anyway, don't feel to bad honey because I can't get home for Xmas, it could be much worse. All I ask is that you take good care of yourself.

I haven't recived any mail for a few days, so I don't no how that big girl is getting along. I suppose she's still learning new tricks every day tho. You no, all the time you've been writing letters to me, telling me about her, I feel that I no her as well as you do. I can never get sick of reading all about her and you, and I think you've done a perfect job of letter writing. However, I'm sure your just as sick as I am of writing and by the time you get this one you'll already have stopped. But I'll keep writing till I leave.

On one of your letters you wanted to no just what I meant by saying you had changed. Well, I didn't really mean you had changed so very much. I guess I haven't seen you for such a long time that's what made me say that. I could still spot you in any crowd by your voice or just looking at your back. And do you think I'd forget that head of hair and black eyes to match? And even tho I don't no that big girl those dark eyes would be enough to tell me she's Breton all over. No, a life time couldn't make me forget any little part of you. I'm still a one woman, man and your it. With that thought in mind I think I'll go to bed and dream until the real thing comes along. Goodnight honey and take care for me.

     Yours Always,
     Willie

No. 474   Nov. 28 - '45

Dearest Face-Faite!

    Another wet and lonely day and also no mail. I figure that I should get mail from you until about the tenth of Dec. Then after that no more. I'll be the rest of that month without mail but I won't mind too much, knowing that I'll be going soon after. But in the meantime I'd like to get all the letters that's coming to me.

    I still haven't got any good news yet so I think I'll answer the two last letters I have of you.

    The way you talk on your letters Elaine can talk pretty good. She must be bigger than I expect and smarter too. You have done a lot of sewing for her and her doll. I wish I could see her face when she sees it. And you'd

-11-

do all your sewing now, because you won't have time for that when I get back. And as for my coming home at night, don't lose to much sleep on that account. I'm pretty sure it will be in the daytime, and you will no in advance just what time. I'll give you plenty of time to get pretty, okay. And I don't care how dirty your room will be either. As long as your in it that will be enough for me. Any old shack will look good to me after living in tents for the past two years. Don't you worry at all about me, I'll be the easiest guy to please you ever saw in your whole life.

Well, I guess I'll cut this short, because there isn't much to talk about. So long until tomorrow honey and take care.
     Love Always,
       Wilke

No. 475 Nov. 28-'45

Hello Face Latte:

Another day without mail, but at least it was nice and sunny for a change. There isn't much to say, so don't be surprised if this turns out to be short.

I wrote to Alice today and told her how I stood on going home. I guess everyone will expect me for X-mas, I haven't written to anyone but you for a long time now.

Well, according to my stoog at headquarters, the General got instructions from Washington today about the 50 point men. He doesn't no everything yet but he did say that we would be released about Jan. 1. I'll probably get more news in a couple of days. I won't get over anxious this time and I won't say anything

-11-

unless I'm sure.

Well, there isn't much work right now, for a change, and it's getting on my nerves again. I hate to work for this army any more but if I don't, I get restless and don't no where to put myself. But I guess I can put up with it for another month.

I really don't no what else to say so I guess I'll close. Take good care of you both honey, Solong

Yours Always,
Willie

No. 476 November 29, 1945.

Dearest Face Laite:

Finally received three letters from you this morning and, although it is just noon I'm going to answer anyway. There should be some more mail this afternoon and I may get some more from you.

From what you say on your letters your not receiving much mail either. But of course it's not my fault as I write the sameas usual. It's the mail service that you can blame and it's the same over here.

Well I got a little bit of news this morning concerning the 55 point men. There's a ship coming in on the 4th, that's next Tuesday here, and it looks like they will probably leave on it. And according to my stoog at headquarters the 50 point men may leave here a few days before the first of Jan. That's the latest news on that deal and I won't say any more because I may say too much. As I get the news I'll tell you about it right away, okay?

I guess Cook will have the chance to go see you yet before I get home.

If Elaine likes ice cream and potatoe chips as well as you say she does, I guess you no who she takes after them. Remember when I used to stop you from eating chips, I like them too but not as much as you do. Quite a girl we have there, and I can't wait to get back to squeeze you both like I want too.

It didn't take long for Laurent to go back to his job. But then I guess there isn't much else you can do in the winter. Take me for instance, I'll be getting back in Jan. in the dead of winter. We can't very well take a vacation at the beach or a lake in that weather. But Just wait till summer comes along, we'll make up for everything.

So your still working over time at that shoe shop huh? Well, I won't give you hell all over again but the minute I write you that I'm on my way home, you'd better quit that job in a hurry.

Well I'm glad some body in the family is finally home. Jerald may be first and then Rene will probably follow and after that ME.

There isn't much more to say so I guess it's time to close. Solong until tomorrow and take care of you both for me.

Love Always,

Wildre'

A World War II Story: Dad's Letters Home

No. 477 Dec. 1 - '45

My Dear Face Suite:

Hello honey, this is saturday night over here, in fact it's just 8.30. I'm in a very sentimental mood right now, but more of that later.

I received another letter from you late last night, and on it you mentioned that, whether I got it or not, here goes. Well, I'm glad you wrote it because I'm sure lonely and just about eat up any letter I can get from you. When I told you a few days ago not to write any more, I should be getting the last letter sometime this week.

There's no more news about my turn yet, and I don't think there will be until the end of this month. So there's not much to talk about in that line for now.

Well, to come back to that sentimental mood

-11-

I talked about at the beginning of this letter, here's what I meant. A french girl was married today to an American soldier. I don't no the soldier but I've known the girl ever since I've been here. You no, in this job we get to no a lot of people, not intimately of course, but in dealing with the french police we interpreters get to no a lot of people. Anyway, this girl happens to be the sister in law of a french policeman I no very well. Her name is Simone Lemaitre (I guess that's the way you spell it). I don't no the soldier tho. Well, there was a reception after the wedding, which was at 5 oclock this afternoon, and I was invited. I hated to go, but I almost had too. Well, I did go with another interpreter. We went at seven oclock and I got so disgusted that

I asked him to take me home an hour later. The reception and everything was alright but I just couldn't have a good time. I kept thinking of you all the time and I couldn't keep my mind on the celebration. I could have got drunk, there was whiskey and champaigne all we wanted, but I couldn't do it. I felt that if you had been there I could have danced all night and would have enjoyed myself, but as it was, nothing doing. In these last few days overseas, it seems that I miss you more than ever. I've been away from you and living for so long that, I'd just like to let myself go and have a good time. You no honey, when I used to go out with you, I always wanted you to stop dancing, well now, it's different. I think I'd like to see you dance the rest of your life. I guess its because I was jealous of you and hated to see you

-IV-

in some body else's arms. And I guess I still am that way, but I'd sure like to see you dancing again. I've had plenty of chances to do you wrong since I've been here, but I can truthfully say that I have done nothing of the kind. But just you wait until I get back. I hope I can make up to you everything that you've missed. Getting back to that french cop, he's going to be mad as hell at me for leaving the reception, but I don't care, I was faithful to you and that's what counts to me.

Well, I guess I'll close for now and will continue tomorrow. Goodnight honey and take care of you both for me. I'm always the same and always will be to you. Goodnight.

-V-

Dec. 7-

It's Sunday night now and I just got back from the show. There isn't much more to add to yesterday's letter. I went to mass this morning and afterwards came right back and read all day. Oh yes, one of the fellows happened to go the post office and I got another letter. But I won't answer it right now, I'll save it for tomorrow. This letter is long enough anyway. ha. ha. After all, I don't want to put everything in one letter and then have nothing to say tomorrow.

Well, I guess I'll close and say goodnight faci laite.

Always Yours,
Willie

No.   2 December 1945.

Chere Face Laite:

Here's a few words in reply to your letter which I received late yesterday. I'm writing this at the office and I don't no the number I'm supposed to put down, so I'll put two numbers on tomorrow's letter, okay?

There still isn't any news to tell you yet, everything is either kept very secret or else theynhave forgotten us altogether. Anyway, we can't say or do anything until we hear from headquarters. But the minute I hear anything I'll let you no as fast as I can. You mentioned on your last letter that it was a long wait and even more so now that the time is getting close. Well honey, it's no easier for me over here, in fact it could be much worse. But my turn will come up soon, it's bound to and this waitng will most probably make that first meeting taste a little better. But who wants to wait, we've done enough of that already.

Was glad to hear that Jerald is on his way out. And I think you did well not to go to Devens to see him. Your mother hasn't changed much in that respect I guess. There are enough people at those separation centers without having the civilians around. When I get there I hope you won't come all that distance for nothing. From what I read in the news everybody is in each ohhers way and yet they don't no enough to stay home.

As for the housing situation at home, I'm not worried yet. And as for staying at the Roys well, we'll look into that when I get back. Personally, I don't think much of the idea, but then again I haven't been home for a long time.

Yes, Fern and I are still doing business as usual. I've already told you what she had bought for you so I won't have to tell you all over again. And by the time you get this letter you won't be able to write me what that some thing was that you had for me, so I'll have to sweat it out until I get back. I'mm still soft hearted I guess, if I wasn't I wouldn't have told you before Xmas. I just mailed the money to Fern this morning so I'm all squared up with everybody. Your the only one I bought anything for Xmas this year, the others will have to wait until another day. Sorry I couldn't make it for Xmas, but next year we'll make up for everything, Xmas tree and all.

Well, I guess I've said my speech for today so until tomorrow, solong and take care for me.

With Love,
Wildre'

No.479 & 480.   4 December 1945.

Dearest Face Laite:

Well, I've finally caught up answering your letters and although there isn't much to say, here's a few lines anyway.

The latest dope on this ship business is as follows. There was one which came in this morning and I think it carried some troops from Guadalcanal here to be processed. These men have 55 points and will probably leave around the 14th. But as for the 50 point men there's still no news. In two weeks I'll start sweating out my turn again, and I hope this time it won't be in vain. I have hopes of leaving before the 1st of Jan. but I'm sure not banking anything on that. I'll let you no when anything is definite.

You mentioned on your last letter about you and Elaine meeting me at the train. Well, I still say that's the way I want it and you'd better be sure there's no one else around either. I still don't like big crowds, only you and me is enough for my money. Of course that includes Elaine too. I'd advise you not to tell any one when I'll be coming off the train. You can tell them when I'm coming home if you want too but I mean when I get off that train in Dover, don't tell any one. It's not that I don't want to see anybody, that will come later on. But for that day only, lets just you and I be by ourselves, okay?

Every day that I stay over here now is getting more on my nerves all the time. Especially with these new kids we have for replacements who are working with us. They don't no shit and don't seem to want to learn either. All they think of doing is play and have a good time. One of them has been in our section only two weeks and already he's made acquaintance with some french girl. I'm afraid they will learn but it will be the hard way. After they get into trouble a few times with these girls they'll probably wise up. I've told them what to do so many times now that I'm sick of telling them any more. So to hell with them I let them go now.

Well I hope you and that big girl are still in tip top shape. Be sure to take good care of you both. It won't be long now you know, I can count the weeks on my fingers now, and pretty soon I'll be able to count my days in the same way. Solong honey and take care,

Yours Always,

Wildre'

No. 481   6 December 1945.

Dearest Face Laite:

        Haven't received any mail for a few days now but I guess that's about the end of it too. If I get any more from you I'll be surprised. But in about three weeks I should be on my way at last, so it won't be too bad being without mail as long as I no it won't be for long.

        There still isn't anything new to report on my case yet and I don't expect to hear anything for another two weeks yet. But don't worry honey, it won't be long now.

        On one of your last letters you said that you had dreamed about having a fight with me and I had just got home too. So that's the way you expect to treat me when I get back huh? Well I'm not worried too much about you and your fights, I've been a good boy for so long now that a real love quarrel would be most welcome I think. And besides you won't have time to fight with me, I'll keep you plenty busy doing some thing else. Get it?

        And about all that fat I have right now, I'm really pretty sloppy to look at. But in the past week tho I've lost some and will lose some more before you see me. I was really too fat and lazy, the least little work I got tired right away. I'M not eating so much now and as of yesterday I started to go swimming every afternoon after work. Being fat is alright but too fat is not so good. Gosh, it will take me six months to get used to hard work again.

        Don't worry about dressing up for me when I get back. From what you've been telling me you haven't bought many new cloths since I've been away, but I'll fix that when I get back. I want to do so many things for you that I won't attemt to write them all down now, but just you wait and see. I've seen a lot of women over here whom I couldn't touch, but when I get a hold of you, just watch me take care of you. It was very tempting seeing all these women and not being able to touch, but when I do touch one it will be you, and I'm not sorry for not having touched behind your back either. I told you before that I'd never wait for another women like I did for you before we were married, but the damn army has been making me wait for over two years now, and for you too. That makes more then five years in all that I've been waiting for you, three before we were married and over two since I've been in the army. If I have to wait for you once more I think I'll give up.

        Well I guess that will be all for now. Take care of you both for me,

        Yours Only,

        Wildre'

No. 482   7 December 1945.

Dearest Face Laite:

      Well, it's just another day over here, there isn't much to do rightnow and the time sure drags along. I haven't had any news from you yet but as I said before I probably won't get anymore letters now that I'm ready to leave. There still isn't any news to report on my turn yet, and until I hear from them there won't be anything new. The 55 point men are supposed to report at the personel center around the 10 or 11, that's next week and will leave here about the 15th. After they go it will be my turn to sweat, and this time I'm sure.

      There hasn't been much work for the past week or more and time is dragging so heavy on me that I simply don't no what to do with myself. I had a chance to go up the island tomorrow but I turned it down. There's a fellow who is absent without leave, or deserter to you, and we are going after him. Three other fellows are supposed to go too. They'll be gone for 5 or 6 days and it will make a nice trip. The reason I turned it down is because if I go, I'll certainly have to appear at his court marshal and it will probably hold me here for I don't no how long. That's not for me, I'm not getting mixed up in anything to hold me here an extra day. So I'm sending one of the new interpreters instead. Speaking of going home, I was reading about that merchant seamen strike in San Francisco. I think maybe that will wake up some of those big wigs in Washington. And I even believe that will help me get back a few days earlier. I won't be officially released before the first of Jan. but they can still send us 50 pointers home before the first, as long as we don't dock at Frisco before then. In other words they could send us from here any time after the 18th and we ouldn't dock before the first. I'm hoping they do that, but only time will tell.

      By next week I'll be the oldest man in my section. The major is leaving then also crazy Jordon and Ritcher, he's the other interpreter. Then I'll be all alone with the new kids until I leave. I hope they call me soon after that.

      Well, I suppose it must be pretty cold in Berwick right now. I imagine that I'll be good and froze for a while after I get back, so you'd better have a lot of loving saved up to keep me warm. But I'm not worrying about the cold, just let me get back, that's all I want. I'm anxious to see how that big girl looks like, she must be quite big now. I don't dare think too much about home right now because I think it would drive me nuts.

      I guess that's about all the gossip for now, so until tomorrow solong and take care of you and you for me.

                    Avec Tendresse,

                    Ton cher epouse avec ces grande jambres,

                      Wilbré'

No. 484 Dec. 10-'45

Dearest Mace Laite!

To my great surprise I received another letter from you today. It was dated Nov. 15 and you didn't mention it being your last, so I may get a couple more from you yet.

The last letter I sent you was last Saturday and since that time I haven't had much time to write. On Saturday afternoon I went swimming at the beach, and at night I was attending the usual movie when I got a phone call to report at the office. Crazy Jordon left last Saturday and Richter also, so I'm the only old hand left here. Anyway I was told that there had been an accident at Thio, that's

-11-

about 160 miles up the island, and a soldier had been killed. Being the only one left who knows this job, I was elected of course. I didn't leave that night but only early Sunday morning. It was a hell of a ride going up there and back, especially driving an army car. I didn't trust the other guy who was with me, because the road was very treacherous and narrow. I didn't feel like going over a 500 foot cliff now that it's almost my turn to go home, so I drove up and back. I investigated the accident and returned late Sunday afternoon pretty tired, and missed mass to boot. But that couldn't be helped. This morning there was only three of us at the office and I had to take crazy Jordon's place. I was so busy all day that

I simply did not see the day go by. The new Provost Marshal told me this afternoon that he was requesting another promotion of staff sergent for me. I don't think I'll get it tho because I have to many points and should leave very soon, and besides, I don't want anything except home.

Speaking of home, I haven't heard anything new yet, but from now on I'm sure looking for something to come up. At any rate, I'm eligible for discharge on Jan. 1, and I hope I leave here before than. But even so, Jan. 1 is only 30 days away. It sure feels good to be able to count the days now, after waiting so long. Even tho I won't be home for Xmas or New Years day, I feel certain that I will be there for Elaine's birthday with bells on.

-IV-

So hold the fort a few days longer honey, I'll get there sure.

Oh yes, I received a Xmas package containing assorted candy from Fern today. I was sure surprised for I didn't expect anything. She must have sent it quite some time ago for it was addressed to me as Cpl. And speaking of packages, I hope you like your new earrings. I hope they help a little in replacing your daddy long legs at Xmas time.

I guess that's enough for now, solong and take care.

     Yours Always,
     Willie

No. 485   Dec. 11-45

Dearest Face Saite:

    Another day bringing us closer together honey. In 20 more days I'll be eligible to leave here, I only hope I'll leave then or maybe sooner. There isn't any news yet, so there's nothing to report.

    I had so much to say on yesterday's letter that I didn't get a chance to answer the one I got from you, so here goes.

    I was glad to hear that Jerald was back home to stay. I can imagine how everybody is asking you when I'm coming home. But pretty soon now you won't have that trouble.

    I see Elaine is still making a hit with everybody she meets. That little shit must be the cutest thing for miles around. I can't wait to get my hands on her, and you too.

-11-

And I see where the old gang were paying you a visit. I seem to be the only one that's missing in the crowd I guess, but once again, it won't be too long now. When I do get there we'll make up for everything, so help me.

And don't worry honey I have that phone number in my head to stay, 566-right?

Well, I guess that's about all for now. There isn't much new here, still the same old grind, only now I'm kept pretty busy, being the oldest man here I have to do most everything myself. These new kids are sure dumb. Solong until tomorrow and take care for me.

Yours Always,
Willie

No. 486 14 December 1945.

Dearest Face Laite:

Hello honey, I didn't get any more letters from you after that last one which was dated the 15th, but then I didn't expect any either. I suppose your still as anxuious as ever to get some news, but no more so them I am. I haven't heard anything new yet. I do no that there are two boat which are supposed to come in here the 19 and 20. That will be next week. It could be possible that I would go on one of them but I doubt it. I have a feeling that they won't release us before the first of Jan. Anyway time will tell.

Well I've been alone here with these new kids all week now and it's sure driving me nuts. I have to do most of the work alone and it keeps me pretty busy. I don't hardly see the days go by. I can't very well say to hell with everything and just let things go wrong, so it keeps me busy all the time. I've been wanting to go swimming but I just didn't have the time.

There's a boat leaving today with about 1200 more men, these are the 55 to 60 point men. There's also a boat docked over herex which is filled with Australian wives and they are supposed to go to the States. There still seems to be plenty of boats for them but not for us. It's the same old run around we're getting. Oh well my turn will come soon now, in twox more weeks at the most I'll no for sure just when I'll be leaving here, maybe before.

I just can't think of anything else to say so I guess I'll close this short letter. Hope you and that big girl are okay. Take care honey it won't be long now.

Love Always,

Wildre'

Dec. 16.

It's about five oclock in the afternoon now and I just got back from supper. There isn't much to add to yesterday's letter. I went to mass this morning and laid around all day. There's plenty of other things I could do I guess, but I don't feel like doing them. Can't get my mind off that foal.

Well, by the time you get this letter, I guess it will be near Xmas. So in case you do get this before then, I hope you have a merry Xmas honey. Enjoy yourself as much as you can and I'll be home soon after.

Solong honey and take care of you both for me.

Yours Always,
Wildré

No. 488   Dec. 17-'45

Dear Face Faite:

I was greatly surprised today by receiving a Xmas card from Alice. She wrote a few words on it telling me the best news that I had for a long time. She told me that you had quit working about the first of December as near as I can figure. Boy, I was glad to hear that. But I think you quit then because you expected me to get home for Xmas. Well, even if I don't get home then I'm glad you finally did quit. You'd better be well rested up for when I get back, because I'm going to keep you busy for a little while at least. The rumors are flying around here. Only today I heard three nice juicy ones, but I won't repeat them to you. As I said before, it's no use telling you

-11-

these rumors and get you all excited for nothing. When the real thing comes along I'll tell you then. And I sure expect something definite in the next few days.

Alice also told me that Andre was expected in the States by the first of the year. She hasn't heard about Medee tho. It's just goes to show you that first come, last served. I came over first and it looks like Medee and Andre will beat me home. Oh well, I still think that we've been lucky thru all this.

Well, I thought I had a lot to tell you but I guess I haven't. I guess I'm happy you quit working, that's why I thought that way. Goodnight honey and take care of you both.
    Love Always,
    Wilde

Norman & Elaine then ...

and now ...

Photo By N.J. Pelletier

About the Authors

Elaine Pelletier was born January 24th, 1943 the same year Dad went into the army. She graduated from Berwick High School, Berwick, Maine in 1960, and later received her diploma in Nursing from the New Hampshire Vocational Technical College (Exeter School of Practical Nursing) in 1962.

Elaine was employed as a Licensed Practical Nurse in College Health at the University of New Hampshire, Durham, NH for thirty years and retired in 2004.

During her career she was elected and served on several state and national professional Boards: The New Hampshire Licensed Practical Nurses Association, The National Federation of Licensed Practical Nurses (NFLPN) and the NFLPN Education Foundation Board.

In 1995 Governor Stephen Merrill appointed Elaine to the New Hampshire Board of Nursing where she served for three years. This is her first time as an author and felt strongly that this story should be told.

Elaine has been married for 42 years to Arnie Holland, and they now reside in Rochester, NH and Zephyrhills, FL.

They have two children: Christine A. Mallahan of South Berwick, Maine and Rodney A. Holland from Gilmanton Iron Works, New Hampshire. They also have three grand-daughters who never knew their great grandfather, and Elaine felt that this book would be a wonderful legacy for them and future generations.

Norman J. Pelletier was born on December 3rd, 1946, a baby boomer. He graduated from Saint Thomas Aquinas High School in Dover, NH in 1964. Four years later, he graduated from Saint Francis College in Biddeford, Maine with a Bachelor's degree in English. His graduation was the culmination of a dream that his father had since Norman was born.

After teaching for one year at Marshwood High School, Eliot, Maine, he served in the United States Air Force during the Vietnam War from May, 1969 to near the end of the war. During this time in service, he earned his Master's degree in Educational Administration from Central Michigan University. He earned one credit at a time as professors traveled to the air force base each week-end and Norman and his classmates studied after work hours. After 30 credit hours, he earned his degree in February, 1973, shortly before his separation from the service.

Norman earned an Honorable Discharge from the service in May of 1973 and he immediately found employment as a teacher of English and French at Gorham High School in Gorham, Maine. While he was Principal at Machias High School, Machias, Maine he earned his Certificate of Advanced Graduate Study in Educational Administration from the University of Maine, Orono, Maine in 1979. He later worked as a teacher and Vice Principal in the Maine communities of Buxton and Sanford. He retired as a public school educator in 1998. Since then he has taught French, Spanish and various English courses at Elan School, a private school in Poland,

Maine. He is married to his wife of 37 years, Joan Vincent Pelletier, and they have resided in Gorham, Maine for 33 years. They have two children: David Pelletier of Portland, Maine, and Lori Pelletier Benham of Concord, North Carolina. They also have seven grandchildren. Norman is also a first time author.

Printed in the United States
65980LVS00001B/19-34